Thinking like a Mall

Thinking like a Mall

Environmental Philosophy after the End of Nature

Steven Vogel

The MIT Press
Cambridge, Massachusetts
London, England

MIT Press books may be purchased at special quantity discounts for business or sales promotional use. For information, please email special_sales@mitpress.mit.edu.

This book was set in Sabon by the MIT Press. Printed and bound in the United States of America.

Library of Congress Cataloging-in-Publication Data

Vogel, Steven, 1954–
Thinking like a mall : environmental philosophy after the end of nature / Steven Vogel.
pages cm
Includes bibliographical references and index.
ISBN 978-0-262-02910-0 (hardcover : alk. paper)
1. Environmental sciences—Philosophy. 2. Philosophy of nature. I. Title.
GE40.V64
363.7001—dc23
2014039752

10 9 8 7 6 5 4 3 2 1

To the memory of my parents

Contents

Preface

This book has been a long time in the writing, and parts of it (or first drafts of parts of it) have been published as independent articles along the way. These include:

"Alienation and the Commons," in *Ethical Adaptation to Climate Change: Human Virtues of the Future,* ed. Allen Thompson and Jeremy Bendik-Keymer (Cambridge, MA: MIT Press, 2012);

"Why 'Nature' Has No Place in Environmental Philosophy," in *The Ideal of Nature: Debates about Biotechnology and the Environment,* ed. Gregory E. Kaebnick (Baltimore, MD: Johns Hopkins University Press, 2011);

"On Nature and Alienation," in *Critical Ecologies: The Frankfurt School and Contemporary Environmental Crises,* ed. Andrew Biro (Toronto: University of Toronto Press, 2011);

"The Silence of Nature," *Environmental Values* 15, no. 2 (May 2006);

"The Nature of Artifacts," *Environmental Ethics* 25, no. 2 (2003);

"Environmental Philosophy after the End of Nature," *Environmental Ethics* 24, no. 1 (2002);

"Nature as Origin and Difference: On Environmental Philosophy and Continental Thought," *Philosophy Today* 42, suppl. (1999);

"Marx and Alienation from Nature," *Social Theory and Practice* 14, no. 3 (1988).

Some of the original work here was done during a semester-long Special Research Fellowship at the Humanities Research Center "Menneske og Natur" at Odense University in Denmark, and I am thankful for that support. I am also grateful to Robert Chapman and to Pace University's Department of Philosophy for providing me with office space and other assistance during part of the writing of this book. Thanks are also due to Clay Morgan, Miranda Martin, Beth Clevenger, and Deborah Cantor-Adams at the MIT Press for their help in bringing it to fruition.

The support, both financial and intellectual, of Denison University has been crucial to me. The book would not have been possible without several grants from Denison's R. C. Good Foundation and the Denison University Research Foundation. I want particularly to thank David Anderson for his support. I would also like to thank my colleagues at Denison, including especially Alexandra Bradner, Barbara Fultner, Harry Heft, Tony Lisska, Jonathan Maskit, Mark Moller, Ron Santoni, and David Goldblatt, all of whom aided in many ways (some obvious and some less so) to help me understand what I wanted to say and how to say it. Others to whom I owe thanks for conversations, arguments, suggestions, or simply moral support over the years include Bryan Bannon, Andrew Biro, James Bohman, Marlaine Browning, Daniel Brudney, Ted Burczak, Dave Bussan, Baird Callicott, Scott Cameron, Lisa Cunningham, Martin Drenthen, Fred Evans, Andrew Feenberg, Janet Fiskio, Simon Hailwood, Ben Hale, David Horn, Andrew Katz, Eric Katz, Laurel Kennedy, Josef Keulartz, Robert Kirkman, Irene Klaver, Ken Liberman, Andrew Light, Thomas McCarthy, Johanna Meehan, Bill Nichols, Priscilla Paton, Stuart Pimsler, Ronald Sandler, Kate Soper, Allen Thompson, Ted Toadvine, Georgia Warnke, Gina Weinberger, Harlan Wilson, and David Wood. Thanks also to my many students over the years, too many to mention here. I want to offer special thanks to the group of my cousins and others whose annual checkups on my work on the beach on (wild) Fire Island have been an important source of inspiration for me over the years, especially Bart Diener, Mick Diener, Lenny Dee, Diane Selden, and Vicky Jaspeado. And particular thanks and love go to my brother Loring, whose clear eyes and remarkable mind have always helped me see the way. That the errors in this book are all entirely mine is something that most of these people have made clear to me on numerous occasions.

The assistance of others at Denison and elsewhere has been invaluable as well: I want especially to thank Kate Tull, Melissa Rubins, and the late Pat Davis for their help, as well as Josh Finnell, Noah Bradtke-Litwack, and Moriah Ellenbogen, all of whom assisted with research. Nick Taggart of the Columbus Metropolitan Library was very helpful in my surprisingly difficult search for images of the City Center Mall, and I thank him. Thanks to Erin Hasley for the cover design, and to Lori Nix for permission to reproduce an image of her diorama, "Mall." I owe special gratitude to June Scrubb. And thanks, finally, to the loves of my life, Jane, Anna, and Jesse, whose patience and support and love have helped me through many difficult patches of this work.

1

Against Nature

Nature and Its End

Environmentalism, both as theory and as practice, has traditionally been concerned above all with *nature*. Its focus is on protecting nature against the harms generated by human action. The "environment" it wishes to defend is not the built environment of cities, or the technological infrastructure that modernity seems to require—although many of us live in urban environments, and the technologies of modernity might be said in a deeper sense to "environ" us all. It is not the nuclear power plants and toxic waste dumps and gridlocked highways surrounding us that environmentalists want to protect but rather the *natural* environment—an environment that these things instead are said to threaten. Environmental protection means the protection *of nature*, and environmental harm means harm *to nature*. The destruction of something built by humans, such as a skyscraper or a dam, does not by itself count as environmental damage. Of course, such destruction may have harmful environmental *consequences*, but this only means consequences that are harmful to nature.

Environmental philosophy reflects this concern. Its central theme is to find an appropriate way to understand and defend the ontological and ethical status of nature. Richard Routley, in one of the essays that founded the field, wrote that an environmental ethic is one concerned with "setting out people's relations to the natural environment."[1] Holmes Rolston in 1988 called for "an ethics that appropriately 'follows nature.'"[2] J. Baird Callicott's first essay on the topic, published in 1989, asserted that "an environmental ethic is supposed to govern human relations with nonhuman natural entities."[3] Paul Taylor began his 1986 book *Respect for Nature* by writing that "environmental ethics is concerned with the moral relations that hold between humans and the natural world."[4] Christopher

Stone in a 1972 law review article anticipated modern concerns by proposing that "we give legal rights ... to the natural environment as a whole."[5] Even Andrew Light, who has criticized the narrow focus of environmental philosophers on the "value of nature,"[6] still offers a defense of environmental restoration projects on the grounds that they help to "restore ... the human connection to nature."[7] Environmental ethicists who want to expand the reach of moral considerability beyond its traditional limitation to humans speak of the "rights of nature"; they do not, typically, worry about the rights of bridges or of toasters. The "environment" spoken of by environmental philosophers is the *natural* environment; the built environment, even though most of us actually live in it, is not generally part of their concern.

And yet to be concerned with the protection of nature, under conditions of modern technological development, is inevitably to worry that it might be too late, that nature might already have ended. This was the famous thesis of Bill McKibben's 1989 book, *The End of Nature*. The real core of the environmental crisis, McKibben claimed, was that nature itself had literally been destroyed. Particularly as the result of large-scale climate changes produced by human technologies, he suggested—especially global warming caused by the burning of fossil fuels and damage to the ozone layer caused by the use of chlorofluorocarbons—we have entered a new historical stage in which no square inch of Earth can any longer correctly be called "natural." Human intervention has affected everything, and so everything in the world is different from what it would otherwise, "naturally," be. The temperature at the top of Mount Everest or in the depths of the Arctic Ocean or anywhere else is now different from what it would have been had humans not transformed the atmosphere; to be in one of these places on a warm day is to be, McKibben writes, "in the equivalent of a heated room."[8] No place is natural any longer, and so the entire environment has become in a certain sense a built environment. "We have changed the atmosphere and so we are changing the weather," McKibben writes. "By changing the weather, we make every spot on earth man-made and artificial. We have deprived nature of its independence, and that is fatal to its meaning. Nature's independence *is* its meaning; without it there is nothing but us."[9] The trees he sees outside his window in the Adirondacks, he sadly concludes, although they look natural, no longer really are. In the context of global warming and acid rain, they are hothouse trees, whose growth and health depend on human action.

But if nature has ended, then it isn't clear any longer what environmentalism is supposed to protect. Without nature, an environmental

theory or practice oriented toward nature's protection has nothing left to do: the game is up, and we (and nature) have simply lost. If McKibben is right, defending nature makes no more sense than defending the Holy Roman Empire or rooting for the Brooklyn Dodgers. His argument appears deeply pessimistic (and self-defeating) in its implications: it can only lead to sadness about what has been lost, but not to any positive environmental policies at all. After the end of nature, it seems, there's not much for environmental thinking to do except to mourn, and perhaps to think about what was lost and why. For nature once ended cannot be restored. The philosopher Eric Katz has made this point quite strongly, arguing emphatically against the idea of "ecological restoration," which in a famous essay he calls a "big lie." Those who work to repair damaged ecosystems or to re-create ones that have been destroyed by human action, he asserts, fail to see that all they are producing are simulacra, artifacts built by human beings for human purposes. Such restoration projects might reproduce particular flora and fauna, and even ecosystemic functioning, Katz argues, but what cannot (ever) be reproduced is the area's *naturalness*. For once humans have transformed an area, that naturalness is gone forever.[10]

The end of nature, then, once it has occurred can never be reversed. And so if environmentalism is concerned with protecting nature, then if McKibben is right environmentalism is simply over; there is no role for it any more. One answer to this might be to suggest that McKibben's point is a rhetorical exaggeration, that nature is not yet *quite* gone, and to take him to be warning us against a potential consequence that is already uncomfortably close to becoming actualized.[11] Yet there are difficulties with this response, not the least of which is that McKibben's argument really is quite convincing, and seems not to involve much exaggeration at all. The temperature likely *is* different everywhere on Earth from what it would have been had humans not spent more than two centuries burning fossil fuels at an unprecedented rate, and so one would be hard-pressed to find those few last remnants of nature that might still exist somewhere, or to figure out how to "protect" them from the influence of anthropogenic atmospheric processes. The impact of human activity on Earth has clearly been enormous.[12]

But a different response to the pessimism McKibben's thesis seems to generate is possible, one that does not deny nature's end but rather wonders why that end should entail the end of environmental concern. Supposing for the sake of argument that his thesis were literally true, one might ask: would the fact that there is no nature any longer mean that environmental considerations had suddenly become irrelevant—for example, that further global warming ought not to be prevented, or that the destruction of atmospheric ozone was no longer something to be criticized, or that the dumping of toxic wastes into waterways was now fine? Wouldn't one expect a good environmentalist to continue to oppose those processes not only for anthropocentric reasons but because of what they do *to the environment*, "unnatural" though that environment would now turn out to be? If the entire environment has become a built environment, would that not then mean that it was time to think about an *environmentalism of the built environment*? Indeed, one might even start to wonder whether the emphasis on the protection of nature—if nature is gone, or even if nature is simply going—might actually be an obstacle to clear environmental thinking: if most or all of the world that "environs" us is not natural, shouldn't it be the built environment, and not nature, that is the focus of our environmental concern? Might not worry about nature seem more like a diversion from the central issues? Such considerations, perhaps surprisingly, suggest that the idea that environmental thought must be oriented toward the protection of nature might in fact be mistaken, and that instead there might be a role for *environmental philosophy after the end of nature*. Thinking through this suggestion is the project of this book.

When Did Nature End? The Problem of Wilderness

The idea that an environmentalism focused on nature finds itself oddly unable to say anything about the real and pressing problems that arise within the environments that humans actually inhabit (and have already transformed) is one that authors such as William Cronon have explored with respect to the notion of *wilderness*. Cronon and others, such as Ramachandra Guha and J. Baird Callicott, have argued against the central role that wilderness and the protection of wilderness have played in American environmentalist discourse. "Wilderness" functions conceptually in that discourse just as "nature" does for McKibben: it refers to that part of the land that has not been settled or transformed by human action. An enormous amount of practical and theoretical energy, these authors suggest, is spent on trying to protect wilderness against its destruction by human alteration.[13] Cronon, Guha, and Callicott all note the uniquely American character of this concern for wilderness and relate it to a national historical narrative that begins with the first European settlers encountering an entirely wild continent and then, decade by decade, taming it and pushing back the frontier. While earlier versions of this narrative emphasized the bravery and heroism of those settlers and celebrated the process whereby nature was "civilized," more recent versions—of which McKibben's can serve as an example—are marked by a palpable nostalgia for the nature that was lost, a nostalgia that is evident in the call to preserve those few remnants of the original wilderness that can still be found. Most other continents have a very different history of human habitation, however, and thus for most other nations, whose connection with the land they inhabit dates from "time immemorial" rather than from a recent date such as 1492, the concept of wilderness does not play as significant a role.[14]

Such an argument shows the culturally bounded character of the appeal to wilderness, relativizing it to a particular kind of historical experience. But furthermore, as Callicott and Cronon and others have pointed out, it is simply false that that the continent encountered by the first European settlers was a wilderness.[15] Tens of millions of people were living in North and Central America in the year Europeans call 1491, with a long history of interaction with the land. The landscapes the first Europeans thought of as unspoiled wilderness had in fact already been transformed by the activities of those humans who lived in them through agriculture, hunting, the building of shelters, religious rituals, and so forth, just like landscapes anywhere else in the world.[16] The forests of New England, the prairies of the upper Midwest, the mounds of the Mississippi Valley, the cliff structures of Arizona and New Mexico, all took the forms they did because of the influence of human activity. Even the wildlife encountered by the colonists showed the effects of the hunting patterns of the aboriginal humans who lived there.[17] The myth that pre-Columbian America was an example of pristine nature, or that the history of European settlement has been one in which a wilderness was humanized, reflects a kind of deep historical amnesia. And, of course, the disappearance of those tens of millions of indigenous inhabitants from the American historical self-understanding is not merely a matter of *conceptual* erasure. One of the most significant environmental effects of the European colonization of North America was the death—especially through European-originated illnesses, to which the aboriginal peoples had no immunity—of up to 90 percent of the indigenous population. (William Denevan calls it "probably the greatest demographic disaster ever."[18]) Arguably it was only because of this massive depopulation that it even became possible to view the North American continent as a pure wilderness: the land seemed unpopulated by humans simply because they had died.

The amnesia here thus has what Callicott calls an "ethnocentric"—perhaps a better word would be racist—element.[19] For whether the history of the American environment is to be understood as the history of the human civilization of nature (as in the positive version of the story) or as the history of the human destruction of wilderness (as in the negative version), the only way such an account can be made consonant with the inconvenient fact that millions of people were already living in, and changing the landscape of, North America in 1492 is by treating those people as themselves "natural" or "wild," as somehow existing on the other side of the human/nature dichotomy—which means: as *not human*. Guha finds this racism also at work in what he sees as an Orientalist tendency in environmental thought to extol indigenous or third world cultures for somehow being more "in touch" with nature than Western ones: when those cultures live on the land, apparently, they do not "civilize" or "humanize" it because they are taken to be natural themselves in a way that Westerners, for better or worse, are not.[20]

But the point of showing that the landscape of 1491 was no wilderness is not to push the moment when wilderness (or nature) disappeared even further back into the mists of time but to raise the question of why finding pristine wilderness should seem so important—and of what the search for it might prevent us from thinking about as well. For as Callicott and Guha and Cronon all argue, to emphasize wilderness protection is at the same time to deemphasize, or even to ignore, the problem of determining a way for human beings to live *in* an environment in a sustainable and ecologically healthy manner. From the point of view of wilderness protection, all humanized landscapes are unnatural, and so talk about what sort of human activity might be best for a landscape is irrelevant or even meaningless. "If we conceive of wilderness as a static benchmark of pristine nature in reference to which all human modifications may be judged to be more or less degradations," Callicott writes, "then we can duck the hard intellectual job of specifying the criteria for land health in four-dimensional, inherently dynamic landscapes long inhabited by Homo sapiens as well as by other species."[21] Guha asserts that in India, the notion of preserving wilderness has led, among other effects, to the displacement of poor farmers from their traditional land as conservation parks are carved out for the protection of wildlife, and thus has "resulted in a direct transfer of resources from the poor to the rich."[22] He contrasts American environmentalists' concern with wilderness, which "is a distinctively American notion, born out of a unique social and environmental history," with Indian or German Green environmentalism, which sees itself as concerned with restructuring a global economic system, and global patterns of consumption, in a way that would allow humans to live and work in ways that are both ecologically sustainable and globally just.[23]

Cronon makes similar points, writing that

> The dream of an unworked natural landscape is very much the fantasy of people who have never themselves had to work the land to make a living—urban folk for whom food comes from a supermarket or restaurant instead of a field, and for whom the wooden houses in which they live and work apparently have no meaningful connection to the forests in which trees grow and die. Only people whose relation to the land was already alienated could hold up wilderness as a model for human life in nature, for the romantic ideology of wilderness leaves precisely nowhere for human beings actually to make their living from the land.[24]

Human beings are by definition left out of wilderness, and so if wilderness is to be our model for environmental thinking, then that thinking will (paradoxically) have nothing to say about human beings and their own activities—except, of course, to insist that they make sure those activities do not encroach on wilderness areas. But then, Cronon concludes, "we thereby leave ourselves little hope of discovering what an ethical, sustainable, *honorable* human place in nature might actually look like."[25]

Indeed, one might even argue that the appeal to wilderness functions as a kind of alibi: by protecting wilderness, we can excuse ourselves from responsibility for the environmental consequences of our own actions within the human, nonwild, world.[26] The built environment is already fallen, and so no work we might do to prevent or remedy environmental damage there does anything to remove the stain of sin, a stain that comes from *not being wild*. And so for this sort of view, as for McKibben's, an environmentalism of the built environment makes no sense. But as Cronon writes, "the majority of our most serious environmental problems start right here, at home, and if we are to solve these problems, we need an environmental ethic that will tell us as much about *using* nature as about *not* using it." The trouble with emphasizing wilderness, he complains, is that it "tends to cast any use as *ab*-use, and thereby denies us a middle ground in which responsible use and non-use might attain some kind of balanced, sustainable relationship."[27]

To recognize that the American view of wilderness is a myth is to realize that the history of the human transformation of nature is an old one indeed, and no less in North America than anywhere else in the world. But that means in turn that the "end of nature" that so worries McKibben might be something that happened a great deal longer ago than he thinks, that it is not the result of modern technological developments such as the burning of fossil fuels and the production of chlorofluorocarbons, or even of the European conquest of a previously pristine wilderness. Rather, the end of nature might be something that, in the Heideggerian phrase that seems relevant here, has *always already happened*. Finding a landscape with no history of human intervention seems difficult indeed, and every search for the imagined pristine landscape before such intervention seems destined to fail. The Adirondack forests whose naturalness McKibben worries is being destroyed because of the effects of acid rain and global warming are not, as he himself acknowledges, primeval ones; the colonists cut down the "original" forests they found in a failed attempt to turn the land into farmland.[28] But those earlier forests, too, as Cronon and others have shown, were not primeval either, showing signs as they did of controlled burnings by the native population before the arrival of the first British explorers.[29] And the history of that native population is itself long and complex, so one would be hard-pressed to specify the moment at which the forests were "first" touched by humans.

It seems as though whatever landscape human beings encounter turns out to be one that they have already transformed, and so the search for the "original" wilderness is always pushed back into the past, always deferred. Or rather perhaps the point is that one cannot encounter a landscape at all without transforming it, which is to say that there is no such thing as a human encounter with a landscape that does not leave that landscape different and hence does not "end nature" in McKibben's sense. What happens, though, if the "end of nature" is something that took place many years ago—or, worse, if it is something intrinsic to the condition of human beings as creatures who live *in* the world, and whose practices cannot help but change that world? If McKibben turned out to be right about the end of nature but wrong about the date on which the end occurred, what would that mean for an environmentalism that saw its goal as nature's protection? Would it turn out that such an environmentalism had always been misguided, having always been based on a mistake—worrying desperately about threats to something that had already ceased to exist millennia before, and perhaps had already, and necessarily, ceased to exist at the moment the first human appeared on the scene?[30] Or would we rather not want to say, in such a case, that an environmentalism *after the end of nature*—which here would mean nothing other than an environmentalism for a world of humans, a *human environmentalism*—would be exactly what needs to be developed?

What Is "Nature"?

But there is another reason why we might want to develop an environmental philosophy that would acknowledge and maybe even approve of nature's "end": because the *concept* of "nature" is one that we *ought* to give up, one whose loss might actually mean an improvement in the quality and rigor of our thinking about the human relationship to the environment we inhabit (and which, by inhabiting, we are always already transforming, have always already transformed). The ambiguity of the concept of nature has been repeatedly noted by those who have written about it: perhaps it is time to admit that the concept is *too* ambiguous, too confusing, too likely to issue in antinomies, perhaps even too intellectually seductive, to be helpful in discussions of how human beings ought best to live in the world.[31] The problem is not merely that nature the *thing* is hard to find—that every claim that such-and-such a landscape really is "natural" might inevitably end in the discovery that no, humans have already been here too—but also that "nature" the *concept* is hard to find as well, meaning that the definition of the term turns out to be so slippery that all attempts to pin it down seem equally doomed to fail. The same logic of deferral operates in this case as in the former one, as each attempt to define nature falls prey to counterexamples that lead the definer to complain "no, that's not what I meant," and then to redefine the term yet again, in an ongoing dialectic that leaves one wondering at the end whether any clear sense can be made of the term at all.[32]

What does "nature" mean, and what does it mean to say that it has ended? McKibben is pretty clear about it.[33] "Nature's independence *is* its meaning," we saw him say, and it's this notion of independence, which is to say independence *from human beings*, that is central to what worries him:

> When I say that we have ended nature, I don't mean, obviously, that natural processes have ceased—there is still sunshine and still wind, still growth, still decay. Photosynthesis continues, as does respiration. *But we have ended the thing that has, at least in modern times, defined nature for us—its separation from human society.*[34]

"Nature" thus here means *that portion of the world that is separate from the human*, or more specifically *from human society*, and "the end of nature" means that that portion of the world no longer exists. The idea of nature here depends on a dualism that distinguishes the natural from the human or social. And it is the violation of that dualism, the encroaching by one side of it on the other, that McKibben is criticizing. Eric Katz quotes William James: "the trail of the human serpent is … over everything," and it is just this that he and McKibben lament: nothing in the world can be found any longer that lacks the trace of that human trail.[35]

In this sense, the protection of nature must be understood to mean something over and above the protection of particular objects *within* nature: it means the protection of naturalness, of the separation between the human world and a world other than us. At the heart of the environmental crisis, McKibben suggests, lies something more than the well-known facts of climate change and acid rain and massive species extinction and the like. In addition to all these is the fact that the world is turning into something *made by humans*. Even if humans could somehow remake the world without extinguishing species and acidifying the clouds and changing the temperature, he thinks, something would be lost—nature, which is to say a world beyond the human one. Thus McKibben writes with persuasive dismay about various technological suggestions for solving the problem of global warming through geo-engineering, such as a proposal to cover the oceans with a layer of white Styrofoam chips to increase Earth's reflectivity, or to place large satellites in orbit to cast shadows on it.[36] His objection to such ideas is not merely that they are ludicrous or ugly, or even that they would likely produce side effects whose consequences may be as bad as the problems they are meant to solve; it is that even if successful they would merely confirm that what had previously been beyond or above or other than the human would itself have been made part of the human world. An ocean covered with Styrofoam, or a shadow deliberately produced by a satellite, would no longer be a part of nature.

To see this is to recognize that McKibben's concern with global warming is not really so much a matter of its consequences as it is of its origin, not so much a matter of the impact of a rise in temperature as of the fact that the rise results from human action. Indeed, on further consideration one realizes that the problem for McKibben really isn't that the temperature is different from what it otherwise would have been, for even if we could somehow ensure—through technologies of Styrofoam or satellite shadows or whatever—that temperatures everywhere were exactly the same, nature for him would still have ended. The problem isn't that the atmosphere is heating up but rather that the atmosphere has now become a human product, its temperature the consequence of human activity. To say that nature has ended, for McKibben, is to say that *a world not produced by human action no longer exists*.

The awkward double negative in the previous sentence is telling. "Nature" here means the nonhuman, and the "end of nature" means the nonexistence of the nonhuman. Nature is defined here by what it is not, by an exclusion, and if nature has ended it is because that exclusion has been breached. No positive definition of nature is provided; rather, it simply functions as the complementary concept to the human. In this sense McKibben's concern with nature is really a concern with human beings, and with the possibility of limits on their actions. The value he finds in nature is really a value in negation—in humans not doing things, not changing things, not acting. What ends nature is nothing other than the human touch, a touch that, rather Midas-like, has the uncanny ability to transform the natural into something outside of nature.

And yet a question worth asking here is how humans could have come to have this special ability to tear things out of their natural state. After all, aren't humans themselves natural? There's something oddly pre-Darwinian about the idea that human action removes objects from nature. The human species and its behaviors presumably evolved through the same sorts of biological processes as other species, and those processes were presumably mediated by the same sorts of chemical and physical forces. If this is so, it is unclear why the consequences of those behaviors deserve to be called "unnatural." If humans are natural, then their burning of fossil fuels, or their use of chlorofluorocarbons, would seem to be natural too, hard to distinguish in terms of naturalness (though doubtless more consequential for the environment) from the activities that other organisms engage in. The dams of beavers and the webs of spiders are presumably natural; why are the dams built by humans or the polyester fabrics they weave not so?

McKibben calls this "a debater's point, a semantic argument" that none of us really believes.[37] But calling it names doesn't actually answer it. And if it is true that even after Darwin, many of us continue to think of ourselves as outside nature, it isn't clear that this is something environmentalists ought to be celebrating, or depending on in making their arguments. Isn't it a sense of separation from nature that is often described as the source of our environmental problems? The issue here reveals an odd inconsistency in the call to protect nature, if nature is understood to mean the nonhuman (and thus to exclude the built environment). For many of those environmental thinkers who worry about the human destruction of nature also believe that humans need to learn to live more in accordance with nature, and indeed that the source of the arrogant anthropocentrism that leads to such destruction lies in the failure of humans to admit their own embeddedness in the natural order.[38] But if the production of a toaster or the changing of a temperature or the restoring of a prairie involves the transformation of nature into something that is no longer natural, then it is not at all clear that humans *are* embedded in nature: they seem rather to be outside it, and if this is so, it isn't clear what living in accordance with nature could possibly mean. There appears to be a contradiction here: if nature is that which is independent from human beings, then humans cannot be natural, nor does it make sense for them to rediscover their role as part of nature. On the other hand, if humans are part of nature, then the built environment would seem to be part of nature too, which leaves McKibben with nothing to worry about: a world of Styrofoam-capped oceans will still be a natural one, and nature is in no danger of (ever) ending.

One way to deal with this problem is to note, as John Stuart Mill had already done in the 1850s, that the word *nature* has (at least) two different meanings, and that the apparent contradiction between saying "humans are part of nature" and "nature is independent of humans" dissolves once one recognizes that the word is being employed to mean different things in each case.[39] On the one hand, we commonly use the word "nature" to mean simply the totality of the physical world subject to the ordinary forces described by physics and chemistry and biology, and in this sense human beings, like every other species of animal, are surely natural. The contrast term to "natural" in this sense would be "supernatural," meaning something that somehow exceeds or escapes the world of ordinary physical processes. (And the extension of the contrast term might well be empty.) On the other hand, we also use the word "nature" in such a way that the contrast term is not "supernatural" but rather "artificial." A person with a taste for natural foods or a preference for natural fibers, after all, is not someone who prefers her meals or clothing not to have a supernatural origin but rather someone who prefers their ingredients not to involve acts of human making. "Nature" in this second sense means exactly what McKibben suggests—the nonhuman world, the world from which human action and its products have been excluded. The first sense of the term is invoked when environmental thinkers worry that humans have forgotten that they are part of nature, but it is the second sense that McKibben calls on when he worries that nature might have ended. The term is simply ambiguous, and what looks like a contradiction is really the result of an equivocation between its two meanings.

Clarifying the ambiguity, however, does not fully solve the difficulties. If environmental theory is supposed to tell us something normative about our relationship to nature—something about how humans ought to treat nature, let's say, and especially how (or simply that) they ought to protect it—it isn't clear that either of these two meanings of the word "nature" will be very helpful. For as Mill pointed out, in the first sense of the word, where nature means everything in the physical world, everything we do and make is natural; in the second, where nature is the nonhuman, nothing is. But then neither meaning has much of a normative force. In neither case can one make much sense out of claims, for instance, that certain human practices or products are more natural than others, or that we ought to live more natural lives. Either we are already guaranteed to be fully natural or else we are guaranteed, by definition, to be nature's opposite.[40]

Protecting nature seems problematic on both meanings, too. If "nature" means the nonhuman world, then humans could protect it only by abstaining from having anything to do with it, perhaps by enforcing the boundary between natural and built environments as stringently as possible. This is an odd conclusion, first of all because if McKibben is right, then it's already too late—the boundary has already been breached and nature is gone—but second because even if he isn't, such a position seems to have nothing to say about what happens on *this* side of the boundary (which is where by definition we actually live), leaving us curiously free to engage in any environmental depredations we wish to undertake here. On the other hand, if "nature" means the totality of the world subject to ordinary physical and biological processes, then working to protect it seems pointless, since in truth nothing humans can do could harm it. The atmospheric consequences of global warming, in *this* sense, are no less natural than those of photosynthesis or respiration; in *this* sense, that is, nature is really in no danger—although *we* might be, and so might some of the other entities (including the built ones!) found within that world.

Still, pointing out that "nature" has two meanings and can refer either to everything in the world or to everything in the world other than human beings does seem to rescue McKibben's argument from the objection that it forgets that human beings are natural, too. Let's use the capitalized "Nature" to refer to the first, broader sense of the word and lowercase "nature" to refer to the second, narrower one. Humans then are doubtless part of Nature, we could say, but still are capable of ending nature. Yet to put it this way is to notice a doubt arising: Is McKibben *really* more worried about nature than he is about Nature? More generally, is the goal of environmentalism the protection of nature, or is it rather the protection of Nature? And which, by the way, do we mean when we talk of the *environment*? Drawing the distinction between the two meanings solves an apparent difficulty with environmental theory's repeated invocation of "nature," but it isn't clear that it leaves environmental theory in a better situation.[41]

For if it is nature in the narrow sense that we are concerned with, then calling certain human actions "unnatural" will no longer depend on discovering that they violate or harm Nature (how could they?) but rather will simply be a matter of definition. Human actions are unnatural (in this sense) not because of what they do to the world but simply because they are actions performed by humans. The word "nature" is stipulatively defined as excluding the human, which means that the claim that any particular human behavior is "unnatural" turns out to be analytic—a tautology. The strong distinction between nature and the human world, and the claim that the latter world is unnatural, turn out to be valid by definition, and not because of the discovery that there are empirically significant differences between the nonhuman world and the human one, or because the former world is somehow more genuinely Natural than the latter. When McKibben writes that "nature's independence *is* its meaning," he certainly seems to be talking about (lowercase) nature, defining it precisely by its separation from human beings, but when he laments the *end* of that nature, it isn't always clear what he has in mind. He writes, for instance, that one of the dismaying consequences of the end of nature is that "we can no longer imagine that we are part of something larger than ourselves."[42] But if nature's independence is its meaning—if it is nonhuman nature and not Nature as a whole that he is worried about—then in what sense could we ever have imagined that we were part of it?

When nature is defined as that which is separate from human beings, the claim that human action harms nature turns out to be an analytic truth. But analytic truths scarcely seem like good candidates on which to found an ethical or political critique; they are not usually things we bemoan or condemn. Nor, of course, are they things that become true, or truer, over time: it makes little sense, for instance, to say that capitalism or technology or anthropocentric arrogance or modernism has made them true. Yet isn't that what much critical environmental thinking wants to argue? Those who criticize the contemporary world for what it does or might do *to* nature, it seems to me, do not intend to be expressing analytic truths: they believe—correctly, I think—that the effects of human activity on the world over the past century or two have been baleful and destructive, and they believe also that different sorts of human activity might produce effects that are less baleful and destructive. But then it cannot be nature in the lowercase sense that they think is being harmed.[43]

One could, after all, stipulatively define a term to refer to the complementary concept of *any* species—"shrature," perhaps, to refer to the world independent of the actions of shrimp, or "bature" to refer to the world independent of the actions of beavers.[44] Then it would surely be true that wherever shrimp swam or wherever beavers built dams, shrature or bature would be destroyed. Yet to make such definitions would be silly, and to lament the destruction thereby defined into existence would be even sillier. Of course, a world that shrimp or beaver had taken over, by spreading and overpopulating like kudzu—so that the trail of the shrimp or beaver serpent (to complicate metaphors) was everywhere—would doubtless likely be ecologically disastrous. But the problem then would be the harm to Nature, to the world that we *share* with beavers and shrimp, not to shrature or bature. Isn't *that* what environmentalists worry about when they worry about the effect of human action on the world—the end of Nature, not of nature? And in warning us about it, aren't they concerned about a kind of destruction that the right sort of environmental policies might prevent or repair, not one that occurs inevitably, no matter which policies we pursue, as a matter of definition?

To be unhappy about the replacement of nature by a humanized world, I am suggesting, one must be able to point to some (presumably valuable) empirical characteristic that the natural world possesses that a humanized one does not. But then (if natural means nonhuman) that characteristic cannot without begging the question be its naturalness *alone*. So it cannot justifiably be simply the end of (lowercase) nature that bothers McKibben; there must be something that the humanization of nature actually harms, and it is that something—is it capitalized Nature?—that he is really concerned to protect. That human beings can (but need not) destroy nature, that they can (but often do not) live in accordance with nature, that nature could (but often does not) serve as a normative model for their actions—these are all meaningful ideas, with substantive content, and yet if "nature" is defined stipulatively simply as that which is independent of human action, then none of these ideas has much content at all, since they all either affirm or deny (pointlessly, in either case) what the definition of nature analytically guarantees to be true.

If nature means the nonhuman, then the "end of nature" through human action can neither be criticized nor prevented, because its occurrence is a matter of definition and not of choice. And so, it seems to me, an environmental theory that wants to protect nature cannot intend by "nature" that second, lowercase, meaning. The assertion that "human action is ending nature" must be synthetic, which is to say there must be some *matter of fact* about human beings that removes their actions and the results of those actions from nature, for reasons that are more than definitional. So "nature" in that assertion cannot mean nature in the lowercase sense. But it cannot easily mean Nature in the capitalized sense, either, because in that sense humans are supposed to be *part* of Nature as "the sum total of all phenomena," and it is hard to see how their actions could end that relationship. We are left with a dilemma. Is there some third meaning of "nature" being appealed to in the claim that humans are ending nature? Or is something else being asserted, perhaps surprisingly: that human beings might not be (fully) part of Nature but rather might turn out to have something of the "supernatural" about them after all?

The Natural and the Artificial

Now, "nature" has at least one other common signification, whereby it refers neither to "the sum of all phenomena" nor to the nonhuman world as such but rather specifically to the world of *life*.[45] We speak of someone deciding to leave the city and move into the country as a person who wants to be closer to nature, and here we clearly do not mean by "nature" either the physical world as a whole (because otherwise she'd already be there, in the city) or the nonhuman world (because otherwise she'd never get there, no matter how far she moved). "Nature" in this sense means the *biological* world, the world of flora and fauna. There's not much nature in the city, we say, with the exception of parks or rats or weeds growing between cracks in the sidewalk. According to this definition it is *living things* that are natural, plus the habitats or biosphere within which they live. But interpreting nature as life in this way doesn't avoid the problems we have seen. For humans are alive too, of course, and have a place in the biosphere, and so they still remain natural even using this third meaning of the word. Nature turns out not to be so hard to find in the city after all: it's a natural habitat of a biological species. If wetlands are natural because of the aquatic creatures who live there, then why not call a city natural because of the (urban) creatures who live *there*?

Does the difference have to do with the way these two kinds of habitat are created? The city, after all, unlike (maybe) the wetlands, is *built*, and built by the very humans who inhabit it. It's hard to deny that humans themselves are natural, but is it possible that the definition of "nature" we are looking for is one in which humans are natural but their *products* are not—are "artificial"? We end nature, in this account, not by making it human but by turning it into an artifact.

To say that humans are natural but their products are not sounds plausible, but a little thought suggests some difficulties. For one thing, among the products humans create are other humans: we call them babies. A baby is a human product, created through human actions, and this fact suggests that not all human products, nor all human actions, are unnatural.[46] When we exhale, when we defecate, when we make babies, the objects we produce are not typically called artificial or unnatural. It seems as though some of the behaviors through which humans produce things are natural while others are not, but it isn't clear on what the distinction depends. We emit carbon dioxide into the atmosphere when we exhale, and we also emit it when we build and drive automobiles powered by fossil fuels. Why is the one sort of emission called natural while the other is termed artificial and said to threaten the end of nature?[47] The carbon dioxide produced by human respiration surely has some (small) effect on the overall heat absorption of the atmosphere: global temperatures are different from what they would be if no humans were around to breathe. Yet those effects are considered to be natural ones, not different from the effects on global temperatures of the respiration of other animals, or of plant photosynthesis.

What distinguishes, then, our natural products from the artificial ones? Is it the distinction between biological and nonbiological products? If by this is meant that our natural products are those that are themselves alive, the examples of respiration and defecation are sufficient to refute the idea. Is the distinction rather between those products made of organic materials and those that are not? But plastics are made of such materials, as are most "artificial" flavorings and colorings. And, of course, there are nonorganic products created by other species that nonetheless are usually called natural: anthills, beaver dams, rodent burrows, and so on.

Or is it the biological character of the *processes* involved that distinguishes natural human products from artificial ones? But much will now depend on what "biological" means. Why is respiration a biological process, and not the extraction and combustion of fossil fuels? The danger of circularity here is strong: why can't technological methods be understood as biological ones? Why not see the use of technology as one of the "biological" behaviors engaged in by the human species, made possible for that species by millennia of evolution? To say that technologically mediated processes are not biological requires having decided ahead of time that technology isn't natural, which begs the question in dispute. (And of course exhalation can be technologically mediated too, most obviously in the case of people who need mechanical assistance with their breathing, but in other cases as well. If the quantity of carbon dioxide I exhale increases because I am running on a treadmill, does the additional carbon dioxide now count as an artificial greenhouse gas?) In the course of biological evolution various organisms have developed various strategies to get around in the world. The processes by which spiders build webs and beavers build dams are surely biological; why not the processes by which humans build automobiles?

Eric Katz falls into the circularity here. Human activity is only unnatural, he writes, when it "goes beyond our biological and evolutionary capacities."[48] Those behaviors for which we are evolutionarily adapted are natural ones, while others are not. But how, one wonders, could it even be possible for us to engage in activities that are "beyond" our biological capacities? (If we engage in them, aren't we capable of them? And isn't that capacity a biological one? What else could it be?) Why isn't the capacity to discover and burn fossil fuels a biological one, developed through evolutionary processes? Katz is following Andrew Brennan here, who also identifies the "natural" for humans with that "for which we are [evolutionarily] adapted."[49] But Darwinians would remind us that species are not adapted *for* anything: they simply find themselves more able to reproduce in some environments and less able to reproduce in others. Humans are "adapted" for whatever they *do*; since they are able to reproduce in the world of global warming and pollution that their own actions have created, those actions, according to Brennan's definition, would seem to be natural ones. Humans may doubtless someday *not* be able to reproduce in such a world, but that won't make them "unnatural," even retroactively (any more than dodoes are). It will simply make them extinct.

Katz and Brennan both employ the example of childbirth to make their point, and it is worth considering. Katz writes that "natural childbirth"—presumably unlike more medicalized obstetric practices—is correctly called natural "not because it is a nonhuman activity" but rather because it eschews "actions designed to control or to manipulate natural processes."[50] But which processes here are "natural" ones, and what is it to "manipulate" them? (And what, one might ask, if the "manipulation" of such processes is precisely what it is "natural" for humans to do, what we have evolved to do?) When a midwife encourages a woman in labor to get into a position in which gravity will assist the birth, or for that matter if the mother decides herself to shift positions because she finds that helps with the pain, don't these actions "manipulate" a natural process? And on the other hand (again), why is the administration of an epidural to a woman in labor *not* the employment of a natural process? Discovering and then synthesizing anesthetics, and using them to minimize pain in childbirth, turn out to be within the "biological and evolutionary capacities" of human beings, and presumably result from natural evolutionary processes. Why is nature being "manipulated" in these cases, as opposed to when a spider uses a web to catch an insect, or a plant attracts a honeybee with its odor, or an animal protects itself from a predator by burrowing into the ground?

To try to distinguish natural from unnatural human activities on the basis of their "biological" character seems doomed to circularity. Might the distinction be drawn differently, perhaps on the basis of the role that conscious intention plays in the action? We can choose whether to engage in technologically mediated actions such as using anesthetics or driving cars; respiration or defecation, on the other hand, seem not to be matters of choice, and that might be a reason for calling the latter sorts of actions "natural" ones.[51] But many children are born because their parents quite deliberately intended to make them, and we would not, I think, want to call anyone whose conception was consciously planned by his or her parents somehow artificial. Furthermore, it doesn't seem clear that intention is reserved for human action alone: other animals may plausibly be said to act intentionally on at least some occasions, and again, it would be odd to suggest that whatever results from such action (a dam built by beavers, bones buried by dogs, nests constructed by birds) is somehow artificial. (Or do we want, like Descartes, to deny animals the possibility of intentional action even in principle?) And in any case it is worth noting that the production of greenhouse gases is not *intended* by those who build or drive automobiles: indeed, the *unintended* consequences of technologies are often the ones that seem environmentally most damaging. It would be strange if as a result at the same time they were the most "natural."

The latter problem can perhaps be avoided by carefully wording the distinction as one not between what humans intend to produce and what they produce unintentionally but rather between that which is the causal consequence (intended or not) of intentional human action and that which is not.[52] But the first problem remains: a woman may choose to become pregnant and bear a child, just as she may choose to drive a car. If the role of human intention in producing an object determines whether that object is natural or not, then it is hard to see why the baby she bears is any less artificial than the carbon dioxide her automobile emits. It's true that sometimes the pregnancy does not come to pass despite the actions the hopeful parents engage in to cause it, but sometimes one's car will not run either, despite one's best attempts to start it. Similarly, although it's true that once the pregnancy begins, processes are set into motion that the mother cannot fully control (but which her intentional acts may still affect), it's also the case that once one starts one's car and gets it moving, processes are also set in motion that are not fully controllable either (but again, which one's intentional actions may surely influence).[53]

Even defecation, sometimes described as "nature's call," is not in truth so entirely lacking in intentionality. Toilet training, for instance, is the process of educating a child in choosing where and when and how to engage in it. It's true that I have no choice as to *whether* to defecate or not, but when and where I do so is typically very much up to me. (And it's equally true that although I may choose which clothes to wear when I walk down the street, I really have no choice as to *whether* to wear clothes or not, without this meaning that wearing clothes is something I do "naturally." To appeal here to a distinction between "natural" and "social" necessities is simply to beg the question, since it is just that distinction we are trying to elucidate.) The truth is that all these actions—becoming pregnant, driving an automobile, getting dressed in the morning, even defecating—involve a complicated mixture of intentional and unintentional elements. The trouble with distinguishing between natural and artificial human behaviors on the basis of intentionality is that it fails to acknowledge this complexity and instead treats intentional actions as though they took place outside the ordinary world of Nature. But the capacity to act intentionally is in fact part of that world; it is a capacity that has evolved in human beings in accordance with standard Darwinian processes, just as the capacity to fly has evolved in birds. Why should the exercise of the former capacity remove an act, or its product, from nature, while the exercise of the latter one does not? Humans act intentionally *in* Nature, not outside it.

The appeal to intention here, however, should be the tip-off as to what is really going on in these repeated unsuccessful attempts to separate "natural" human products from "artificial" ones: the territory we have entered is the familiar territory of Cartesianism. The dualism being posited between humans and nature seems to derive from a dualism within human beings themselves. We humans, it turns out, are inwardly divided: we have two sides, a "bodily" side that connects us with the rest of the world of Nature and at the same time another side, associated with thought and intention, that removes us from that world. The distinction between natural and artificial human products is really the distinction between those products we produce using our *minds* and those we produce using (merely) our *bodies*. The human body is natural, and so too are that body's products: babies, exhalations, feces. But the mind is something other than the body; its products are different, and somehow stand outside the world of nature. When *thought* is employed in the production of something, the product is thereby rendered "artificial," not natural.

The familiar dualism at work here is one that has been pretty thoroughly discredited, and that few philosophers explicitly hold today. It is also, as I have repeatedly pointed out, pre-Darwinian: rather than seeing thought or intention as themselves capacities that have evolved naturally, it treats them from the start as ontologically distinct from nature, as if they had arisen independently of the processes that have led to the capacities of all the other species in the world. Yet despite its philosophical and biological deficiencies, such a dualism really does seem to underlie the conception of nature as something whose "independence *is* its meaning" that we have been trying to understand. Such a conception, it turns out, functions less as an account of what nature is than as an account of what human beings are—creatures who transcend nature, and transcend it because of their minds.

But then those who employ that conception of nature (such as McKibben and Katz) are not using the word "nature" in any way different from those who use it to mean what I have called Nature. For them the two meanings of the word mentioned above—Nature as everything in the world and nature as everything other than the human—collapse into one: "nature" *does* mean everything in the (physical) world, only now it turns out that humans live, in part anyhow, in another world. And so when such thinkers worry about human beings harming "nature," it is indeed Nature that they must mean. I said above that the contrast term to "natural" could be either "supernatural" or "artificial," depending on which sense of "nature" was being employed, but now the two latter terms turn out to be connected: the reason that (some) human products are called artificial is that human beings are (in part) supernatural. Human activity, or at least that kind of human activity in which we employ our conscious, thinking minds (and not just our reproductive organs, or our digestive or respiratory systems), is somehow *outside Nature*—outside, that is, the ordinary physical world. And so the claim that human action harms nature, or that human action could conceivably end it, is indeed a synthetic claim about Nature in the sense of the "sum of all (physical) phenomena" (a sum from which mental or intentional action is excluded) and not the sort of definitional or analytic claim about nature we have discussed earlier.

More specifically, it is a metaphysical claim. If the harm to nature that humans are said to do were any sort of empirical harm, anything that scientific investigation could uncover, then for just that reason the harm would itself be part of "the sum of all phenomena," and so would in fact be no harm to *nature* at all—though doubtless perhaps a harm to particular entities *within* nature. (And here I've dropped the Nature/nature distinction, because for the thinkers I'm considering it turns out to be no distinction at all.) Thus, for instance, when it is suggested that human action is unnatural because it violates the finely tuned balance characteristic of nature, the suggestion only makes sense if nature is indeed characterized by such a balance; but if human action violates that balance, then apparently nature is *not* so characterized, unless we have decided beforehand and for other reasons that the effects of human action on nature are not themselves natural. (It would be like saying that birds are unnatural because nature—with the exception of birds, of course—is marked by flightlessness.) Or if it is asserted that the transformative impact of humans on nature is on a scale so radically different from that of other species as to render it unnatural, again this only makes sense if the global impact of natural species can be shown always to remain within certain limits—but apparently it cannot be shown to do this (since human actions by hypothesis exceed those limits) unless we have decided *antecedently* that the impact of human actions is not to be counted in the determination of what the limits are.[54] The argument here is perfectly general: we can't decide whether humans are natural or not by observing nature, since before engaging in the observation we would need to decide whether humans themselves are part of what is to be observed. But if the dualist claim that humans are at least in part unnatural cannot be a matter of empirical observation, then (if it is not merely a matter of definition) it must be a matter of a metaphysical assumption. *It is not a discovery about the human impact on nature but rather a metaphysical presupposition about it.*

When thinkers such as McKibben or Katz distinguish nature from the human, I am suggesting, this is not because it is possible to discover *in the world* some ontologically significant difference between those things human beings have transformed and those they have not. Rather, this dualistic conception of nature begins by *assuming* the existence of such a difference—begins, that is, by assuming that humans are distinct from nature, typically because of their rational/mental/conscious capacities—and then uses that assumption to justify the claim that that which humans have made or done (the "artificial") can be ontologically distinguished from the "natural." The position does not (although it often claims to) posit a species-neutral criterion of naturalness and then notice with regret that the actions and products of one particular species, our own, fail to satisfy it. Rather, it starts by assuming that humans are (partly) unnatural and then looks for a criterion that confirms the assumption. Far from being a discovery about nature, I would argue, the claim that certain acts and products are unnatural is in fact the expression of a certain a priori metaphysical view about human beings. The dualism here is presupposed, not argued for. That's why beaver dams will never be described as unnatural—not because they possess some fundamentally distinctive character compared to the dams humans build but simply because humans do not build them.[55]

It is hard to avoid the conclusion that the dualism here is also—as surely Descartes' dualism was—fundamentally anthropocentric, surprising though such a suggestion might be with respect to a view that is so common among supposedly antianthropocentric environmental thinkers. Humans stand in an absolutely unique and distinctive relation to nature, according to this view: alone of all the species in the world, their acts have the special ability to move something out of the realm of nature and into a different, specifically human, realm. Although humans are part of nature in one sense, the specific difference between humans and all other animals (indeed, between humans and everything else in the world) is that in another sense they stand over and against nature, separate from it and capable of ending it through their acts, because they possess qualities of reason and consciousness that themselves transcend nature. This surely is an impressive species, one set off ontologically from every other: a metaphysically unique species, we might say. Why should this sort of view not be called an anthropocentric one?

It is true that this is an anthropocentrism with the signs reversed, in which humans turn out to be unique in that they are uniquely *dangerous*, capable of visiting a kind of ontological harm on nature of which no other species is capable.[56] The human mind no longer looks here like the crown of creation, but rather like a dangerous exotic whose appearance poses a metaphysical peril to nature and its independence.[57] Yet underneath the misanthropy (and, to use a Kantian term, misology) here, this view of human beings remains remarkably similar to that found in traditional triumphalist anthropocentrism: here too we humans are viewed as metaphysically distinctive, as uniquely capable of transforming the ontological status of those things with which we have to do, as constructing a world of "artifice" that is utterly unlike the world of "nature," as possessing extraordinary characteristics (in particular those associated with mind and conscious agency) that render us singular among all living creatures. The human mind, seemingly *not* a product of ordinary evolutionary processes (because how otherwise could it allow us to "transcend" nature or make possible acts that go beyond our "biological capacities"?) appears to this dualism as something sui generis. Aldo Leopold described the land ethic as calling on us to see ourselves as "plain member" of the land community, not as its "conqueror," but isn't it exactly as a conqueror, although now a dangerous conqueror who must be resisted, that human beings appear on this account?[58]

The distinction between humans and nature, I am suggesting, that seems crucial to McKibben's concern about nature's end, and that more broadly seems central to the environmentalist desire to protect nature from destruction at the hands of human beings, depends on a philosophically and biologically untenable dualism that forgets that human beings themselves are part of nature and instead treats them as exceptional creatures who somehow transcend the natural. And the problems here are not solved—as some, such as Katz, seem to think they are—by asserting that the human/nature dualism should not be understood as a sharp dichotomy or polar opposition but rather is meant to refer to points along a continuum, or as admitting of degrees.[59] It's surely true that while employing the sense of nature as independent of the human we tend to speak of degrees of naturalness—so that a rural landscape, despite the role of humans in helping shape it, might appropriately be described as more natural than a fully groomed suburban one or a park, and the latter might in turn be understood as more natural than, say, midtown Manhattan. But although this fact is frequently mentioned as if it showed that the dualism posited by such a view of nature does not perniciously remove human beings from the natural order, it shows no such thing. Recasting a binary opposition as a continuum doesn't render it less dualistic, it only extends the dualism along an axis whose poles (even if reached only asymptotically) remain fundamentally opposed to each other. Why is "naturalness" measured along an axis whose negative pole (so to speak) is the human and not, say, the shrimp or the beaver? Human beings here are still being anthropocentrically picked out here as animals with the remarkable ability to remove items from nature. That this removal is always partial and takes place by degrees does not transform the fundamentally dualist (and anthropocentric) character of the position.[60]

That's what
this is about

Against Nostalgia

So where have we ended up? I began this chapter by noting the importance of the concept of nature for much environmentalist thinking. And yet the centrality of that concept turns out to face significant difficulties. The idea that environmental philosophy can (or must) base itself on the defense of nature against human depredation confronts at least three problems, as we have seen. One is that McKibben might turn out to be right: nature has already ended, and therefore environmental philosophy comes on the scene too late. An environmental theory concerned with protecting nature against its replacement by a built environment has nothing to do if that replacement has already taken place, and furthermore by its own admission has nothing to say about the actual (unnatural) environment within which most humans live. But a second problem, as our consideration of various arguments in the wilderness debate revealed, is that the end of nature might not be a recent event but rather something that has always already taken place: human beings have always transformed the world they encounter, and they transform it *in* encountering it, a fact that might well be part of their "nature." The search for a real piece of pristine nature—if that term refers to something like an untrammeled wilderness that shows no sign of human activity—might turn out to be a difficult one indeed, and the harder it is to find such an environment the more the nagging question might arise as to why finding it is so important. If environmental philosophy is supposed to think about how humans do and should relate to the environment, and if the environment humans inhabit in fact is, always already, a built one, then shouldn't *that* sort of environment be the focus of environmental thinking, rather than the fetishistic (and almost Sisyphean) search for that magical piece of ground that no human being has ever touched?

But both these problems presupposed that at least we knew what "nature" was, and knew in particular how and why it was to be distinguished from the human. The third problem we have seen, however, raised questions even about this. Not only, that is, might nature have ended, or have always already ended, the *concept* of "nature" might be such an ambiguous and problematic one, so prone to misunderstanding and so riddled with pitfalls, that its usefulness for a coherent environmental philosophy turns out to be small indeed. We have seen the difficulties in the concept, especially when it is employed dualistically to mean something like (but not exactly, it turns out!) "that which is independent of the human": it seems to require continual modification, it issues almost inevitably in antinomies, it produces a series of paradoxes, and most of all its employment seems to commit one to an essentially Cartesian anthropocentrism that fits very uncomfortably with the other theoretical commitments most environmental philosophers typically defend. If we find ourselves unable even to define what we mean by the term "nature," and if our attempts to define it involve us in metaphysical thickets that philosophers over the past two centuries have found it much more reasonable to avoid, then it might indeed be worthwhile to consider whether environmental philosophy might be better off if it dropped the concept altogether.

An *environmental philosophy after the end of nature* might then be understood as one that recognized that McKibben is right, nature is gone, and yet we still need an environmental theory of the "postnatural" world, *and* at the same time one that recognized that nature might *always* have been gone, that "postnaturalism" is simply the (natural) human condition, and so environmental theory ought to take that condition as its starting place, and finally one that recognized that the concept of "nature" is itself so confusing and ambiguous and even intellectually dangerous that any coherent environmental theory would be well advised to eschew it in any case. This book is intended to investigate what such a philosophy might look like. But it is worth asking, at this juncture, why the idea that environmental theory would be better off if it dropped the concept of nature is such a disturbing one—which means also asking why "nature" seems like such an important concept for environmental philosophy at all.

I think the answer has to do with yet one more meaning that the word "nature" frequently has, one that Mill mentions as well in his essay: nature as a *normative standard*.[61] The implicit connections between the natural and the *right*, and between the unnatural and the *wrong*, are strong ones indeed. In contemporary usage, what is "natural" somehow seems to be good, while the "unnatural" or artificial has something inevitably suspect about it. But as Mill points out, to take nature more broadly as a normative standard leads to pretty dangerous ethical waters. "In sober truth," he writes,

> nearly all the things for which men are hanged or imprisoned for doing to one another are nature's every day performances. Killing, the most criminal act recognized by human laws, Nature does once to every being that lives, and in a large proportion of cases, after protracted tortures such as only the greatest monsters ... purposely inflicted on their living fellow-creatures.... Nature impales men, breaks them as if on the wheel, casts them to be devoured by wild beasts, burns them to death, crushes them with stones like the first Christian martyr, starves

> them with hunger, freezes them with cold, poisons them by the quick or slow venom of her exhalations, and has hundreds of other hideous deaths in reserve.... All this, Nature does with the most supercilious disregard both of mercy and of justice.... A single hurricane destroys the hopes of a season, a flight of locusts, or an inundation, desolates a district; a trifling chemical change in an edible root starves a million of people.[62]

Trying to act more "naturally" in this sense scarcely seems like a good idea. Mill is pretty clear about the difficulties, both moral and logical, with the notion that nature should be the model for our behaviors, and it is doubtless true that most good environmental philosophers recognize these difficulties and attempt to avoid making this mistake. Yet the idea that human action ought to "follow nature," or that the natural is at least prima facie the good and the unnatural the bad, remains a powerful one in environmental thought.[63] And the view that the destruction of nature—and its replacement by an artificial or built world—would involve a clear disvalue, and that nature therefore deserves our protection, surely involves a version of this idea.

This is particularly the case for any sort of "deep" environmental theory characterized by a fundamental commitment to antianthropocentrism. For if the moral value of an action is *not* to be determined anthropocentrically (not by the consequences of that action for human beings, not by its implications regarding the character of the human actor who performs it, not by the possibility of willing its universalization over all human actors, etc.), then there needs to be some external, nonhuman standard by which the determination is to be made. And the obvious candidate for that standard is nature. Whether it be the consequences for individual natural entities that are considered or for species or for ecosystemic functioning or for "biodiversity" or simply for nature as a whole, antianthropocentric environmental thinking hopes to be able to answer the normative question by appealing to nature instead of to human beings. But an environmental philosophy that has given up on the appeal to nature would seem to have no options left except to return to humans as a normative standard, and thus apparently to give up its antianthropocentrism as well.

I will return below to the question of what options are available to a postnaturalist environmental theory in terms of its normative foundations, and to whether and in what sense such a theory might be appropriately called an anthropocentric one. But at this point it is worth noting simply that the attempt to use nature as a normative standard faces some pretty serious difficulties. For beyond the problems with defining nature or with dealing with the fact of its apparent (and perhaps long-standing) demise that we have already considered, the problems that both Hume and Moore (and in his own way Mill as well) point out with such an attempt remain a significant obstacle. *Ought* cannot be derived from *is*; a descriptive account of a state of affairs tells us nothing about the value of that state; evaluative terms like good and bad and right and wrong function in accordance with a different grammar than do the sorts of terms with which we describe the characteristics of nature. Any catalog of the difficulties posed by the concept of nature for a philosophically coherent environmental theory must surely include the *naturalistic fallacy* as among the most acute ones.

This is so particularly in a Darwinian (and one might also say a post-metaphysical) context, where appeals to final causes in nature seem dubious at best. Nature has no goals, or even in the strict sense any tendencies: its apparent directionality is an illusion, the consequence of prior processes of adaptation and evolution. Thus nothing of a normative character can justifiably be said to follow from descriptions of Nature's current structure—and, for the reasons I have been outlining, such descriptions in any case cannot without begging all the questions involved exclude descriptions of phenomena such as urbanization, pollution, global warming, massive increases in human population and extinction of other species, and so forth. These latter too must be part of a description of what Nature *is*; to leave them out of that description is to begin with a set of presuppositions about what Nature *ought to be* (hidden as presuppositions about what Nature is *really* or *authentically* or *in essence*). And if it is nature in the narrower sense, as the nonhuman, that is meant, then even this choice of meaning itself, as I have been arguing, involves a set of significant normative presuppositions and can scarcely then be used to ground any normative claims. The worry that the elimination of the concept of nature from environmental theory would rob that theory of its central normative standard is therefore deeply misplaced; rather, the worry ought to be that the *employment* of that concept serves as a constant temptation to find a normative significance in it that it is unable actually to bear. That dropping the concept altogether might help avoid that temptation is thus yet another reason why it might be the right strategy for environmental philosophy to take on.

As many have noted, the concept of nature has been used historically to defend much that has been reactionary and oppressive. The notion that some people are naturally slaves, that women are naturally different from and intellectually and morally inferior to men (because women's bodies reveal them to be "closer to nature"), that homosexuality is sinful because it involves "unnatural" acts—the examples are many, and should give pause to anyone who wants to find in nature a normative standard for human action while remaining committed to modern ideas of human equality, liberty, and dignity. Is the problem with these notions that "nature" has been misunderstood, that, rightly grasped, its standard points in a different direction? Or is it not that nature in fact provides us with no answers about how humans ought to act and ought to be treated, because all it can tell us is what happens in the world and not what *should* happen, or what a human life *should* be? When nature is used as a standard the danger always is that what we think we have learned from nature may really be what we ourselves have already presupposed, and so the standard we claim to find there is merely an expression of our own social context and our own social prejudices claiming for themselves the authority of the "natural" and therefore not to be questioned. This last danger, I think, would be reason enough to try to develop an environmental philosophy without appeals to nature, or Nature.

Can we learn to think the end of nature *without nostalgia*?[64] McKibben's book is drenched in nostalgia and regret, and these seem to be the guiding emotions behind so many appeals to nature and the importance of its protection. And yet, as I have suggested, if the end of nature is something that has already happened, such nostalgia seems to stand as an obstacle in the way of serious thinking and serious choices about environmental questions today. Even more clearly, if the end of nature turns out to be something that happened long ago—so long ago that we cannot even fix the date, so that it might be more correct to say that it has always already happened—then nostalgia seems even less appropriate. Whether the end of nature is a product of the human condition or only a product of the condition of modernity is not so important; in either case we might prefer an environmental theory that begins with where (and who) we are, begins, that, is by accepting our condition and trying critically to understand and to improve it, rather than one that pines nostalgically for an Edenic age that it knows all too well can never be recaptured.

There is no nature: can we acknowledge this and indeed assert it confidently without succumbing to the temptation to bemoan it, and—more important—can we do so without thereby having to give up the goal of developing an environmental philosophy that remains true to the our strongest intuitions about the terrible dangers to us and to the world we inhabit that present-day technological practices so obviously pose? Within the "fallen" world described by McKibben, the world where nature has ended because every inch of it has already been transformed by the acts of human beings, can we nonetheless continue to make moral distinctions between those sorts of transformative acts that are justifiable and those that are not? Can we find a normative standard for those distinctions, and more specifically can we speak of ethical obligations toward the environment even after we have admitted that that environment is no longer (and maybe never was) a "natural" one, or after we concede that terms like "natural" or "unnatural" are useless under present conditions, more trouble indeed than they are worth? Can we develop an environmental ethic, and an environmental philosophy, that take the environment (a word that simply means "what surrounds us") to be the built one we actually inhabit, and no longer concern themselves with "nature" at all?

What I have been calling an environmental philosophy after the end of nature seems to me not only possible but also necessary. Without it, environmental theory will remain stuck—on the one hand in a series of antinomies stemming from the conceptual ambiguities about what nature is, and on the other in the impotence of a romantic nostalgia for a lost and possibly imaginary world beyond the world of human action in which we actually live. To show the value of the sort of postnaturalist environmental philosophy I have in mind, though, I need to show both that there are still questions of environmental significance to be raised at a philosophical level about the built or "unnatural" environment we inhabit and that without the appeal to nature, a normative standard can still be found that can help answer those questions. Environmental philosophy cannot separate itself from environmental critique, but for critique to be possible, something like a normative foundation for that critique and for its justification—and for that matter also for the attempt to offer positive solutions to the problems, and to show why they are positive—must be available.

The first of these tasks, showing that environmental problems still arise *after nature* (or that they even only truly arise then), I have begun to undertake in this chapter. That they do still arise might even be said to be obvious, as any glance at the newspaper will reveal: the problems of pollution and toxic waste and water shortages and global warming and resource depletion that we face today are all problems that arise *here*, in the human, "non-natural" world. They are problems of the built environment. The second task, however, requires more investigation, and is the focus of the next chapters. In the course of this investigation it will become clear that the appeal to nature turns out not merely to be unhelpful for environmental thinking but may in itself be harmful to that thinking. I will argue that the view of nature as something that needs to be protected because of its independence from human beings may itself be a central part of the environmental problem we face today. The conceptual framework out of which that view arises, I suggest, is at some deep level the culprit in the contemporary crises of the environment, and not at all the direction in which we ought to look for a solution to those crises. In that sense, an environmental philosophy after the end of nature is more than just a conceptual corrective to the older forms of environmental thinking. By offering what might be called a "critique of nature," I will try to argue, such a philosophy may in fact show those older forms to be associated with a worldview and a social order that are themselves complicit in the environmental horrors of today and of the future; and in so doing, it might provide the opportunity for a deeper understanding of the relation between humans and the world they inhabit that could serve as an alternative to that worldview, and could perhaps also offer a model for imagining a new and different social order where those horrors would not come to pass.

2

The Social Construction of Nature

On the Very Idea of a Social Construction

The idea that nature is a "social construction" has been the subject of much controversy in environmental philosophy, and perhaps some of what I argued in the previous chapter suggests something resembling that idea. But what I have called postnaturalism in environmental thought actually stands in at best an uneasy relationship to that oft-criticized claim, which, after all, gets its shock value precisely from its use of the very concept I am suggesting we should eschew. An environmental philosophy after nature's end would not be particularly interested in whether nature is socially constructed or not, since it wouldn't be particularly interested in describing what nature *is* at all. If nature is already gone, or if we can make no coherent sense of what "nature" actually means, then it scarcely seems helpful to call it a social construct. And yet there is a sense—quite different from the standard one—in which I am indeed talking about something like the social construction of nature here. Understanding that sense, however, requires thinking in more detail not just about the tense and difficult word "nature" but also first about the (equally?) difficult word "social," and then second—and even more important—about the key word "construction."

What does the idea that nature is a social construction really mean? One of the things it has most frequently meant is (as Georg Lukács put it) that "nature is a social category": that the meaning of the word "nature" has changed over time, that what counts as natural, and the relative values placed on the natural and the artificial (or "unnatural"), have varied from society to society and from historical period to historical period (and indeed, that in certain societies that distinction doesn't even arise), that views of nature have always reflected facts about the social order in which they occur, and so forth.[1] More broadly, the claim has frequently been that the way in which we experience the natural world is always affected in profound and ineliminable ways by the social organizations and habits and mores and worldviews that structure our perception of everything that surrounds us. The "nature" experienced by modern inhabitants of a thoroughly industrialized world in this sense is different from the one that was experienced by medieval peasants in Europe, or by hunter-gatherers in Africa thousands of years in the past. If this is so, then "nature" is no single thing but rather many different things that appear in different societies at different historical periods. But then when people such as McKibben or Katz talk of "nature" as something fundamentally *separate* from the social—as something whose "independence [from the human] is its meaning," as McKibben puts it—they are being naïve: whatever we experience as nature is ipso facto *not* separate from the social or independent of the human because our experience of it is always filtered through our own social framework.

Something like this sort of argument was at work, for example, in Cronon's discussion of "wilderness" and the role it has played in American environmentalism. The point of his discussion was precisely to historicize and "socialize"—and thus also, inevitably, to relativize—the concept of wilderness: to show how the concept itself has changed over time, and thus to indicate that the value Americans have come to see in wilderness is not really something they *find* there, in a world beyond the social, but rather something that derives from the social world itself. Although "wilderness" is supposed to refer to that which exists on the other side of the frontier, the very idea that there *is* an "other" side to it, and for that matter the very idea of a frontier itself, are the products of a particular social history and structure, which is to say (paradoxically enough) that its provenance lies on *this* side, the social one. Americans have "created wilderness in their own image," Cronon writes, adding, in criticism of those who fail to understand this, that "those who have no difficulty seeing God as the expression of our human dreams and desires nonetheless have trouble recognizing that in a secular age Nature can offer precisely the same sort of mirror."[2] Thus, while the appeal to wilderness—and more generally to nature—is intended precisely as an appeal to something that escapes history and society, in fact there is no such escape: our views of nature and of the wild cannot help but express and reflect the particular historical and social contexts in which those views are formed. Far from being something other than or beyond the human, that is, "nature" and "wilderness" are revealed on close historical examination to be concepts that are created by humans—which is to say, they are social constructions.

Yet if the thesis of social constructionism is put in this bald way, those who reject it have a perfectly good and persuasive response.[3] That *concepts* are created by human beings, and that this creation occurs in a social context and therefore has a history, is unquestionably true, they will point out, but it does not follow that the *referents* of those concepts are so created.[4] One has to be very careful to distinguish, so to speak, between "nature" and nature—between the socially constructed concept of a realm independent of the human and the social, that is, and that realm itself. The former is social and historical, but that does not mean that the latter is. That our *ideas* about nature are social and have a history is obvious, and is indeed a commonplace. But that does not make nature *itself* social, or a "construction." Similarly, while it is doubtless true that the way in which nature is experienced changes over time and is closely related to changes in social structure and worldview, this does not mean that nature itself, the thing that is experienced in different ways by different societies, changes. The *idea* of nature is socially constructed, we might say, and perhaps it is true that our experiences of nature could be said to be socially constructed as well, but that does not in any way suggest that *nature* is socially constructed. To think that it does is to make the mistake of confusing epistemological issues with ontological ones. And one could go further here, to suggest that this mistake is not an innocent one but rather is symptomatic of an anthropocentric failure to acknowledge nature's independence. The confusion of ontological with epistemological questions is characteristic of a modernist or Western reason that systematically mistakes itself for the world, unable to acknowledge the difference between its own conception of things and the things themselves. It is just this difference that the concept of nature is supposed to mark, making possible as it does an appeal to a world that is neither identical to nor mastered by the human or the social—a world that in fact escapes, necessarily, the domination by human purposes hidden within the notion of a "social construction."[5]

There is something quite persuasive about this line of argument, and it seems clearly true that a certain amount of contemporary social constructionism about nature does indeed fall into this (essentially idealist) error. (Whether that error is itself truly associated with modernism or Western reason is a separate question; I will argue later that although there is much to be criticized in the modern conception of the relation between nature and the human, its real mistake is a very different one, and even in a sense the inverse of the one it is accused of making here.) Ian Hacking's book *The Social Construction of What?* does a nice job of showing the complexities involved in the idea of a social construction, and offers a sympathetic but critical discussion of how easy and tempting—but wrong—it is to mistake claims that *our experience* of X is socially determined or historically variable, or that *our concept* of it is, for the (typically much stronger, and in any case clearly different) claim that X *itself* is a social construction.[6]

Hacking's discussion helps us think more clearly about social constructionist arguments in general, not only about nature. He points out that social constructionist claims are often motivated by a critical or "unmasking" impulse, oriented toward questioning some element of the status quo. The general form of the claim that an entity X is socially constructed, Hacking argues, seems to have as its precondition that X's existence is typically taken for granted as obvious, unquestionable, and eternal. That X exists—indeed, that it must exist and has always existed—is simply assumed to be an inescapable fact of the world. The social constructionist then adduces evidence to show that this assumption is false: X's existence is the result of particular social processes that occurred (or continue to occur) at a certain historical moment in a certain social context, and without those processes X either would not exist at all or would exist in an entirely different form. Its existence, as Hacking puts it, is thus "not determined by the nature of things."[7]

The point of social constructionist arguments, in other words, is a debunking one: they aim to show that that which appears to be a necessary fact of the world actually has a contingent social and historical origin. Thus to say that something is socially constructed, in this unmasking or debunking sense of the term, is to say that it is not something we found in the world but rather something we have put there—something we have "constructed." What is unmasked by this sort of argument is precisely the hidden processes of production—of social "construction"—through which the thing has come to be, processes that we had apparently forgotten in our too quick assumption that the thing was simply given, an unquestionable part of the universe's furniture. Once such an unmasking has taken place, we can recognize, further, the contingency of the object that we at first mistakenly took to be necessary and eternal: having discovered that it was constructed under certain specific historical and social conditions, we realize that under other conditions it might have been constructed differently, or might never have been constructed at all. And this in turn raises the question of its value, for if a world without X might have been, or might still be, we can ask whether such a world would be a *better* one.

Still, this isn't quite right. To say that something is socially constructed simply means that social practices were necessary for it to come into existence. This doesn't by itself entail its contingency: perhaps all functioning societies necessarily produce some particular institution, for instance, or perhaps the evolution of human sociality inevitably moves toward some particular structure. What's really debunked by these unmasking versions of social constructionism isn't the claim for the necessity of X or even the value of X itself, but simply the assertion that X's existence owes nothing to human social doings. The unmasking social constructionist reveals this assertion to be mistaken by showing the ways in which X *is* the product of such doings, and it is precisely this mistake itself that this kind of social constructionism is concerned to criticize.

It is important to notice that to say that X has been socially constructed is not to say that it doesn't exist, or doesn't "really" exist. Often the claim that something has been socially constructed is taken to mean that it's "merely" a social construction and therefore somehow not real—as if something's being socially constructed means its existence is an illusion, or that we're deluded if we believe in it at all. But this seems confused. Something can surely be both socially constructed and perfectly real. Money is socially constructed, and so is the Electoral College, and yet to claim these things aren't real would be to misunderstand powerfully important facts about the world. That something was socially constructed suggests certain facts about how it came into existence but does not in any sense suggest that it doesn't "really" exist or has no causal efficacy. Society is perfectly real, and so are the things it constructs. And what it constructs, it is important to note, are not merely nonphysical "ideas" or "meanings." Being socially constructed and having concrete physical existence are not mutually exclusive. Physical things can surely be socially constructed: houses, for example, are physical objects, and yet they come into existence as the result of socially organized processes of construction—of literal construction, first and foremost, engaged in by carpenters and masons and so forth, but second, processes engaged in by developers and realtors and county clerks and the like as well. Similarly, there could not be money without physical objects to be exchanged—whether coins or bills or bytes on a hard drive—or an Electoral College without voting machines, written constitutions, meeting rooms, communication devices, and so on.

Is something being debunked or criticized in the assertion that houses or money or the Electoral College are socially constructed? Sure: in each case the assertion attempts to counter a kind of amnesia about the actual historical and social processes that made it possible for those objects to come into existence. In our ordinary experience of the world we tend to forget the fact that the existence and shape of the houses we inhabit are the product of complex social operations—not just of carpentry but of banking, taxation, schooling, and so forth; we forget that money is not founded in the intrinsic value of some precious metal or, for that matter, in the intrinsic value of the objects it can buy but rather arises out of the socially organized productive activities in which human beings engage, and in particular out of a particular form of organization those activities can take; we forget that the Electoral College was originally developed to prevent direct democratic election of the president, and more generally we forget that constitutions are pieces of paper and that obedience to their requirements is something that has to be reproduced daily by the acts of each citizen. By reminding us of these social processes, and thus of our own complicity in the creation of these institutions and objects, the claim that they are socially constructed in turn might lead us to question them, by coming to realize that they could be constructed *differently*.

But where is nature in all this, and what might the "social construction of nature" mean? One way to start to think about this is to consider what it would mean for something *not* to be socially constructed—to think, that is, about the contrast term. The socially constructed, I have suggested, can be perfectly real, and perfectly physical; I have also noted that it can also, at least in principle, be perfectly necessary or inevitable. What it cannot be, though, is *natural*, at least not in what I have called the second, lowercase meaning of the term. When social constructionism unmasks something whose existence has been claimed to be an obvious and eternal fact of the world and reveals instead the social processes through which that thing has come into being, what it denies above all is the claim to *naturalness* of the thing. The processes that built it, such a constructionism insists, are social ones, meaning human beings were involved in them, and so they are not natural processes at all. This is the real structure of what I have called the debunking form of social constructionism: it is concerned to show that that which appears to be natural actually isn't. To say that X is socially constructed, that is, is precisely to say that it is "not determined by the nature of things," as Hacking says, but rather by a set of social processes. Thus the very idea of social constructionism seems to involve the assumption of a distinction between that which is natural and that which has been produced by social forces; its goal is to unmask institutions and phenomena that misleadingly appear to belong on one side of that distinction and to show that in truth, they belong on the other one. The point thus isn't that socially constructed things aren't real, it's that they aren't *natural*. To criticize something for being a social construction is to criticize it for appearing to be natural (and therefore eternal, inevitable, obvious) when it really isn't.

We are back, in a word, at the question of nature. The very notion of social construction seems to depend, both for its structure and for its critical force, on the notion of nature—and more particularly on the very dualism between the natural and the human to which I objected in the previous chapter. Indeed, it seems as though the critical strategy of what I have called the debunking form of social constructionism might turn out to be entangled in precisely the sorts of categories that I suggested environmental philosophy would be better off dropping entirely. If showing something to be socially constructed means showing it not to be natural, and if "nature" as a concept is something we ought to try to do without, then social constructionism would seem to be a bad idea in general—not simply the notion of the social construction of *nature* but the very idea of a "social construction" as such might need to be given up. But there is more to be said here, I think, and perhaps more value to be found for environmental thinking in the idea of a socially constructed nature than might at first seem to be the case. A little more analysis is needed.

The first thing to note is that if debunking social constructionism about X takes the form of arguing that X is not natural but rather has been socially produced, then social constructionism about *nature* would take a form that is quite radical, if not indeed so paradoxical as to be incoherent. For it would mean that *nature itself isn't natural* but is rather socially produced; and of course, the moment such a thing is said, the distinction between the natural and the social seems to disappear. For McKibben and Katz the problem would look like a matter of self-contradiction: "nature" *means* that which exists independently of social processes, and so if some X is successfully shown to be socially constructed, then by definition that X cannot be nature. The idea of a socially constructed nature for them would be simply impossible, and this point would be a conceptual one, not the result of a difference of opinion about empirical matters. Nature can't be socially constructed, because the natural and the socially constructed are mutually exclusive and opposing categories.

To unmask something as socially constructed, which is to say as produced by people, as having an origin in history, as contingent, and so forth, seems to require assuming the existence of something that is *not* so constructed, *not* produced by people, *without* a historical origin, *not* contingent—something whose obviousness and permanence *cannot* be unmasked because it really possesses those characters—and that, of course, is nature. Thus the very possibility of a debunking social constructionism apparently depends on the assumption that something like nature exists as the antipode of the social. That nature is not itself socially constructed, then, seems to be a necessary presupposition of the debunking use of the concept. On the other hand, we could turn this argument around, if the considerations I raised in the previous chapter are correct, and suggest that precisely because the notion of a socially constructed nature, or for that matter a socially constructed *anything,* requires this sort of presupposition, we need to give up the notion of social construction just as much as we need to give up the notion of nature, since the former no less than the latter presupposes the dualism we should be trying to overcome. The very idea of a social construction involves us in the use of categories that do not stand up to conceptual analysis.

Yet this isn't quite right: one can, I think, employ the notion of social construction, even in a debunking sense, without assuming a distinction between the natural and the social and hence committing oneself to the sort of conception of nature that I criticized in the previous chapter. One can argue in a witch trial (to choose an admittedly odd example) that such-and-such a person is not a witch—has never showed herself to have paranormal powers, has never bewitched anyone, and so on—without thereby committing oneself to the claim that some people *are* witches. One might instead believe, say, that no witches exist, that no one has paranormal powers, that the category of "bewitchment" refers to no real process, and so on, and therefore be prepared to argue, about any particular individual accused of witchcraft, that that individual too is no witch. Similarly, if claims about the social construction of X are interpreted as meaning that X is not a "natural fact of the world," it doesn't seem that making them commits one to the assertion that some things *are* natural facts of the world: the claim about X might just be a special case of a more general claim, namely that there are *no* such facts. Everything, one might say, is socially constructed, and so X is, too.

This last might seem too strong, not least because we have offered no analysis yet of what the social is. But it could provide a clue as to what the social construction of nature might mean. Rather than interpreting this idea simply as yet another debunking form of social constructionism—which on the one hand produces the paradox of asserting that nature isn't natural, while on the other hand seems to commit one to the sort of dualism between the natural and the human that I have argued environmental philosophy needs to abandon—we might instead interpret it as something much broader and more radical. To say that nature is socially constructed would then be not to debunk yet another particular entity, simply adding it to Hacking's list of the sorts of X's that social constructionists have shown to be "social" and not "natural," but rather to debunk the very dualism between the social and the natural *itself*. The "social construction of nature" might then be the shorthand name for a program raising questions not about whether this or that entity is natural or social but instead about the very idea of this opposition as such, and whether it bears up to any conceptual scrutiny at all. In that sense it might turn out to be the same as what I called, in chapter 1, postnaturalism. Applied to environmental issues, then, it would itself be part of an *environmental philosophy after the end of nature*. Its goal would be to show that the distinction between that which exists independently of human beings and that which is the product of human beings is not a tenable one, not because there is nothing beyond human beings but because the very notion of independence here needs to be reconsidered. "Independent of us" and "produced by us" are not mutually exclusive categories; our products *are* independent of us, on the one hand, while on the other, there is nothing in our environment that we have not, in some sense or other, had a hand in producing. Understanding this last point, however, requires thinking more carefully about what "construction" means.

Construction as a Physical Process

"After the end of nature," of course, there might be other reasons why the notion that nature could be socially constructed would turn out to be questionable. The problem wouldn't be that the very idea makes no sense but rather that it makes no sense *any more:* how could nature be socially constructed if it no longer exists? If McKibben is right—and I have suggested there is a serious sense in which he is—there's simply no nature left either to be socially constructed or not, and so the very debate about whether it has been constructed looks silly. For McKibben, we might say, the most pressing problem for environmental thinking to consider is the social *de*struction of nature, not its social *con*struction.[8] Our actions to transform the environment do not construct nature so much as they threaten to end it. McKibben, further, is not concerned with something like a mental change, or a transformation in our "experience" of nature, or a "paradigm shift," or something like that: the end of nature that worries him is the result of real physical acts, the ones that have increased the carbon dioxide in the atmosphere, torn a hole in the ozone layer, and so forth.[9] Human beings effect a change in the world when they transform it through their physical actions, which is to say through their socially organized practices, and this change for McKibben is an *ontological* one: the objects so transformed move from being part of nature to part of the human realm, and the realm of the natural accordingly shrinks. Ultimately, as technology becomes global in its effects, the latter realm dwindles away to nothing. Nature, we could say, has been socially destroyed.

But notice also that as the natural realm shrinks, the human one grows. The destruction of one thing is always at the same time the construction of something else. If nature is being socially destroyed by modern industry and technology, as McKibben says, this must be because something is at the same time being socially constructed—a postnatural world in which everything we encounter turns out to be the consequence, one way or another, of human action. What is really socially constructed, one might want to say, is precisely the familiar urbanized humanized environment that most of us inhabit. And here the word "construction" is being used in a very literal sense, referring to the actual physical (and socially organized) processes of construction and transformation that human beings engage in and through which their day-to-day environment comes to have the shape it does. What *is* socially constructed, that is to say, explicitly and uncontroversially, is the built environment: that's what it means, obviously, to say that it's built. (And the prime example of a socially constructed object would then be something like a house, rather than money or the Electoral College. For that a house has been socially constructed is, once one stops and thinks about it, obvious: people built it, and did so socially.) And then, since McKibben is surely right, and the "environment" we inhabit today simply is, overwhelmingly, a built one, it follows that it might make the most sense if we spoke about not the social construction of *nature* but rather the social construction of the *environment* (by which term we will now mean the actual postnatural world we inhabit). The interest of a postnaturalist environmental philosophy in "social constructionism" would then mean this: an interest in the social processes through which the actual environment we currently inhabit—which is above all a built one—came to be built (constructed). Such a philosophy would thus be concerned not with the social construction of something like nature but rather with social construction *as such:* the construction of the built environment. It would be especially concerned, further—in accord with the debunking motivation typical of social constructionism—with unmasking the ways in which the built environment comes to seem as though it were *not* built, as though it were a natural environment whose status as the product of human transformative practices has been forgotten or otherwise occluded. Thus it will be key to such a view that "nature" and "environment" are not taken as synonymous: "environment" simply means "that which environs us," and what I have been arguing (and as McKibben and others have pointed out as well, though with more dismay than I think is warranted) is that what environs us isn't nature at all but rather a world that human action has helped build.[10] Environmental philosophy should be about *that*, about the built world that we actually inhabit and that actually environs us, and not about the chimera called "nature."

But if our focus is then on the social processes through which human beings construct the built environment they inhabit, the first thing to notice is that such processes are much older, and much broader in scope, than the technological ones that have constructed the particular modern urbanized environment most people inhabit today. I noted in chapter 1 that McKibben's "end of nature" might have happened much earlier than he acknowledges, so that even the "wilderness" of 1492 turns out not to have been so wild but rather already to have exhibited the consequences of earlier human transformative practices. The landscape encountered by the first European settlers in that sense was already a built environment, if by that term we mean an environment that human actions played a role in producing (or constructing). Indeed, one might argue that the environments human beings inhabit are *all* built ones: building an environment, which is to say transforming the world around them through their practices, is what human beings do ("by nature," so to speak). And they do it socially: the transformative practices through which humans construct the environments they inhabit are themselves socially organized ones, by which I mean that they are normatively and intersubjectively structured. If this is so, then the social constructionism of a postnaturalist environmental philosophy would mean above all an examination of the ways in which human beings transform their surroundings and thereby build the environments they inhabit.

The point I'm making here might help to clarify why the dualism between nature and the human discussed in chapter 1 turns out to be so problematic. Positing nature as something separate and ontologically distinct from the human makes no sense, not merely because we human beings are ourselves natural but also because—as is true of all other natural organisms—our position in the world is fundamentally active and transformative, and so the "nature" (or rather the environment) we inhabit is always one we have already helped form. This is a key point for me. Rejecting the distinction between nature and the human is not simply a matter of noting that humans are themselves natural in the sense that nature "produces" them but, more important, of recognizing that *humans actively produce nature*, or more precisely produce *their own environment*. In saying this, I do not mean that humans are "masters of nature" and can remake the world technologically in their own image. Rather, I am merely saying something that should be an anthropological—and biological—commonplace. An organism comes to be what it is through its environment and can only be thought of coherently in that environment, but by the same token the environment of the organism too itself comes to be what it is only through the activities in which that organism engages. And this is certainly true of those remarkable organisms called human beings. To understand what humans *are* we must understand them as beings *within* an environment. What would it be, one might ask, for a human to exist *not* in an environment, outside an environment? This is the Cartesian dream—the dream that somehow humans are *not* in the world, that the world is other than them and outside of them. (For Descartes, of course, this dream becomes a nightmare.) But to be in an environment is to be active in it, and with every act in it we change it. There is nothing we do that does not change, and therefore build, the environment.[11]

This is what I mean by saying that the world surrounding us is always already something that human beings have transformed, and so has always already been socially constructed. (Further, it is always already *under construction*, as Tim Ingold points out.[12] We have not merely *already* transformed the world, we are always doing so *now*. As I write this text, the bytes in my computer change; as you read it you turn the pages or scroll down on the screen; we both exhale, and thereby change the carbon dioxide concentration in the air around us; furthermore, we likely both use electricity and thus depend on large transformative processes taking place at far distances from where we sit. With all these acts we change the world, and thereby construct—socially—the environment we inhabit.) The world is not something we *find* ourselves in; it is something we have helped to *make*. But at the same time it is something that helps to make *us*: we are who we are because of the environment that we inhabit. The environment is socially constructed; society is environmentally constructed. Humanity and the environment cannot be separated from each other—a conclusion that does *not* mean that we are masters of the world, or that it masters us either, but rather that "world" and "we" are so deeply interconnected that there is no way to tell where one leaves off and the other begins. All this is what I meant, in the previous chapter, by proposing that the "end of nature" might not be something that occurred so recently as McKibben suggests, or even something that occurred within any sort of historical or even anthropological memory, but rather that it might turn out to be something that has *always already happened*. If nature means a world independent of human action, then the end of nature might have taken place already, as soon as those world-changers called humans, whose nature it might be to change—yes, to end!—nature, appeared on the scene.

Knowledge and Construction

The anthropological point I have been making is at the same time an epistemological one. To be a human being, I have suggested, is to be in an environment (a Heideggerian might be inclined to write: in-an-environment), and to be in an environment is to be *active* in it. The human condition is fundamentally an active and world-changing one: all we do is act, and to act is to change the world. But one of the things we do in the world is to know it, and so (if I am right) knowledge too must be understood as an active process: we come to know the world only through transforming it. In this section I want to examine the idea of knowledge as active and show its significance for the notion of an environmental philosophy after the end of nature. The difficulties about nature we have been tracing, I will suggest, bear instructive similarities to a set of traditional difficulties in the history of epistemology.

Kant, of course, is the key figure in the history of philosophy who emphasizes something like an activist account of knowledge in his response to the dilemmas engendered by empiricism. The empiricist model of knowledge according to which a receptive knower passively takes in information from an external world that (actively) produces that information, Kant saw, led inevitably to insoluble problems of skepticism. His insight was that for knowledge to be possible at all, the knower had to be *actively* involved in "constituting" the object of knowledge: only in this way, he realized, could the knower be certain that the object was truly grasped.

The story is a familiar one, but it is worth telling again, because so many of its themes are directly relevant to the problems involving the concept of nature that I have been outlining. The empiricist conception of knowledge, found in Locke and Berkeley and Hume—and for that matter, going back in its essence to Descartes—involves a knower confronted with an external world of objects and trying to come to know them. "Knowing" here means "having a correct representation of" in the knower's mind—or, since the knower is identified with the mental (the subjective) and not the physical, simply in the knower. Information about the objects in the world comes in to the knower through various sense organs, with the sense of sight serving as the paradigm. The knower's task is to receive this information as it is, and then to develop an internal representation of the world of objects that is homologous to ("corresponds to," "accurately represents") that world. The content of the representation, if knowledge is to be achieved, must be entirely the product of the objective world; anything originating from the knower herself is denigrated as "subjective" and does not count as knowledge. Locke's version of this conception involves the key distinction between primary qualities, representations in the mind that directly resemble the real characteristics of the object, and secondary ones, representations that resemble nothing in the object and hence are irreducibly subjective. True knowledge of an object thus consists in knowledge of its primary qualities, which is to say it is knowledge from which reference to secondary qualities has been removed. To know something is to know it as it (objectively) is, not as the knower wishes or fears or imagines it to be. Knowledge must be *objective* knowledge, knowledge of the object itself—a knowledge from which any admixture of the subjective has been removed.

The knower here is conceived of as essentially distinct from the world. Subject and object are ontologically separated from each other. The knower sees (or otherwise senses) the world of objects, but is not herself—insofar as she is a knower, anyway—an object in it: rather, it is laid out as it were in front of her, as something she observes.[13] She receives information from it, and does so passively: to *act* so as to transform the information would be to illegitimately contaminate it by tainting it with subjectivity. Anything the knower *does* to the information, that is, destroys it, changing it from true knowledge to mere subjectivity. This model of knowledge thus begins by assuming that objects and subjects are distinct, and then insists that knowledge must protect that distinction. Any blurring of the distinction, any injection of something from the subjective side into the intended representation of objectivity, appears in this account as inimical to the possibility of knowledge.

The model of knowledge involved here, I would like to suggest, mirrors—or does it depend on? or does it underlie?—the conception of nature and its relation to the human examined in the previous chapter. Just as subjects and objects are ontologically distinct in this model, so too we saw humans and nature there as distinct, and humans as fundamentally "unnatural," outside nature. Just as human action was seen there to be something that ended nature, that turned natural landscapes or wildernesses into something artificial and unnatural, so too here the insertion of subjectivity into a representation of the world transforms that representation from knowledge to error. Human activity, in both accounts, appears as destructive: the right approach to nature (on the one hand) and to the goal of achieving knowledge (on the other) appears in each as a passive one. Knowledge involves receiving information from the world and letting that information arrive exactly as it is, without transforming it (or forming it). So too, in the model we saw above, environmental virtue consists in "letting nature be," in protecting wilderness against human transformative acts, in preserving nature's independence.

We have seen the difficulties and antinomies such a view of nature and of our place within it leads to. The "nature" that it wants to defend (and whose existence it simply assumes) turns out to be remarkably difficult to find, not least because wherever *we* go, *it* is not, and so the problem of how we could ever find or otherwise encounter it seems intrinsically insoluble.[14] And similar antinomies, interestingly, arise for the empiricist account of knowledge. If knowledge of the world consists in nothing other than what our senses report about it, and if we are prohibited—on pain of the dreaded introduction of "subjectivity"—from *doing* anything to or with those sense-reports, then sense-reports turn out to be all that we can know. In particular, we have no warrant for concluding from the reports anything about the existence of a world beyond or behind them. The sensory experience the knower has of an object, it turns out, itself forms the outer limit of what the knower can know about that object. But that means the object *itself*, the self-identical and independent thing being experienced, which by definition stands outside that outer limit, can never itself be known. But then even our assumption that there *is* such an object whose qualities (whether primary or secondary) we are experiencing turns out to be unjustified. The substance that underlies the experienced properties, Locke famously (and tremulously) concludes, is "something, I know not what": a mysterious X that somehow gives rise to our experiences but cannot itself be known (since it is by definition unexperienced).[15] If nature is defined by its independence from the human, we saw in chapter 1, then we never live in it (it can never form part of *our* environment), and so the idea of living in accordance or consonance with it makes no sense. Locke's situation is the epistemological version of the same problem: if material substance is something that underlies our experience, it can never itself be experienced, and so there is no way it could ever be known, or even be known to exist.

Berkeley famously bites the bullet here. The idea of a material substance that is not itself experienced, he says, is simply nonsensical: to be is to be perceived. There is no object behind or beyond or underneath sense-experience; all there are are the experiences, and their unity is not a unity in some sort of mind-independent substance but rather precisely a unity *in a mind*. His position has the advantage of being more rigorously consistent with basic empiricist assumptions than Locke's is, but it has the corresponding disadvantage of having moved considerably further away from common sense. Empiricism thought it was eschewing metaphysical speculation and sticking close to a common sense that would both avoid Cartesian skepticism and make it possible to ground knowledge in straightforward observation. But taken to its logical conclusion, as Berkeley shows, it ends by rendering our knowledge of those truths we (prephilosophically) thought were most unquestionable—for example, that objects exist when unperceived by any knower—in fact deeply problematic.

Berkeley's view is perhaps analogous, in environmental philosophy, to a kind of caricature of social constructionism (one that I am not sure any actual social constructionist ever held) that identifies "nature" in a naively idealist fashion with whatever human beings believe it to be at a given moment.[16] His mistake is that, faced with the conflict between the empiricist model of knowledge, on the one hand, and our strong sense that objects exist unperceived on the other, he gives up the latter rather than the former, not recognizing that it might be that model itself that is at fault here. Hume sees the problem more clearly, though he does not see a solution—and sees, too, that the difficulty goes deeper than Berkeley realized, and is worse. For it is not only the unity *in the object* of the experiences we have of it that the empiricist model renders impossible, their unity *in the mind* of the experiencer is just as endangered. To assert the existence of a material substance in which the experienced qualities of the object inhere is to make an unjustified inference from those experienced qualities; but the same thing is true of the assertion of a "spiritual" substance—a mind—in which those qualities are experienced. Thus, just as my experience of an object is not sufficient to give me knowledge of that object as it is independent of experience, so by the same token it is not even sufficient to call that experience mine: if the empiricist model is correct, then all it is possible to have knowledge of (and whose knowledge is it?) are the experiences *themselves*—neither the objects supposed to be producing the experiences nor the subjects supposed to be experiencing them turn out to be knowable.[17]

No longer knowable as unified in an object or a subject, the experiences are left, as it were, floating freely. They cannot even be known as cohering with each other, or indeed as being collectively structured at all, Hume realizes: even the notion that one event or experience *causes* another turns out to depend on the illegitimate imposition of the putative knower's subjective expectation upon the data provided by experience. Nothing in experience, Hume notoriously argues, shows the connection between one experience and another to be a *necessary* one; indeed, necessity of this sort is no more something itself experienced than is "substance" or "self." And so our sense that events in the world are causally connected one to another turns out not to be something we discover in the world but rather something like a construction we put on the world—and since for the empiricist model knowledge must be passive, and that which is subjectively imposed can never count as knowledge, it follows that no knowledge of the world's causal structure (or that it has one!) is possible at all. Thus is "common sense" laid low: the empiricist attempt to develop an account of knowledge that leaves out anything of the subjective ends up making it impossible to know anything about a world of objects, a world of selves, or a world in which causal relations play any role. Not only physical science and psychology but any sort of standard realism at all turns out to be impossible.

It was Kant who saw the way out of the problem here, and saw that it consisted precisely in giving up the model of the knower as a passive receiver of information. Knowledge, Kant realized, had to be understood as *active*. The subject does not receive knowledge but rather constructs it, by actively forming the inchoate material furnished by sensation into the structured and meaningful unities that make up the world we do in fact inhabit: a world of objects, of selves, and of causal relations. Far from representing the introduction of an illegitimate subjectivity into knowledge, such formative activity is what makes possible objectivity as such. The history of empiricism serves as a kind of reductio ad absurdum of the passive model of knowledge: if *that's* what knowledge is, then knowledge by a subject of a causally structured objective world is impossible. Yet knowledge by a subject of such a world *is* possible, as the very fact that we live in such a world and know lots of things about it proves. And so knowledge must be active, must, that is, result from the subject's active synthesis of sensory material. This is Kant's "Copernican Revolution": just as the observed motion of the sun turns out to have its origin not in the sun itself but rather in the motion of those who observe it, so too the structured and causal character of the world we experience has its origin not in a realm independent of us that we passively observe but rather *in us*, the subjects who experience it. It is structured because *we* structure it, not because it comes to us prestructured in itself.

The world we experience, whose structure we do not find but rather make, is what Kant calls the phenomenal world, counterposing it to the noumenal world of things-in-themselves—a world, that is, that we have not structured but that is rather the source of the sensory material on which our formative or structuring activity works. About things-in-themselves, Kant says—returning to something like Locke's formulation—there is nothing that can be said; since knowledge requires a knower's activity, and since things in themselves are not formed through such activity, it follows that they cannot be known. It doesn't take much reflection about this doctrine to suggest the question as to why, then, they need to be posited at all, or rather how this positing could ever itself count as knowledge. The noumenal realm functions quite like the notion of wilderness, or perhaps the notion of nature itself, in much environmental thought—as that which somehow underlies the built (phenomenal) landscapes we actually inhabit, but which despite our best efforts we can never actually attain. The more we insist that something like noumena, or like wilderness, *must* exist, the harder it seems to actually find it, and the more (eventually) one starts to wonder why proving the existence of something so fundamentally—indeed, definitionally—unknowable ever came to seem so important. Isn't our knowledge inevitably about the *phenomenal* world? Don't environmental issues arise in *humanized* environments? Again, the epistemological issues here are directly analogous to the ones faced in the previous chapter.

Hegel's critique of Kant faults the latter for the unnecessary and indeed incoherent appeal to a noumenal realm "behind" the one we actually inhabit. The world we live in *is* the real world; there is neither any need for nor any advantage in contrasting it to some other unknowable world that would somehow exceed it in reality, or in describing the one we inhabit as "merely" the phenomenal world of appearances. The key Kantian idea is not the distinction between noumena and phenomena but rather the idea of knowledge as an active process, through which the object of knowledge comes to be constructed or "constituted." Yet this notion of constitution remains a pretty mysterious one. How exactly does it take place? What specifically does it consist in? Hegel took an important step by *historicizing* and *socializing* the process of constitution. The processes through which subjects come actively to know the world are historical processes: they change over time, and with them the world these subjects come to know changes as well. And these processes, crucially, are social ones: knowledge is not merely a matter of a solitary knower somehow magically constituting a world but rather is marked essentially by *intersubjectivity*. We come to know the world *together*. The empiricist model of a solitary knower passively receiving information from the world is thus doubly mistaken: not only is knowledge not passive, it is also not something that happens in isolation from others. We have to learn how to know, have to learn (one might say) how to constitute a world—and we do so from each other, in a social context.

Yet even in Hegel's version, the process by which we knowers come to constitute the world remains obscure. Both Kant and Hegel are still prisoners of a set of assumptions that go back to Descartes, whereby "knowing" is something done with the "mind" and the subject or knower *is* a mind. Under such assumptions the "active constitution" of the world is hard to grasp as anything other than some magical process through which a disembodied spirit somehow imposes structure on a world still conceived of as outside it. The activity involved is mental activity, and the conception projected is an idealist one. But if the dualist/Cartesian assumption is dropped, and the subject is understood to be a real human being living in a real world, a physical organism inhabiting a real environment and active within it, the mystery (and the idealism) begin to dissipate. The early philosophical work of Marx plays an important role in this story; he can be understood as one of the first to see that the process of constitution should be understood as a matter of concrete physical *practice*. "All mysteries which mislead theory to mysticism," he wrote, "find their rational solution in human practice and in the comprehension of this practice."[18] This is the basis for the centrality of the concept of labor for Marx: its moral and political significance derives ultimately from its epistemological significance. Labor—or "practice"—plays for him the same role that the mysterious process of world-constitution played for Kant and Hegel.[19] To say that we can come to know the world only insofar as we constitute it—which is to say, only insofar as we prestructure it—is to say that we know it because we *build* it, through the actual processes of labor, of physical acting and making, that are fundamental to who we are. It is only to the extent that we are actively involved in transforming the world that it can come to be known by us.[20]

But of course, to say this requires rethinking what is meant by knowledge. No longer a relation between subjective mind and objective world that somehow just occurs, knowledge itself now appears rather as a form of *activity*, as a way in which an organism gets around in the world it (necessarily, and always already) inhabits. Marx—whose central interests, of course, lay in different directions, and who mistakenly rejected philosophy itself as irremediably marked by idealist "mysticism"—never developed this idea fully, and provides only hints of what a materialist, practice-based version of Kantian and Hegelian epistemology might look like. An alternative approach, coming out of a tradition with much less of a direct connection to classical German idealism, appeared in the twentieth century in the work of Heidegger, and might help here to elucidate the concept of practice and its relation to knowledge further. Heidegger rejects the dualist conception of the subject as standing outside the world, first coming to know it and only afterward deciding how to act in it.[21] Instead, for Heidegger being human has to be understood as being-in-the-world: I am *always already* in a world, always already active in it, and so am always already practically involved. I do not begin as some sort of disembodied and unworldly mind who then finds itself confronted by a world; to be me *is* to be actively at work in the world, busily concerned with it. My concernful involvement in the world is thus prior to any conceptual or representational "knowledge" of it; indeed, that sort of knowledge itself requires and depends on my previous involvement. Knowledge does not precede practical engagement with the world but rather is conditioned and made possible by it. Heidegger calls knowledge a "founded" mode of being-in-the-world, meaning that its possibility rests on (and can neither precede nor even be independent of) our ordinary modes of practical involvement.[22]

Indeed, what empiricism traditionally saw as "knowledge" requires a *stepping back* from that involvement; Heidegger describes it as a "just-tarrying-alongside [*Nur-noch-verweilen*]" the objects with which one had previously been engaged. "Knowing" something in this sense is not preparatory to acting on it but rather involves a fundamental modification of the way one had previously been actively engaged with it.[23] Typically this modification arises when one's ordinary mode of practice fails—when the car won't start or the printer won't work, say. The concernful involvement with those objects one had been engaged with—one's concern with getting to work on time, or with making a copy of the assignment—had involved what could almost be called a blindness to the objects involved, although Heidegger interestingly describes it as "circumspection," not blindness but a different kind of sight. But when the practice fails, suddenly the circumspection shifts into a mode of direct examination: one ceases to engage in the practice one was involved in and instead changes over into a new one, searchingly examining the broken object and attempting to determine where the problem lies. Now one is concerned not with the job or the homework but rather with the object itself: one wants to *know* it, to understand how it works and how it can be fixed. Once the problem is solved, of course—the starter turns over, the paper jam is removed—one shifts back immediately to the previous mode of engagement, and the object returns to the dimness of circumspective concern.[24] Knowing thus involves holding oneself back from one's ordinary involvements, typically because something has happened to hinder or short-circuit them. But it does not require an *end* to involvement as such, as though it might attain a kind of "objective neutrality" from which all personal goals and engagements had been removed. To know something is to be involved with it in a *different way*, making it the center of one's concern—while at the same time, of course, other objects (the driver's seat one rests on as one tries to start the car, the monitor one stares at while trying to diagnose the printer problem) continue to function as "un-known," which is to say as circumspectively but not directly grasped, elements in the new practice of coming to "know" the starter or the printer. Thus to know something is still to *do* something, still involves an active engagement—is still, that is, a mode of being-in-the-world.

Heidegger by this argument recasts the passive or receptive account of knowledge that was central to the empiricist model, showing it to be an account of what he calls a deficient form of being-in-the-world. "Knowing" in the traditional sense turns out to be merely a special case of active and concernful coping—a special kind of practice, not something that "underlies" practice or is prior to it. Knowledge here again turns out to be an activity, just as it was for Kant and for Marx. The epistemological trajectory that begins by identifying the human being with the "subject" or "knower," and that takes knowledge to be the passive reception in the knower's "mind" of information from an external world, is transformed here into a recognition not only that knowledge is not passive but also that knowing is merely *one* of the forms of human active engagement in the world. The privileged role for knowledge, both within philosophy and as an account of what it is to be human, thus gives way to a broader understanding of human being as *active and concernful involvement*—an involvement to which I am giving the name of *practice*.

Kant, I am suggesting, was right to see that knowledge has to be understood as an active process, but the activity involved has to be understood as *real physical* activity—as practice, or as what Marx called labor, which in my interpretation has much in common with what Heidegger describes in his account of concernful being-in-the-world. The traditional model of knowledge as involving a passive relation between a receptive knower and an independent world, and the Kantian revision of this model that inverts the relation into an (obscurely) "active" one between an immaterial transcendental ego and a constituted phenomenal world (mysteriously resting on an unknowable noumenal base), thus *both* have to be given up. The right model is of an active bodily participant *in* the world (or: in-the-world), necessarily and always already engaged in concrete physical practices that change that world, whose knowledge of the world arises and is expressed within those practices (and whose achievement of the specifically "theoretical" knowledge examined by traditional epistemology is itself simply one of those practices). Not a disembodied mind at all—neither a passive one nor an active one—what used to be called the "subject" of knowledge is rather an *organism-in-an-environment*: and to be in-an-environment is to be in it *actively*—there is no other way to be. And here we return to the conclusions of the previous section. In its activity, the organism changes the environment, or, to put it more correctly, the environment itself *comes to be what it is through that activity:* the organism "constitutes" it, or we might say it "constructs" it. (But it is not just the environment that comes to be what it is through these practices of construction: so too does the organism itself. My practices make me who I am—teacher, parent, male, and so on—just as photosynthesis makes the plant, and web-weaving makes the spider.) There is no such thing as an organism separate from an environment, but by the same token there is no such thing as an environment that is not the environment *of* an organism: both "environment" and "organism" are relational terms. And the relation between them involves activity and change: they are both dynamic terms as well. "Constitution" is a form of practice, of activity, not a form of theory—it means *construction*.

Furthermore, if understanding knowledge requires seeing the human "subject" not as a mind but as an active participant in the world, it also, and just as crucially, requires seeing that subject not as solitary but rather as *together with others*.[25] The political version of Lockeanism had imagined isolated private individuals in a state of nature who only afterward organized themselves into a social whole. But this conception is as fraught with difficulties as Locke's related epistemological one. Both Marx and Heidegger emphasize the (Hegelian) point that the practices I engage in are always already social ones. I do not first exist as this private individual and then find other people around me; rather I have come to be the individual I am through and because of those others. Two of them made me, first of all, and they and others taught me and formed me into the person I am. The very language I speak and in which I form my conceptions of myself and of the world is one that preceded me and would not exist were it not for those many others who spoke it before me as well. The practices I engage in are social too, in the simple sense that I typically engage in them *with others*: most of my practices are cooperative ones. Even when I engage in a practice that appears to be solitary—writing these words, for example—the mark of others is not hard to find. The computer I use, the software it runs, the room in which I sit, the heat that keeps me comfortable—all these are necessary for me to engage in the practice at all, and none of them would be here and available for my circumspective concern were it not for the active practices engaged in, some at this very moment, by thousands or perhaps millions of other people. (And, of course, I am writing for others, too: you, for example.)

My practices are social, furthermore, not simply because they typically use tools that depend on the existence of others but also because being social is part of what it is for something to be a practice at all. Practices are *normatively structured:* to engage in a practice is to make implicit reference to a set of norms about how to engage in it, about what counts as engaging in it well, and what counts as engaging in it poorly or not at all. And such norms are always social norms—a normatively structured practice that is essentially solitary makes no more sense (and for exactly the same reasons) than a private language. One has to learn how to engage in a practice, and such learning requires reference to others—to teachers, often, or else at least to other practitioners whose acts serve implicitly to determine the norms involved. Just as I could not have come to be who I am without the mediation of other people, so too in particular I could not have come to engage in the practices I engage in without the mediation of others who taught me to engage in them, and without whom indeed those practices themselves would have no meaning and so would not be the practices they are. In this sense, the post-Kantian move from the idea of knowledge as requiring some sort of mysteriously transcendental act of "constitution" to the idea that humans come to know the world by acting in it requires one more crucial step: when they act in it, they do so in ways that always *involve others* (and that therefore also involve norms).

Social Construction as Practice

This digression into the history of epistemology brings us back to the question of what "social construction" means. If Kant's epistemological advance consisted in understanding knowledge as activity, I have been arguing, the next advance (represented in different ways by Marx and by Heidegger) consists in understanding that activity as *real* activity, as *practice* (and not as theory), and then furthermore in coming to understand our practices as always social and normatively structured ones. Practices are our way of coming to know the world—they are, one might say, our way of being-in-the-world. But precisely because they are real, they are also ways of *changing* the world, and of doing so socially.[26] The Kantian "constitution" of the phenomenal world here turns out to mean simply the practical physical construction of it. The world we inhabit comes to be what it is through our practices, just as we come to be who we are through them too—and through our practices we come to know the world, and ourselves, as well. Indeed, on this account, knowing the world and constructing it cannot be distinguished. And this suggests how the term "social construction" should best be understood: as referring to the active, physical, socially and normatively organized processes through which we build the environment we inhabit. Social construction, that is, should be meant *literally*: to say that X is "socially constructed" would mean that socially organized human beings have built X, through processes of labor. In this sense—which is surely not the standard one—social constructionism as a program would involve above all an examination of human practices and of the ways in which those practices transform and (in so doing) make possible knowledge of both the world we inhabit and, at the same time, ourselves. If *that* is what social constructionism means, then I am happy to accept it as a description of my view.

Such a notion of social construction shows both what is right and what is wrong with the interpretation considered earlier, whereby the "social construction of nature" referred to the socially variable and historically contingent character of our *experiences* of nature—the interpretation that easily fell prey to the response that while our experiences of nature might be variable and contingent in this sense, nature itself is not. For the previous considerations have shown what is problematic about this response, and about the conception of experience on which it depends: experience of the world is not something passive but rather is itself a transformation of the world—we cannot experience without acting, and we cannot act without changing. And so if our experiences of the world are historically variable, this means that the world-transforming practices we engage in are historically variable as well, which means that as our experience of the world changes, *the world itself* (as transformed through our practices) *does too*. Thus the distinction between the "experienced world" and the "real" one begins to collapse: the world we experience *is* the (real) world.

This last point is not meant in some idealist sense, whether Berkeleyan or Kantian, but rather in the literal and practice-oriented sense worked out above. Historical or social changes in "experience" are nothing other than changes in practices, in the way in which human beings act within the world, and so, since human action in turn changes the environment, they are changes in that environment itself. Changes in experience are distinct from changes in the world only if "experience" is understood passively or theoretically, as involving the reception of information from the world in a way that leaves it unaffected. But if experience is understood actively, as world-changing, then changes in experience mean changes in the world, because changes in experience transform the world. The mistake in the simplistic kind of social constructionism that emphasizes the historical variability of "views" of the world derives from its failure to recognize that we don't simply "view" the environment, as if we were separate from it and merely observers of it; rather, we *act in* it, and through our actions are constantly building and rebuilding it. Thus although it is doubtless true that people have "seen" or "understood" or "conceptualized" nature differently at different historical moments and in different cultures, the deeper point is that they have *acted* differently at different historical moments and in different cultures, and so have transformed the environment they inhabited in different ways—and so have in quite a literal sense inhabited different environments, all of which have been (again, very literally) socially constructed.

The point should be an obvious one, but somehow its lesson is frequently ignored: the different "views" of nature found in hunter-gatherer or agricultural or ancient urban or feudal or industrial or postindustrial societies are not simply "conceptual schemes" that fell from the sky or just happened to arise at certain historical moments. Rather, they are expressions of the fact that hunter-gatherers and agriculturalists and ancient city-dwellers and inhabitants of feudal or industrial or postindustrial societies *engage in different kinds of practices,* and so live in different (built) environments. Hunter-gatherers viewed nature differently (or, as has frequently been suggested, had no view of "nature" in the contemporary sense at all) from nineteenth-century Europeans (who saw nature as something to be conquered) because their modes of action *in the world* were (very) different, and hence so too were the worlds they were "viewing," or rather acting within. Similarly, if Cronon is right about the different ways wilderness was viewed in the United States after the closing of the frontier, this would be because certain modes of practice—those associated with explorers in the first place, and then with cowboys and other "frontiersmen" after that—were no longer possible, and hence could only be engaged in as modified by the rich in their highly artificial wilderness camps, or by those taking part in Buffalo Bill–style reenactments.

I have been suggesting that the form of social constructionism appropriate to a postnaturalist environmental theory would be one that emphasized the literal and concrete processes of construction through which the environment we inhabit comes to take the form it does, processes that are social and normatively structured ones through and through. The central claim of such a social constructionism is therefore not, in the first instance, that our conceptions of nature are socially and historically determined but rather that the environment we encounter and live within is always already a built environment, because we cannot be in-an-environment without acting in it, and cannot act in it without changing it. And so the environment we inhabit is, in this sense, always already socially constructed.

Is *nature* socially constructed? I have carefully spoken above of the social construction of the environment, by which I mean the world we actually inhabit, the one that environs us. In the context of the epistemological story I've been telling, the relation between "nature" and "environment" could be seen as analogous to the Kantian one between noumena and phenomena. The environment is *this* world—the one you see around you as you inspect that which surrounds you right now: a world that is *built*, and thus one that comes (just as it does for Kant) already prestructured by previous human activity—while "nature" might stand for the world prior to or underlying that activity, the material substratum, perhaps, that makes such activity possible or "upon" which it acts. But just as in the Kantian case, if nature is understood in this way, then by definition nature is something we can never know or experience, or even encounter, for if my arguments above were correct, then to "know" or "experience" or "encounter" a world requires acting in it and therefore changing it, and hence any world we have to do with in any of these ways would be one that we have already built, and so would be what I have called the environment and not "nature." And thus the conception of nature as noumena would seem to fall prey to the standard Hegelian response to this kind of Kantianism, as one begins to wonder what role such a nature could ever actually play in our environmental theorizing. We never encounter nature, it turns out, and can never know it: if this is so, then in what sense is it something we ought to defend or protect? What would defending or protecting it mean? And, even more important, if there is no way to know it—if we have no access to it at all—then in what sense could it serve as a normative standard for judging our actions? Our actions, it turns out, can neither "harm" nature nor "help" it or "accord" with it; rather they have no effect on it at all, since by definition nature as noumena is a realm entirely independent of human action. To posit nature as something that can actually function as a goal or standard for environmental philosophy is to fail to grasp the radicality of the Kantian point that *nothing whatsoever can be said or concluded about noumena*—a point that is radicalized even further by the quasi-Hegelian corollary that therefore *it has no serious philosophical significance*.[27] There is no nature in itself, no noumenal nature, that can be known, or inhabited, independently of human practices. "Nature" is not socially constructed on this view but rather turns out to be a philosophically empty concept; *nature in this sense simply does not exist for environmental philosophy*. And so, once again, I conclude that environmental philosophy would be better off without it.

Have I gone too far with this argument? It might seem that I have. When nature is contrasted to the built environment (which is what I have been calling simply the environment), one might protest, it is not being thought of as *noumenal* in the strong (and philosophically impossible) Kantian sense. Rather, what is being pointed to is something like the natural substratum out of which all things are built. If we take the notion of construction in the term "social construction" literally, as I have suggested, don't we then also have to acknowledge that things are not constructed ex nihilo but rather that anything built is built *from materials*—and hence that there could not be anything like a socially organized practice of constructing the environment unless there were also something like a "nature" *out of which* the buildings that make up the environment are constructed? We *do* encounter this nature, the argument would run, for without having previously encountered it, we would not even be able to get the process of construction started. And indeed we *know* things about this nature, too, for the technical skills required for construction themselves require knowledge about the raw materials on which the practices of construction act. Something is transformed in construction—and that which is transformed we could call nature. My house is surely part of the built environment, but it is made of wood—and wood comes from trees, and *they* are not built but rather are part of nature.

Nature here means something like "matter," the material on which construction works. Yet the unhappy experiences of the concept of "material substance" in the history of empiricism should give us pause here and make us worry about how well this definition will fare. My house is built of wood, it's true, and if we trace the shingles (say) back through the construction processes that produced them, we doubtless will find trees somewhere, yet the trees very likely did not come from a primeval forest but almost certainly were planted and tended by human beings engaging in the socially organized practices of forestry. Timber plantations too, that is, are part of the built environment, and hence so are the trees that grow in them. Perhaps those planted (and planned) trees had ancestors that came from somewhere else; perhaps the trees that were felled to make the cedar shingles on my house had genetic ancestors that were growing in the Northwest before any European lumbermen arrived. But now we are back at the problem of wilderness, thinking about old-growth forests and what the impact on them was of Native American logging and burning and other practices. We've returned here to what in the previous chapter I called the logic of deferral, searching backward in time for some *Ur*-tree that could be truly called a natural one, and wondering at the same moment *why* it is important to find such a tree, and noticing how far we've moved from thinking of nature as the matter out of which and on which construction occurs. *This* wood, the wood my shingles are made of, surely does not come from such an *Ur*-tree.

For a house to come to be requires there to be the social practice of homebuilding, and so as I have already noted a house is (uncontroversially) a social construction and not a piece of nature. The "matter" on which the practice of homebuilding works includes shingles—but of course, they are not nature either, since they arise out of the social practice of shingle construction. *Its* matter, one might say in turn, consists of wood, but the wood requires the social practice of lumbering. The matter on which lumbering works consists of trees, but these trees too come to be through the social practice of forestry. It isn't clear where this process ends (or rather begins): the question of which comes first, social practice or matter, looks instead like the question of the chicken or the egg, which is to say it has the structure of the Heideggerian "always already." It's doubtless true that all practices of construction work *on* something, and so whatever is built is built *out of* something, but there is no reason why that which it is built out of should not itself be something built (as houses are built of shingles, and shingles are built of lumber, and lumber is built of logs, and logs are built of trees, and trees are built of other trees, and so on).

Is the social practice of forestry closer to the end (or rather the beginning) of that regress, requiring as *its* matter something like a "raw material," something "natural" like a tree? It isn't, as a little thought will make clear. For the practice of forestry does not depend on only one material, and indeed it depends on other practices too. Our fascination with the "something, I know not what" of material substance leads us to imagine that the story of a house's "origin" can be told via a hierarchical or tree-like structure, with branches of various sorts (the roof, the windows, the plumbing system, etc.) each being made out of other more "natural" entities (wood, glass, copper), which can all in turn be traced back to some *Ur*-entities that would be purely natural. But the real structure is more like a web, or a rhizome, which is to say it has no point of origin, no privileged point that could be identified with nature, from which and on which construction could be said to begin.[28] And so the process of tracing back the history of the shingles on my house does not involve moving in only one direction, back toward logs and tree farms and old-growth forests and *Ur*-trees and so forth. Producing the shingles itself requires tools—lathes and saws and sanders—and those tools themselves have histories that would need to be traced back; the logs that play a role in the shingles' history had to be moved from the locations where the trees they came from fell, and that required trucks and grappling machines, and therefore gasoline and steel. The gasoline that moved the trucks had to be refined, and in turn transported to the locations where it was pumped into the trucks, which required more and different trucks; the refineries themselves had to be built and maintained and operated, which in turn required other tools, made of other materials. And none of the practices involved in building these various objects could have taken place without lots of other ones, since managers and bankers and stockbrokers and janitors were all necessary to make it possible for those processes of logging and trucking and shingle construction to take place, and those people used tools too—copying machines and computers and ink and electricity and plumbing—and those tools themselves had to have been built.... And where exactly in this infinitely complicated web of practices and materials do we ever arrive at something like an origin, at something like nature?

The logic of deferral keeps returning, as we keep thinking that somewhere, just around the corner, we'll arrive at "nature," and yet no matter how close we think we're getting to it we always seem to be ... not quite there yet. This is the logic, of course, of the search for noumena—which we somehow feel *must* be there and yet which we never actually can find a way to reach; it is the logic that leads Locke to his forlorn appeal to "something, I know not what." (It is also, one might remark, the logic of a certain familiar sort of dream.) Wouldn't we be better off to leave it behind, and admit that the matter on which our practices work is always itself in part a product of other, previous practices, and so is itself just as much an element of the built environment we inhabit, and just as little "natural," as anything we explicitly build within that environment? Shouldn't we rather admit that there is no *first* practice, no practice that takes place upon some virginal Edenic world without requiring *other* practices and other constructions for its own possibility—and hence no *original* matter, no nature, either?

A dualistic distinction between matter and practice is at fault here. Matter and social construction are not separate poles but rather are intertwined and mutually implicative: there could not be a social construction without a matter on which it works, and there could not be such a matter without processes of social construction that make it possible.

Just as the dualist conception of "minds" outside the world that then somehow "encounter" it (and struggle to know it) has to be replaced by a conception of the human organism as in-the-environment (or being-in-the-world), meaning there could be no organism without its environment and similarly no environment without the organism whose environment it is, so here too we have to find a way to stop viewing matter as something external to practices. Rather, we have to see that all practices are themselves *material* practices, which means on the one hand that they surely do always work on matter, always have a matter that they transform, but also, on the other hand, that what they *produce* is itself always material, and can and does therefore serve as the matter for other, further practices. To say that they are material practices is to say that they are the practices of a material organism and involve the application of processes in the world that are themselves material and physical processes.

But insisting that practices are always material requires also understanding that *matter is always practical*—that the "matter" we have to do with is always already *the matter of a practice* (a matter, one might say, that *matters* to us). This means not merely that the matter is the "object" of that practice, some external thing on which the practice works: that's still the dualist view that separates matter from practice and imagines there could be some pure matter (some "nature") on which practice has not yet worked and that could therefore be the object of a first or original practice. Rather, its role as matter of *this* practice is part of what it *is*: it would not be this matter were it not the matter of this practice, and so cannot even be imagined independently of (or prior to) this practice. Kant might say that we have preconstituted it as the matter for this sort of practice, but, as I have argued, this notion of constitution itself has to be understood practically: and so to say that the matter of a practice would not be what it is were it not for the practice means that it has itself already been *built*, in other practices, to be the matter that it is. The "always already" functions here too, and deeply: nothing could be the matter of a practice were it not already prepared to be that matter by other practices. And so anything that functions as matter for construction must itself already have been constructed. There are no raw materials, no "natural resources," that have not themselves already been the object of prior practices of construction.

The view I have been developing here is thus a kind of materialism, but a materialism that takes the idea of practice seriously: it begins not with matter as some sort of substance separate from and prior to the practices that "employ" it but rather begins with *practice*, always understood as *material practice*. The "material" in materialism, one might say, necessarily functions here as an adjective, reminding us that practices are always real practices that take place in a real material world, but without suggesting some noumenal "matter" *upon* which practice acts. In the next chapters I try to show in more detail what the implications of such an activist materialism might be for postnaturalist environmental thought.

3

Alienation, Nature, and the Environment

Are We Alienated from Nature?

I have argued that the concept of nature ought to be dropped by environmental philosophers because it is too ambiguous and prone to lead to antinomies, because "nature" in the sense of a world unaffected by human action doesn't exist any longer (and arguably never did), and because the very idea of distinguishing the natural from the human or the social involves a metaphysical dualism that treats human beings as somehow outside the world instead of acknowledging them as simply another organism within the world. Our environment is not something we passively *confront* or *experience* or *perceive* or *know*; rather, it is the *object of our practices*. And since nothing is a practice unless it changes the world (because all practices are transformative), it follows that the environment is the product of our practices as well. In this sense we construct the environment, and do so socially.

But to call the environment the product of our practices is not to see it as something we somehow invent or imagine or idealistically constitute through our thoughts, nor to view it as something we control. It is simply to note that the environment comes to be what it is *through* our practices, just as it comes to be what it is through the actions of beavers, honeybees, earthworms, trees, and all the other organisms that make up the world. (And not just organisms: it comes to be what it is through the actions of water and soil, and for that matter of subways, airplanes, and incinerators, too.) Furthermore we humans come to be who *we* are through those practices as well: what we do, the behaviors we engage in and the objects we produce, help to form us into the people we are—indeed they help to form our "selves." Practice here, I am suggesting, is *prior* to what philosophy has traditionally seen as subjects and objects: it is only through practices that subjects and objects come to be what they are.

And yet the idea of nature as something distinct from and underlying our practices, something that is independent and outside of us, something that modern industry and technology have put into danger—but something that is also capable of taking a cataclysmic "revenge" on us through the unanticipated consequences of that technology—is unquestionably a familiar and powerful one. When I call for an environmental philosophy that does without the concept of nature, it is the very familiarity and power of that idea that make the call seem quixotic or paradoxical, no matter how many antinomies I point to as following from the attempt to take the idea seriously. Where does this notion of a nature separate from us, threatened by us, but also potentially dangerous to us, come from? What undergirds our sense that "nature" is fundamentally different from the human, what motivates that almost compulsive search for the Really Real, the Originally Original, the deep wilderness that no human has ever transformed or even walked through, the discovery of which (as I've argued) is always deferred, but which nonetheless we are always convinced we can find? Why, in a word, do we believe in nature? Why is the myth of a world distinct from the human one (and better than it, always better, in the modern version of this myth!) so powerful, and where does it come from?

In chapter 1 I suggested that part of the answer had to do with the desire to find a normative standard outside human practices that could be used to evaluate those practices. But there's more at work, I think. In this chapter I want to return to this issue by coming at it from a slightly different angle, examining first an idea almost as familiar as the idea of nature itself—the idea that something is *wrong* with our modern attitude toward nature, and in particular that we suffer today from an *alienation from nature* that underlies our environmental problems. According to this idea, we have lost a connection to nature that we once had or ought to have, and we are thus separated from nature in a way that makes it possible for us to ignore the impact of our actions on it. We suffer, in this view, from what Richard Louv calls "nature-deficit disorder."[1] Having lost our connection to nature, we see it merely as a kind of raw material at our disposal, as something we could (and should) master, and the upshot is that we destroy it with technologies that attempt to reshape the natural world into an artificial one structured for human purposes. Yet such attempts are never successful, this line of argument continues, because in truth we depend on nature, and so it takes its revenge on us as our technologies consistently produce dire consequences. To overcome our alienation would be to give up anthropocentrism and to reintegrate ourselves within the natural order, abandoning the impossible dream of replacing the natural world with one created by humans and learning instead to live in harmony with nature.

This notion of alienation from nature should be familiar. Versions of it can be found both in popular discussions of environmental problems and in the environmental philosophy literature itself.[2] And yet there are real difficulties, it seems to me, with this idea. I have already referred to Marx in the previous chapter; he was the great theorist of alienation, and looking at his views might help clarify the notion of what it might mean to be alienated from nature, and might also reveal some of the problems with such a conception. In fact, I'll argue, according to Marx's account it makes very little sense to say we are or could be alienated from nature at all—but it *does* make sense to say, and indeed it is true, that we are alienated from the *environment*, by which I mean the socially constructed, built environment discussed in the previous chapter. Furthermore, I will suggest, the unquestioned identification of environment with nature, and the view of the latter as a realm independent of human beings and human practices, is itself a symptom of our alienation. My answer to the question of why the idea of nature is such a powerful one, then, will be that it is what Marxists used to call a piece of ideology: a mistaken view that nonetheless expresses a truth about the contemporary world, one that reveals what's wrong with that world, and thus has a critical significance.

It will already be clear from the last two chapters that the idea of being alienated from nature is problematic. One might first ask which conception of nature is employed when we are accused of suffering from such alienation: are we alienated from Nature as the "totality of all phenomena," or from nature as that part of the world that is separate from human beings? To ask the question is to see the difficulty: on the one hand, we can scarcely be said to be alienated from the totality of phenomena, since to be alienated from *x* presumably involves being separated from it, and if there's something separate from *x*, then by definition it surely couldn't be a "totality" (since there's something separate from it!). This suggests that we are alienated from nature in the lowercase sense, the sense in which the natural is defined as that which humans have not changed or affected. But how can one be alienated from something from which one has been excluded by definition? If it *is* nature in the lowercase sense that is meant, the statement that humans are outside of nature is an analytic truth, but analytic truths scarcely seem like the sort of thing it makes sense to criticize. To be alienated from something, further, isn't merely to be separated from it, it is to be *illegitimately* separated from it; but if our separation from nature is a matter of definition, and hence of conceptual necessity, it's hard to see how it could be said to be illegitimate. And if it is nature in this second sense from which we are alienated, it is difficult to imagine what overcoming our alienation could possibly mean, or on what basis it could be hoped for. Of course, alienation might be a tragic part of the human condition, in the sense that to be human is to be separated from something with which there is no possibility of reconciliation, but even in this sort of case one would have to imagine reconciliation as at least logically possible and our inability to achieve it as in some sense a tragic fact of the actual world. To see tragedy in that which is true *by definition* seems excessively romantic, even somehow comic: it makes no more sense to deplore our alienation from nature in this sense than it would to deplore the lack of any married bachelors. How can we find tragedy in the meaning of a word?

Or might the alienation consist in a failure to recognize a connection that really does exist but is somehow hidden or unseen? This interpretation would return to the idea of Nature as a totality, as something of which humans are necessarily part, and would understand our alienation from it as consisting in our failure (refusal?) to acknowledge our connection to it. We live *as though* we were separate from nature, the idea would be, but we are mistaken about this, and the result is a set of behaviors and attitudes—and ultimately of technologies—that end up expressing our felt unconnectedness from a world that in fact we are not only connected to but embedded within. But wait: *do* we live or feel as though we are separate from nature, if by that word we mean Nature, the totality of everything that exists? Do our technologies express a disconnectedness from *that*? (Do we think of them as supernatural, as outside the physical world?) Surely not. This interpretation once again trades on the ambiguity in the concept of nature we have repeatedly noted: when it says that we are "part of nature," it means Nature, but when it says that we live as though we were "separate from nature," it means nature—the green world of living things that exists (supposedly) *beyond* the human one. But if it's beyond us, how could we possibly overcome our separation from it?

The idea that we are alienated from nature in that we are part of it but have forgotten this fact, and that the "unnatural," human-built world we inhabit is a symptom of that alienation, can again best be understood as a metaphysical idea about humans, who turn out to be *more* than natural, since they're able through their building activities to transcend nature. Once again, the anthropocentrism of such an idea is striking, not least because it presents itself as a critique of anthropocentrism: humans are the one species that is (naturally) able to escape nature. The antihumanism here remains tied to a deep human exceptionalism, but with the traditional signs reversed. We are (originally) part of nature, the idea seems to be, but we are also capable of going beyond it, yet we *ought not* do so. Transcending nature, in this view, is wrong, and involves a kind of alienation from what one really is. But there remains an incoherence here, because the claim that we are part of nature is also supposed to mean that escaping nature is impossible (and not just immoral)—yet if it's impossible, then how have we been able to do it? And if we haven't been able to do it, in what sense is the world we have built a symptom of alienation?

This whole idea of alienation from nature, familiar and common as it is, turns out to be intellectually defective. It attempts to ground a critique of contemporary human attitudes and behaviors—those associated with technology and "instrumental rationality"—by showing how those attitudes and behaviors are expressions of alienation, but it is not finally able to make that critique good because of the antinomies and ambiguities inherent in its idea of nature. And yet I believe the concept of alienation *is* a useful one for thinking about our relation to the environment. The problem is that it is the environment, and not nature, from which we are alienated. By "environment" I mean the world that actually environs us; and as I have argued earlier, that world is always already one that we have changed, and in that sense is a built or socially constructed environment. *We are alienated from the built environment, not from nature.*

Marx and Alienation

The conception of alienation I want to employ derives from the tradition of Hegelian Marxism, whose key idea—already discussed in the previous chapter—is that the human relation to the environment should be understood as an *active* (and social) one in which the environment comes to be what it is by being transformed. In Hegel's thought, this process of an active forming of the external world is interpreted as *overcoming its externality,* and in this sense therefore as a kind of negation. The otherness of the world, its independence of the subject, turns out for Hegel to be a false otherness: the subject's activity in the world is an activity that proves the falsity of this supposed otherness by overcoming and negating it. (The proof, that is, is not a "theoretical" proof but rather, in accordance with the central conception of knowledge as active, one that takes place through *practice.*) All living things, Hegel points out, engage in this sort of activity: life itself requires the constant introjection of apparently external substances—food, water, sunlight, air—into the living organism for it to continue to function. Eating, one might say, is itself a form of "negation" of the otherness of the world, in which something that is "other" than the organism is transformed, through activity, into something that is no longer other but rather is quite literally part of the organism itself.[3]

But of course, once eaten, the food disappears. This is characteristic of what Hegel calls "desire": it wants to take something that is external to it and entirely negate that externality in a way that leaves nothing behind. But as a result, desire is insatiable, since once it achieves its goal it is by definition faced with nothing, and so has to start all over again. Hegel's dialectical logic points him instead toward a different and "higher" form of negation, in which the object negated nonetheless and at the same time continues to exist outside the negating subject: a negation in which the object's independence from the subject is both canceled and preserved. And he finds that sort of negation, in his famous discussion of lordship and bondage, in the labor of the slave or bondsman who transforms external nature so as to produce an object not for his own consumption but rather for the pleasure of the master. "Work ... is desire held in check, fleetingness staved off," Hegel writes. Rather than entirely destroying the external object, work forms and transforms it, producing a humanized object in which the worker can potentially come to recognize himself.[4] Instead of the external object disappearing and becoming part of the (insatiable) subject, as occurs in the case of satisfied desire, in work it is the subject who externalizes himself, producing something permanent and substantial in the world in which he himself is expressed. In transforming externality into a *humanized* externality, the bondsman both changes the world and changes himself: he *real-izes* himself, makes himself into something real in the world.[5]

And yet it remains true that he is a bondsman, *Knecht*. The object he has produced through his transformative labor ends up being consumed, and therefore destroyed, by the master whose slave he actually is; his slavery consists precisely in the requirement that he produce such an object. And so he is "alienated" from the object, which appears to him not as his realization but rather as the very chains that bind him to the master. The object appears as "alien," as other—and indeed in this case as more profoundly other than that untransformed world of nature that was merely the object of simple hunger or desire. No longer simply external to him, it now holds him in its power. Rather than offering him a literal self-realization, in which he can see his subjectivity as a really existing thing in the world, his labor instead produces an object in which he *cannot* see himself but rather is the basis of his bondage.

There is more to the story of the master and the slave, of course, and more too to the remarkable narrative that Hegel recounts in the later chapters of the *Phenomenology of Spirit.* But I have said enough here, I think, to indicate some key strands in the Hegelian conception of alienation, strands that become even more important in Marx's early work, where the notion of alienation plays an enormously significant role. Marx removes the discussion from the semimythical context of the curious Beckettian drama between Master and Slave and resituates it within the rapidly industrializing Europe of his day; the philosophical fascination of Marx's *1844 Manuscripts* arises from the way in which he combines abstract elements of Hegelian philosophy with the results of a detailed investigation of contemporary economics (both economic theory and economic reality) and shows how each side of that combination can help elucidate and illustrate the other. In the famous section on estranged labor in those manuscripts, he defines alienation in a way that clearly derives from Hegel's account, but also explicitly associates it with an economic system based on private property and wage labor. Alienation arises, Marx writes, when

> the object which labor produces—labor's product—confronts it as an *alien being*, as a *power independent* of the producer. The product of labor is labor which has been embodied in an object, which has become material: it is the *objectification* of labor. The objectification of labor is its realization. But under contemporary economic conditions this realization of labor appears as the *de-realization* of the laborer, objectification appears as *loss of the object* and *bondage* [*Knechtschaft*] *to it,* appropriation as *estrangement,* as *alienation*.... The worker puts his life into the object, but now his life no longer belongs to him but to the object.... The *alienation* of the laborer in his product means not only that his labor becomes an object, something *external*, but that it exists *beyond him*, independently, as something alien to him, as a self-subsistent power over and against him. It means that the life which he has conferred on the object confronts him as something hostile and alien.[6]

For Marx as for Hegel, alienation thus has fundamentally to do with the relation of humans to objects that they have produced—that is, to objects of labor. Under alienation, these objects turn into alien and independent powers over and against humans, achieving a kind of sham self-sufficiency in which they paradoxically become the masters of those who produced them and thus "realized" themselves in them. And the paradigm case of such alienation, Marx argues, occurs in the current economic system when the objects produced by the workers are counted as adding to the wealth of their capitalist employers, and in this sense make possible the workers' continued exploitation. It is the workers' own products, he argues, that come to enslave them. "The worker becomes all the poorer the more wealth he produces," Marx writes. "The *devaluation* of the world of men is in direct proportion to the *increasing value* of the world of things.... So much does labor's realization appear as loss of realization that the worker loses realization to the point of starving to death. So much does objectification appear as loss of the object that the worker is robbed of the objects most necessary not only for his life but for his work."[7]

The account of alienation in the *Manuscripts* thus directs us to consider the realm of "produced objects," objects that have been built by human labor—that is, the *built environment*. By making labor into the central category of both his epistemology and his social theory, Marx draws our attention to the fact that most of what we call the "objective world," the world of objects surrounding us, is a world of *human* objects, objects produced by human beings through their labor. We are alienated from that world, Marx's account suggests, when we fail to recognize its humanness, when we are unable to see it as something we have produced, and when it accordingly begins to appear as an alien power over and against us. In the *Manuscripts* Marx describes this as an alienation from what he calls (following Feuerbach) human "species-being":

> In the practical creation of an objective world, in his work upon inorganic nature, man proves himself a conscious species-being.... Through this production, nature appears as *his* work and his reality. The object of labor is thus the *objectification of man's species-life:* for he duplicates himself not only intellectually, as in consciousness, but also actively, in reality, and therefore sees himself in a world that he has created. In tearing away from man the object of his production, therefore, estranged labor tears from him his *species-life*, his real species objectivity.[8]

It is precisely in this failure of humans to "see themselves in the world they have created" that their alienation consists.

Marx is quite explicit, in passages like this, that the "nature" surrounding us should be seen as something human beings have built. That's what it means to say that "nature appears as *his* work and his reality": "nature" here does not mean a world stipulatively defined as independent of the human but rather what I have been calling the environment, the (built) world that environs us and that our own activities have helped produce. In the *Theses on Feuerbach* and *The German Ideology,* Marx emphasizes the difference between his view and the earlier materialism of Feuerbach, which Marx claims failed to grasp the material environment as itself a product of concrete human activity and hence fell into a simplistic naturalism that treats human beings merely as the passive product of external circumstances. Feuerbach, writes Marx in *The German Ideology,* does not see that the sensuous world around him is not a thing given direct from all eternity, remaining ever the same, but is rather the product of industry and of the state of society, in the sense that it is the ... product of the activity of a whole succession of generations, each standing on the shoulders of the preceding one, further developing industry and trade, and modifying the social order in accordance with changed needs.... Even the objects of the simplest "sense-certainty" are only given to him through social development, industry, and commercial trade. The cherry-tree, like almost all fruit-trees, was as is well-known only transplanted by *commerce* into our zone, and therefore it is only *through* the action of a specific society at a specific time that it is given as "sense-certainty" to Feuerbach.[9]

Marx's version of materialism instead views the human relation to the world as an active one. The "material circumstances" that human beings encounter in the world are themselves the product of previous human activity, and so the "matter" of which materialism speaks is always a matter that humans have built.[10] And that process of building is an ongoing one, and in fact is a precondition for the possibility even of philosophical reflection on the nature of "matter" or of "sense-certainty": "So much is this activity, this unceasing sensuous labor and creation, this production," Marx writes, "the foundation of the whole sensuous world as it now exists that, were it interrupted for only a year, Feuerbach would not only find an enormous change in the natural world, but would very soon find that the whole human world, his own faculty of perception, even his own existence, would be missing."[11] For this activist version of materialism, the insistence on the priority of matter over spirit means not that humans are dependent on nature but that they and the environment they inhabit are both dependent on *practice*, labor—not on ideas, not on theories or on the self-development of *Geist* but on concrete, transformative physical activity. The necessary material basis of my life, and of the world I inhabit, is always the product of the previous labor of others.

To say this, Marx writes, is not to deny "the priority of external nature"; clearly, nature existed before humans did. But today a nature entirely independent of human action is scarcely to be found, Marx points out, "except perhaps on a few Australian coral islands of recent origin."[12] Rather, it is "the nature which develops in human history" that is "man's *real* nature," he writes. "Industry is the *actual* historical relationship of nature ... to man. If, therefore, industry is grasped as the *exoteric* revelation of man's *essential powers,* we also gain an understanding of the *human* essence of nature or the *natural* essence of man." Thus "history itself is a *real* part of *natural history,*" Marx writes, "of nature developing into man."[13] "Nature" here is used to mean "that which environs us," or the environment, and the point of Marx's repeated inversions (very

Feuerbachian in style) is to emphasize how the distinction between the natural and the human is overcome in an understanding of the key role of practice (labor) in forming each. Distinguishing between nature and history (or between the natural and the social) is incoherent: history is a natural process, both in the (passive materialist) sense that it results from human beings' "natural" material characteristics and needs and in the (active materialist) sense that it is nothing other than the process of nature becoming humanized, being transformed by human practices into an environment that is more and more a built one. And this applies above all to the history of "industry," which is to say of technology.

Alienation, according to this account, arises when humans fail to recognize themselves in the world that surrounds them: when the objects they produce through their labor, instead of appearing as the "exoteric revelation" of their "essential powers" or as expressions of their self-realization, become powers over and against them. It is a process, Marx writes in *The German Ideology*, whereby "man's own deed becomes an alien power opposed to him, which enslaves him instead of being controlled by him."[14] And it is explicitly the working class, in Marx's view, that bears the brunt of this alienation. It is the workers' labor that quite literally produces—builds—the entire world of industry, and yet this world, argues Marx, comes to appear to the workers as an alien and hostile power, and indeed as the source of their oppression. The objects the worker builds become part of the capitalist's wealth, and hence—as in Hegel—become the material fetters that keep the worker in bondage. The wealth and power of the capitalist appear to the worker as intrinsic to the former; he does not recognize that the world they both inhabit is a world he himself produced.

At one level, alienation thus means "loss of the object": the worker is alienated in the simple sense that the object he has produced does not belong to him but rather to his employer. A system of wage labor, Marx seems to suggest, in this sense is inherently alienating. The worker does not "recognize himself" in the object, which appears to him as something external to him and not as something his own. But this way of putting the story is misleading, and still owes too much to the Hegelian myth of the lone master confronting the lone slave. For it is not merely the *produced* character of the object that alienation hides but also and simultaneously its *social* character. Under alienation, the problem is not just that I fail to recognize that the object is one that I produced, or that under capitalist economic conditions it does not belong to me. The problem is rather that *we* fail to recognize it as something that *we* have produced, and that we have produced *for each other*. For production under modern conditions is always social production, both in the sense that it requires the cooperative activity of many workers to produce one object and in the sense that the users of the product are other than the ones who actually produce it.

The subject who actively produces a world through labor, for Marx, in this sense is a social subject, not an isolated individual. Practice, and the world transformation it entails, are never private. *We* transform the world through our practices, and one of the reasons we do so is for the satisfaction of *our* needs, needs that themselves are never purely private either. The "self-realization" that labor makes possible is the realization of a social self, of a community. Labor is thus always implicitly social labor—socially organized, and oriented toward social goals. But under capitalism, Marx argues, this implicit sociality is hidden, and labor appears merely as something engaged in by an individual for individual purposes. He emphasizes this line of argument more directly in *The German Ideology* than in the *1844 Manuscripts*, explicitly associating alienation in the former with the division of labor under capitalist conditions.[15] Instead of seeing one's own labor as something that directly satisfies the needs of others, Marx suggests, under capitalism the worker views it merely as a means to an individual end, a troublesome necessity requisite to obtaining the money for the satisfaction of his or her own needs. Thus, whereas from an external standpoint one can see the worker's labor as part of an overall system of mutual and interdependent production, in which the labor of all functions to satisfy the needs of all, this implicitly social and cooperative element to the act of production is obscured to the worker, who produces the object only because he or she has to in order to be paid.

Marx describes this as a contradiction between the worker's "particular" interest and the "common" interest of the society of which he or she is a citizen, a contradiction that is itself a form of alienation. Since the interdependence and mutuality implicit in social production are never explicitly recognized as such by the producers themselves, the "common" interest comes to appear as an alien interest, as a power external to and separate from any of the individual producers. It appears, in fact, in the form of something impersonal, such as "the market" or the "laws of supply and demand," which seem to rule over human productive activity although in fact they are its result. Adam Smith's "invisible hand," Marx suggests, operating behind the backs and beyond the intentions of those who engage in the capitalist market, is itself nothing other than the alienated form of their own practices, which have now turned into an external power that comes to direct those practices.[16] Instead of all explicitly and intentionally working together cooperatively to satisfy each other's needs, each one works independently for his or her own self-interest. The interdependence and cooperation between them are mediated not by their own conscious and mutual decisions but by something "objective" and apparently external to their work, a price (either of the goods being produced or of the labor they sell). That price is itself merely the consequence of their own activity, and yet it appears as something independent of them to which they must adjust: it *is* their own activity, Marx would argue, but in an alienated form.

Marx uses the word *Sichfestsetzen* in this context, which is hard to translate but suggests the idea of an activity that settles into something entrenched.[17] He describes the process as a "consolidation of what we ourselves produce into a material power above us, growing out of our control," and then continues, in an important passage, as follows:

> The social power, i.e., the multiplied productive force that arises through the co-operation of distinct individuals brought about by the division of labor, appears to those individuals, since their cooperation is not voluntary but has come about naturally [*nicht freiwillig, sondern naturwüchsig*], not as their own united power, but as an alien force existing outside them, of the origin and goal of which they are ignorant, which they thus are no longer able to control.[18]

Until the implicit sociality of production is recognized and made explicit, that is, production ("man's own deed") will continue to appear in the form of an opaque and independent social system that humans are unable to master, and as a set of "economic laws" operating behind their backs. Abolishing alienation is thus not a matter of abolishing the sociality of production by abolishing the division of labor but rather of explicitly recognizing and acknowledging this sociality by asserting conscious and voluntary social control over production through the democratic planning Marx associates with communism: rather than production decisions being left to the workings of external and unknowable forces of the "invisible hand," they would be made consciously and democratically by the community as such. As long as the cooperative character of production remains only implicit and unconscious, it appears *naturwüchsig*—which is to say, like something that has grown up "naturally," the way weeds do, without any human intervention and planning—and hence comes to seem an independent and alien power.[19]

In *Capital* and the notes that form the *Grundrisse*, the account of alienation takes a somewhat different form. Marx's earlier emphasis on labor as the central philosophical category reappears in his later and more explicitly economic analyses as the assertion of a labor theory of value.

Central to his argument in those analyses is the idea that since labor is the only source of value, capital itself (labor's antithesis) *is* simply labor, "dead labor," as he sometimes calls it, the labor of past workers embodied concretely not only in the capitalist's wealth but in the machinery and the factories that serve as the environment in which and through which current workers are oppressed. The power of capital over labor under contemporary conditions thus turns out to be the power of dead or objectified labor, labor that has turned into things external to the laborers, over living labor, which is to say over the laborers themselves. Capital is thus itself nothing other than alienated labor.[20] And Marx extends this analysis to the economic system as a whole: the mysteries he investigates at the heart of phenomena such as profit, money, prices, and so on reveal them ultimately not to be primary phenomena at all but rather precisely the reified form in which human productive activity appears under conditions of alienation—when, as he famously writes, "a definite social relation between men ... assumes, in their eyes, the fantastic form of a relation between things."[21]

Marx's analysis centers in the early chapters of *Capital* on the commodity, that "very queer thing, abounding in metaphysical subtleties and theological niceties."[22] A commodity is first of all the product of human labor, and this labor is the source of its value. But under conditions of capitalist production, Marx points out, it does not appear as such. Rather, the value of the commodity seems to be a natural fact about it, an "objective" characteristic independent of human action. He writes that

> a commodity ... is a mysterious thing simply because in it the social character of men's own labor is reflected back to them as objective characteristics of the product of that labor itself, as socially natural properties [*gesellschaftliche Natureigenschaften*] of the thing itself, and thus also because the social relation of the producers to their collective labor appears to them instead as a social relation, existing independently and outside them, between objects.[23]

The commodity, he writes, is a "social hieroglyphic" in which the truth about contemporary social relations is written, but in an initially unreadable form.[24]

As he did in *The German Ideology*, Marx claims here too that it is above all the sociality of production that is hidden under capitalism. A relation between humans—the implicit mutuality and cooperation of their labor, the way in which production is always *social* production, conditioned on and oriented toward others—appears under capitalism only in the distorted and alienated form of a relation between things—that is, between the prices of external objects whose source in human labor, and thus whose connection to us, has been lost. In the *Grundrisse* he writes that

> The social character of activity, as well as the social form of the product, and the share of individuals in production here appear as something alien and objective, confronting the individuals, not as their relation to one another, but as their subordination to relations which subsist independently of them and which arise out of collisions between mutually indifferent individuals.... In exchange value, the social connection between persons is transformed into a social relation between things; personal capacity into objective wealth.[25]

Money itself is the clearest form of this transformation of a social relation into a thing: "The individual," Marx writes, "carries his social power, as well as his bond with society, in his pocket."[26]

In this analysis of the "fetish character" of commodities, various strands of the earlier discussions of alienation are brought together. The commodity is something built—a product of labor, and hence part of the "built environment," not a naturally occurring object. The labor that produces it is implicitly social: the commodity is produced because it satisfies (or is hoped to satisfy) the needs of others, and it is produced in a cooperative way, not by a single artisan but through the coordinated labor of many workers. But its sociality remains only implicit, concealed in a market-based economic system by structures of private property and private exchange. And so the sociality of labor finds explicit expression only in an alienated form, in which (as Marx writes) the laborers' "own social action takes the form of the action of objects, which rule the producers instead of being ruled by them."[27] The human world of objects produced by social and cooperative labor comes to appear in the form of an independent, external world that functions as a power over and against the producers. It takes the form of a "second nature"—a social and economic system that humans take as "natural," that they cannot change but to which they must adjust themselves. Individual prices, but also larger items—the level of unemployment, the rate of inflation, the Dow Jones Industrial Average—all of these are simply the product of a series of actions and transactions we all engage in, and in that sense they are something we *build*, yet they appear to each of us as natural facts of the world, as given states of affairs we are each powerless to affect. The overcoming of alienation, then, would consist in the recognition and the explicit assertion of the sociality of labor by the associated human community. This is why it is central to Marx's vision of the future communist "realm of freedom" that the anarchy and *Naturwüchsigkeit* of the market be replaced by a system of conscious and democratically controlled social planning of production. Only in this way, he thinks, can humans regain control over their own objects, reassert their power over that which had come to seem alien and independent of them.

Alienation from the Environment

What are the implications of this analysis of Marx's notion of alienation for the question of alienation from nature? At one level, it seems that there aren't many. Alienation, for Marx, turns out to mean the failure to recognize the human origin of objects (and institutions) that have been produced by human activity. And this means in turn that we can only be alienated (in Marx's sense of the term) from things that we have ourselves built through our practices. But if this is so, then obviously the concept of being alienated from nature makes no sense, since—no matter whether it is nature or Nature that one has in mind—neither one is something that we ourselves have built. It looks, therefore, as though there is not much in Marx's view of alienation that can be helpful here. If we are alienated from nature, apparently, it must be in some other sense of the word. Perhaps Marx, committed (as he is sometimes described as being) to a "Promethean" and "productivist" conception of humans and labor, has little of value to provide to environmental philosophy; certainly this is the conclusion that a number of environmental philosophers have come to.[28]

But the arguments of the previous chapters might suggest more of interest in Marx's conception than appears at first. Those arguments have cast doubt, after all, on the very idea of nature as an unbuilt world independent of and prior to acts of human transformation that underlies the claim that alienation from nature in Marx's sense isn't possible. A postnaturalist environmental philosophy would note that the world we inhabit, the one directly environing us, is indeed a world that we have built. Even if we leave the word "nature" to the side, or let it mean (stipulatively) that which human beings have not transformed, and therefore acknowledge that in Marx's sense, humans *cannot* be "alienated from nature," it still remains possible that they are alienated from their *environment*, meaning now from the (socially) built character of the world they actually inhabit. And this, I will argue, is in fact the case.

There is an obvious similarity between Marx's account of alienation and the unmasking or debunking form of social constructionism (as Hacking calls it) examined in the previous chapter. Such a form, as I reconstructed it, consists in showing that what appears to be natural, eternal, built into the structure of the world, and, most important, not produced by human social forces is in fact the result of such forces and hence is not "natural" in the ordinary sense at all. This is clearly the structure of Marx's account, in which the objects shown to be socially constructed are first of all those "queer things" he calls commodities (or more precisely their exchange values), but also second and more broadly, the entire world of institutions, such as the market, the economy, and so forth, whose properties are the result of human actions but that appear under capitalism as unalterable givens to which one must simply adjust as if they were facts of nature. What is particularly interesting and important about Marx's account is that it connects social construction in Hacking's sense with the literal acts of construction engaged in by workers under capitalism—that is to say, with the labor he describes in *Capital* as the source of value. And the difficulty about how, according to this account, it is possible to be alienated from nature itself repeats the question discussed in the previous chapter about what the social construction of nature might mean. In both cases it is precisely the appearance of something as "natural" that is being unmasked as an illusion, and at first it seems difficult to see then how nature *itself* could be the object of such an unmasking. But we saw above a way in which this could be understood: the social construction of nature, I suggested, could be interpreted as referring to the project of trying to show (to put it bluntly) that *nothing* is natural, or rather that the very distinction between the natural and the social—that is, between that which has been "produced" by humans and that which is "independent" of them—is an untenable one.[29] In Marx's case too, then, although in one sense nature is by definition something from which we cannot be alienated, still, in another and deeper sense, our alienation might be said to consist in our mistaken belief that there *is* anything like "nature" distinct from the (built) environment we inhabit at all.

Thus, although Marx's view seems to entail that we can't be alienated *from* nature, the sort of alienation we do experience (on his account) nonetheless has a great deal to do *with* nature, and more specifically with the processes by which things show up that *seem* to be natural. It is the *illusion of naturalness* that his account of alienation is concerned to unmask: alienation has to do with the appearance of something as natural, eternal, untouched by human action that in reality is built through human practices, and so is socially constructed. For Marx, as we have seen, alienation consists in our failure to recognize the human, social, and, most important, the practical origin of the world we inhabit. There are two senses in which the contemporary world is marked by such alienation. On the one hand, we view social institutions as if they were "facts of nature": this is so above all with respect to that crucial institution called "the market," which is treated in much contemporary discourse as though it were the only "natural" form for human economic transactions and whose implicit pronouncements about social value are treated as unquestionable truths. Each one of us as an individual faces "the market" in the same way we face forces such as climate, gravity, or for that matter even time itself: the world of commodities, prices, employment opportunities, and wage scales that we confront is simply *given* and beyond our control. Such and such *is* the price of milk, the interest rate on thirty-year fixed mortgages, the prevailing salary for associate professors of English, the types of available hybrid vehicles, the size of a sheet of legal paper and so forth. All these things result, of course, from an almost unimaginable series of transactions in which all of us take part, and in this sense they are our social product. And yet to each one of us they appear simply as facts, in the determination of which we have no role to play, and in that sense like facts of nature. We cannot choose to change them, nor would we even know how to do so, although it is our own acts that produce them. They seem "natural"—and this isn't simply an illusion, since it is true that to each individual they're unalterable facts; and yet it remains true that they're not natural but rather result from the choices and actions of all those individuals together.

But it is not only the market that appears like a fact of nature in this way; many other social institutions have the same alienated character. They are the ones that are ripe for Hacking's unmasking social constructionism: norms and behaviors that are treated as "naturally" or intrinsically valid but that in fact are the result of the operation of social forces. Gender roles are an example whose significance has been widely discussed; other examples include norms of etiquette or of cuisine or of dress. It's striking, for instance, that dress codes for certain professions or certain sorts of events are routinely explained by the assertion that being dressed a certain way—elegantly, professionally, appropriately—makes the wearer, or the wearer's clients, or the wearer's fellow attendees feel better or more productive or more serious. This is often stated as if the effect of the clothing on those who wear or see it were intrinsic to that particular style—as if wearing an expensive suit and tie in itself made one a more productive or more serious lawyer, for example, or as if the very fabric and cut of t-shirts and cutoff denims themselves harmed the experience of someone eating in a fancy restaurant. These effects of "appropriate" or "inappropriate" clothing, I hasten to say, are perfectly real, and I don't mean to deny them, but my point is that they follow from nothing other than the very (social) appropriateness or inappropriateness of the clothing *itself:* it's not the design or fabric of the suit that makes one a better lawyer and therefore is what lawyers ought to wear but rather that caring about wearing what lawyers ought to wear itself shows one to have the kind of skills that make one a better lawyer. Wearing cutoffs to Per Se makes fellow diners uncomfortable not because of something intrinsic about cutoffs but because, simply, one doesn't wear cutoffs to Per Se, and diners are uncomfortable when in the company of those who do what one doesn't do. For any one of us, these rules of dress—which are complicated but which we all to one degree or another know and comply with—appear, again, like facts of nature: one simply does not wear cutoffs to a fancy restaurant. But in truth it's the very fact that we all know and obey these rules that provides them with their (perfectly genuine) validity. The sociality of the process by which they become valid is hidden, and appears in alienated form as a "natural fact" about the clothing itself.

There may be somewhat less alienation with respect to political institutions (in the United States) than with respect to norms of dress or gender or etiquette. Citizens tend in general to be aware that the political structures of our society are the result of social choices and social actions: no one believes any more that kings are divinely ordained, and the idea of a constitutional agreement as something that was entered into by particular "founding fathers" at a particular moment in history is fairly well understood. Still, even the significance of that historical moment is typically interpreted in an alienated way, as if a set of undertakings entered into by a group of eighteenth-century landowners inevitably and without argument bound the inhabitants of a twenty-first-century nation. In that sense, for us the Constitution no longer functions as something chosen and constructed, the way it presumably did for members of the founding generation; rather, it appears to be something like a fact of nature (though perhaps a fact of *moral* nature), with our obedience to its strictures something that cannot be questioned. In truth, of course, just as with norms regarding dress, it is only through our acts of obedience to the Constitution, our willingness to follow its procedures and submit to its requirements, that its validity is contemporaneously maintained. But we do not see those acts and that willingness as daily choices that we make but rather as things to which we are bound, as it were by natural bonds of filial obedience to the undertakings of one's ancestors.[30]

In other ways, too, the political structures of the American system appear to citizens as unchangeable facts of nature. A clear example is the two-party system. The situation here has a structure very similar to the one involving dress codes. Faced with two candidates, one Democratic and one Republican, each holding unacceptable views—perhaps both agreeing that a president has the right unilaterally to label an American citizen an enemy combatant and order that citizen's murder, for example—a voter might try to find a "minor" party candidate to support, but then would surely confront the (persuasive) argument that a vote for such a candidate is wasted or, worse, effectively aids one of the two "major" party candidates by making it harder for the other one to win. The fact that only Democrats and Republicans have a real chance to be elected, even though many voters frequently express significant unhappiness with both parties, appears as a fact of nature, the denial of which is said to indicate a lack of realism on the part of those who support third-party candidates. And there is no doubt that this objection to third-party adventurism is correct. Yet if all those who were disappointed in the two major candidates in fact supported a third or a fourth one, the "fact of nature" here might well turn out to be not so unquestionable and eternal as it seems. It's only the fact that people believe it, one might say, that makes it true. (And yet it *is* true!) The structure here is again the structure of what Marx called alienation.

But Marx's materialist turn also reminds us that the "construction" through which social norms and institutions of the sort just discussed are created and sustained must be understood in a literal and physical sense. Dress codes are expressed in actual garments, woven and sewn by workers using machines that themselves had to be built; political structures require physical structures—buildings and voting booths and prisons and passports. Social institutions are not ideas or attitudes or expectations in people's heads; they are elements of the physical world, parts of what I have been calling the environment, and therefore are always things that have been (literally) built. And this suggests a second sense in which we might be said to be alienated (in Marx's understanding of the term) in the modern world. For the built character of the environment, the fact that the actual physical world we inhabit was built through human labor, although it is certainly not something anyone would explicitly deny, still remains something we fail to genuinely acknowledge in our relations to and interactions with it.

I ask the reader here, for instance, to consider the objects in her or his immediate vicinity right now: the book or other device on which these words are being read, the chair or other item of furniture on which the reader sits, the floor upon which that furniture itself rests, etc. Each of these items, of course, had to be built. The paper had to be printed, the e-reader's screen had to be assembled, the chair had to be upholstered, the floor had to be laid. And for the printing to take place ink had to be produced; for the assembly of the screen glass needed to be formed into the proper shape; upholstering the chair required fabric to be woven; nails or glue were employed to put the floor into place. Each of those other processes in turn required tools, whether simple or complex, that themselves had to be produced, and so on. At each of these stages people were involved—printing, assembling, nailing, weaving, but also transporting, cleaning, performing maintenance tasks on machines. (And every stage also required financing, organizing, etc., and so managers, lawyers, bankers, and so forth played roles as well.) None of the work involved, probably, was very easy, nor was it necessarily pleasant, though doubtless for some of them it was done with some enjoyment or at least without much in the way of discomfort. But in every case it took labor—effort, physical action, the expenditure of energy. The total number of people directly involved in producing the objects in my own immediate visible environment right now must be in the tens of thousands—and that's leaving aside those involved in producing the environments within which those people labored. If I don't leave those others aside, the number must quickly rise to millions, or (if we start to trace back *their* tools and buildings and finances) so large as to be practically limitless.

This point has been noted repeatedly: John Locke and Adam Smith, for example, both come up with lists in some ways not that different from the one I just gave. "It is not barely the plough-man's pains, the reaper's and thresher's toil, and the baker's sweat, is to be counted into the bread we eat; the labour of those who broke the oxen, who digged and wrought the iron and stones, who felled and framed the timber employed about the plough, mill, oven, or any other utensils, which are a vast number, requisite to this corn, from its being feed to be sown to its being made bread, must all be charged on the account of labour, and received as an effect of that," wrote Locke, and later Smith asked us to consider "what a variety of labour is requisite in order to form that very simple machine, the shears with which the shepherd clips the wool," mentioning "the miner, the builder of the furnace for smelting the ore, the feller of the timber, the burner of the charcoal to be made use of in the smelting-house, the brick-maker, the brick-layer, the workmen who attend the furnace, the mill-wright, the forger, the smith," who "must all ... join their different arts in order to produce them." "The number of people of whose industry a part ... has been employed" in producing the goods required for the "accommodation" of a "common laborer," Smith says, "exceeds all computation."[31]

And yet as a phenomenological matter we do not typically experience the objects in our environment this way. They are *mere* objects, things we simply find around us, things we use, enjoy, ignore, without thinking about the processes through which they came to be, and most importantly about the people—real flesh and blood people, just like us—whose effort and labor helped to bring them into existence. The objects that surround us are *built*, employing techniques and procedures we almost never consider and rarely can even imagine. This envelope that happens to be lying on my desk: how was the paper folded and cut to form it? How was the adhesive applied, and what was it made from? The pattern printed on the inside for security, to mask the contents: Who designed it? How was it tested? How is it printed? Where does the ink for the printing come from, and what methods are used to produce that ink? What machines are needed for the cutting, folding, applying of adhesive, and printing? How are *they* produced? And what about the paper itself? How is it made—and sliced, and smoothed, and bleached? In our ordinary relation to these sorts of items, such questions never arise; the items are treated as if they had simply come into existence of themselves, or as if they had always been in existence. They appear, that is to say, like *natural* objects—"natural" both in the sense of ordinary, not to be questioned, unremarkable, but also in the sense of not having an origin in human labor. They simply *are*. If the question of where something of this sort came from ever arises, it does so as a question about where it was bought: "How did those envelopes get here?" "I got them at Staples, last week." Their origin, that is, is treated as if it occurs with the financial transaction in which they came into one's possession, and not in the processes of labor that produce them.[32]

There is a kind of fascination, for many people, in watching a large building being erected in the middle of a city: the clearing of the land, the digging of a hole, the slow laying of the foundation, the pounding in of girders, the careful placement of crossbeams, the installation of pipes and other utilities. At each stage the complexity and effort involved (and the difficulty of designing and planning the procedures employed) are obvious and impressive. And yet those who end up inhabiting the building—using it as a place of work or just of dwelling—typically have no sense of that; for them the building is simply the "natural" environment in which they carry out their daily activities, something to which they rarely give a second thought. The builtness of the world they inhabit, so striking as one watches the construction that makes that inhabiting possible, recedes for them as they begin to inhabit it, becoming for them something natural and taken for granted.

This process of building, whereby the activity of human beings—activity that is difficult, complex, and requires skill and effort as well as planning and organization—quite literally produces the environment in which we live, the homes and offices within which we work, the objects with which we have to do in our daily lives, the very clothing that we wear and the food we eat, could be called a process of *reification*. In it our own labor, the expenditure of our energy and our time, takes the form of things. A human process—dynamic, socially organized, involving duration and effort—appears as a static thing: ordinary, external, nonhuman, permanent, and above all *given*, simply there, not built or produced. We fail to notice the close and complex relationship between the things around us and *us*: they appear simply as the things that surround us, like things of nature. It's striking that philosophers when discussing issues about our knowledge of "external" objects almost always choose as their examples things that are *built*: a chair, a book, a piece of chalk. Descartes is in his heated room, in his dressing gown, with a piece of paper in his hands and a candle nearby whose wax he examines. Hume watches billiard balls and worries about how he can be sure of the nourishing properties of bread. Husserl looks around his office, and takes us on a tour of his house. Heidegger picks up his hammer. The objects involved in these examples are always treated as paradigmatic cases of things that are entirely independent of and external to the subject whose knowledge of them is then put in question. But the fact that the examples themselves are always constructed objects, always the product of labor, and therefore always already the result of a *preexisting relation* between "subject" and an "objective world," is rarely noted. The chair is *not* a "mere thing" that the human philosopher stumbles upon and then tries to know; it is something that some other humans have already built, and built in fact *as a chair*. The relation between subject and object, in these examples, is one in which practice or labor *has already occurred*: practice is prior to and presupposed by the examples themselves, and so is prior as well to the raising of the question of knowledge. I could not ask how I, a professor in a classroom, come to know the chair had not a whole group of humans already labored to build the chair, and the desks, and the classroom itself. To abstract from those prior practices and those prior workers, and treat the chair as though it were something absolutely independent from those of us, teacher and students, now suddenly faced with trying to "know" it, is to fall prey to reification, treating as a mere object what is in fact the result of a human process—which is to say, it is to fall prey to what Marx described as alienation.

But again, it is not only the builtness of the objects that surround us (and of the objects we use as examples in philosophy classrooms) that we fail to notice when we treat them as mere objects, it is also the sociality of the practices through which that building takes place. Although neither Locke nor Smith take it that way, what's crucial (and startling) in the realization one gets from considering the immense amount of labor and the vast number of laborers necessary for the production of even one item in one's environment is the image of human *mutuality* and (implicit) cooperation it reveals. I could not be here writing, and you, reader, could not be there reading were it not for the previous labor of literally hundreds of thousands or more people who were needed in order to make our "natural" comfortable unnoticed environments possible. My effort in writing and yours in reading depends on the effort (and it is substantial) of all those others. Recognizing that fact, it seems to me, ought to evoke a sense of deep gratitude—an appreciation of the complexity of the processes that underlie the possibility of whatever one is doing at any given moment, and the enormous numbers of one's fellow humans from across the globe who were involved in bringing that possibility about. And yet we rarely recognize that fact and certainly rarely feel that gratitude. Our mutual dependence is expressed in the very objects that surround us, objects that we have all built *for each other,* but again, we do not see those objects that way, we do not see them (as Marx puts it) as social hieroglyphics that, when correctly read, would reveal how much our practices are always social and cooperative ones in which we construct, together, a world that we all share. Instead, once more, they seem like *things,* dumb objects of property, not expressions of solidarity or community. Under our social and economic system those hieroglyphics remain illegible. Mutual dependence and cooperation appear only as mediated through the market, expressed in the prices of the goods we buy and sell and the wages our labor commands; within the market, as economic theory teaches, each one of us works only for ourself, concerned only with maximizing personal utility while minimizing the expenditure of labor-power. Our work *for* each other, and our dependence *on* each other, are expressed only in the form of those market transactions in which the goods we produce are exchanged. As Marx says, a social relation between people takes the fantastic form of a material relation between things.

What would it be like to experience the world we inhabit differently? Is a social order imaginable in which we would recognize and appreciate the builtness and the sociality of the objects that surround us, actually experience them as objects that fellow members of our community have constructed with effort and care, for us? Is a social world imaginable where the communal and co-operative character of our practices and their products would be explicit, so that we would engage in labor fully and intentionally aware that those practices were helping to produce the environment that we mutually inhabit, helping to improve the lives of all members of the community? This surely sounds wildly utopian, and I don't mean here to suggest that such a social order is in any sense in the offing. But I think it is the goal—the regulative ideal—toward which Marx's account of alienation points, and helps to clarify what on his account an unalienated relationship to the environment would look like. It would be a relationship in which the environment was recognized *by* the community as *ours*, as something that is produced through our practices, and not as something external to or independent of those practices.

Nature as Alienation

In chapter 7 I will have more to say about the vision of politics that such a regulative ideal points toward. But for now I want to return to the question of alienation. I have been arguing that for Marx. alienation arises when objects and institutions that are really the product of social practices come to seem as though their existence is independent of such practices, and so they appear to be unquestionable, eternal, given, pure Things in whose origin human actions played no role. And I have emphasized that this appearance is always associated with what might be called the illusion of naturalness: these reified objects and institutions come to seem "natural" in all the varying senses of that word—ordinary, to be expected, part of the given structure of the world, unalterable, not subject to ethical or political choice, and so forth. We might then say that Marx's account of alienation should be seen as in a certain sense a *critique of nature*. The key role played by labor in his account points us toward noticing both the builtness and the sociality of the world—the fact that the institutions that surround us are the result of our socially organized practices, and that these practices are literal physical ones that produce the actual material environment we inhabit. In doing so, it points us as well toward a distrust of assertions that such-and-such is "natural." Instead, we have always to ask about the hidden processes through which the putatively natural was constructed, a deconstructive procedure in which the human and social practices that make it possible are revealed. For Marx's view, *the appearance of "nature" is itself a symptom of alienation.*

But then the identification of the "environment" with "nature" that is so characteristic of much contemporary environmentalism is itself a symptom of alienation as well, not so much part of the solution to our alienated relation to the surrounding world as simply another example of that relation. For the world that actually environs us, the real "environment" that we inhabit, as I have been arguing, is *not* "nature" at all—at least not if nature is meant in Mill's second, lowercase sense as something beyond or outside human practices of building—but is rather a world that is indeed always already built, a world that human beings have always already transformed and constructed, and thus a world where nature, despite McKibben's worry, has always already ended. An environmentalism that takes "environment" and "nature" as synonyms and that emphasizes the destructive effects of human action on a realm marked by an original (and mourned) independence from the human, I am suggesting, is an *alienated* environmentalism; it treats the world that we inhabit and (because this is what inhabiting *is*) are therefore always transforming, always building and rebuilding, as though it were *other than*, *alien to* us—as though it were an external and unalterable object to which we must simply adjust ourselves. By identifying the environment with "nature" and therefore viewing it as separate from the human—and then criticizing humans for encroaching upon it—such a position sees the world we actually inhabit in the same way that Marx says that alienated workers see the capitalist social order: as an externally given reality they cannot change but must simply accept, instead of something that their own practices have helped to produce.

Indeed, the similarities between the way this sort of environmentalism speaks of "the environment" and the way members of capitalist societies view the market is striking: both must be accepted as they are, both are beyond our understanding, both require us to act in certain ways without any possibility of moral objection or appeal, both serve as constraints it is pointless (or arrogant) to question. Nature, we're told, always takes its revenge: it can't be fooled, its laws are unalterable, and efforts to intervene in and manipulate it to improve its effects on us always end in disaster. Attempts to alter its workings are doomed, just like attempts to intervene in market processes. Environmentalists with this sort of view are like Austrian economists in their skepticism about the possibility of intentionally adjusting or modifying market mechanisms to achieve particular results. We do not know enough, they say; there is more at work here than we could ever understand; it's an act of hubris to try to steer these massively complex processes; the attempt to do so expresses a desire for social domination over forces that rather ought to be allowed their freedom; the effort to manipulate the operation of these processes always leads to unintended consequences that are worse than the problems they were meant to solve.

But the environment that surrounds us, I keep insisting, isn't nature at all; it's a world we have built, and as such it is a world that we can question and can change. The environment is our product.[33] The world that surrounds us has the shape it has and consists of the objects it does because of our activities, our institutions, our social and economic structures. We have built it. But there's more to say about it, for the sad truth is also that we have built it *badly*. The world we inhabit is something that has come to be what it is through our practices, but what it has come to be, clearly enough, is pretty awful: polluted, ugly, toxic, dangerously warming, and harmful to many of the creatures that live within it, including ourselves. It is our own actions that have led to these results, although those results were never really intended by anyone. Yet *our practices* produced them—practices of building factories, developing suburbs, extracting and burning fossil fuels, spreading pesticides on the land, paving over wetlands, and so forth. None of us intended the negative results—no one wants the world to warm dangerously, no one wants pollution, no one wants to harm future generations—and yet our own actions seem likely to lead to those consequences. The negative effects on the *environment*, desired by no one and yet the result of our own practices, appear to each of us like facts of *nature*. And here is where Marx's account of alienation seems to me to be helpful to environmental thinking, precisely because it focuses on the question of how the things we produce can become independent and threatening powers opposed to us. We are alienated from our environment when we fail to recognize it as the product of our own actions and thus fail to acknowledge our own responsibility for it, and so instead it starts to look like a natural fact about which there is nothing we can do: global warming simply part of a natural cycle, pollution an inevitable byproduct of technology, urban sprawl the inexorable consequence of market forces. It is exactly when our environment comes to look like nature, and when the problems it faces come to look like things about which there is nothing we can do, that our alienation from it occurs.

I began above with the familiar claim that we're alienated from nature in the sense that we don't acknowledge our embeddedness in it and instead try to dominate it, replacing the natural world with a human-made one that forgets that we too are part of nature. That view of alienation from *nature*, it should be clear, and the view of alienation from the *environment* that I am proposing are quite different, even opposed; indeed, on my view that more familiar one is marked by the very alienation I think we need to overcome. By emphasizing nature's independence from us, by talking of our embeddedness in it in a way that emphasizes its largeness, its indifference to and its power over us, and by proposing that the appropriate relation to nature involves a kind of submissive obedience, it treats humans as impotent objects of an external force whose structures they must acknowledge but can never question or change; in doing so, I have been suggesting, it treats the environment in the same way that capitalism treats institutions and commodities whose origin in human action is systematically forgotten or ignored.

What such a view of nature misses is what Marx called the "active side" of materialism. We *are* embedded in nature (more specifically, in Nature), but not simply in the sense that it forms us and we depend on it. We are embedded in it *actively*, which means that that *we* form *it*, that *it* depends on *us*—except the "it" here should no longer be thought of as "nature" but rather the environment, the world we actually inhabit. The dualism between humans and nature that environmental thinkers frequently say must be overcome is not overcome by viewing humans as simply part of some larger whole to which they owe obedience and respect—that is, to which their relation is understood as entirely passive. Rather, it is overcome by understanding that humans and their environment are mutually transformative, that to be human is to be formed *by* the environment *in the course of* actively forming and reforming it.

The view of alienation I am criticizing ultimately thinks that we alienate ourselves from nature whenever we transform it, which is to say that an unalienated relation to nature would be one in which we simply (and passively) obeyed its strictures and hence avoided its revenge—as if we had any choice in the matter, as if transforming the world were not itself *our nature,* as it is the nature of everything else in the world. Alienation, I am suggesting, arises not from our transformation of the world but rather from our failure to recognize ourselves in the world we have transformed—a failure, that is, to acknowledge responsibility for what we have done and what we have built. That means, first of all, not recognizing that the environment that surrounds us—our sprawling suburbs, our paved-over wetlands, our rapidly warming atmosphere, and more generally the social and economic arrangements that we take for granted as given—is something that results from human practices, *our* practices, and is not anything like a "fact of nature." And second, it means not recognizing that the practices that produce that environment are always *socially organized* ones. They have social preconditions and social consequences, and operate in accordance with socially defined norms; and further, they are almost always engaged in alongside other people. Our responsibility for the environment, therefore, is social, not private.

We mistake the environment for nature, failing to recognize that what surrounds us is not "natural" at all but rather a world that we have built and for which we are therefore responsible, in both the causal and the moral senses of that last word. But talk of a failure to recognize facts about our environment, or about the importance of "acknowledging" our responsibility for it, should not be understood as referring merely to attitudes or beliefs. The practice-oriented epistemology I outlined in the previous chapter implies instead that recognition or acknowledgment is not primarily a "mental" state but is rather itself a practice: to overcome our alienation from the environment by recognizing that the environment comes to be what it is through our practices, that is to say, *is itself to engage in different practices*. We can genuinely acknowledge our active involvement in transforming the world only through action, which is to say through actively transforming the world in new ways. Similarly, the recognition that the practices involved are always social practices requires a new sort of sociality. Practices that are self-conscious about their significance—aware that they do transform the environment, and aware that they are always implicitly social in their preconditions, their normative structure, and their consequences as well—will be *different practices* from the ones we engage in under conditions of alienation. This point is a crucial one, and I return to it in chapter 7. But it should be clear enough that under contemporary alienated conditions the practices through which we construct the world are not self-conscious, do not know themselves as social and world-building, and that as a result the environment they build is—well, the awful one we find around us today. Again, this is exactly what Marx says about alienation: when humans don't recognize themselves in their products, the products become powers over and against their producers, out of their control and dangerous to them. Today as a society we do not choose our social practices self-consciously: we leave the question of what our practices should be up to the vagaries of the market, that ultimate fetish we worship and obey as the most powerful external and independent force there is. It's no wonder that the result of those practices is environmental disaster.

I began this chapter by asking why the idea of nature as something separate from and independent of (and superior to) the human is so powerful and attractive, and why it seems so hard to give up. It should now be clear what my answer is. The idea is an ideological one, in the sense that it expresses a mistaken view of the world that at the same time reveals something deep about *our* world, the particular social order that we inhabit. We are alienated from our environment, I have suggested, in the sense that we fail to see it as built and fail to see it as social, and so it *looks like* nature; and thus the strength of our belief that it *is* nature, that the world around us is other than us, unchangeable by us, and more powerful (and more dangerous) than we are, is in fact a symptom of our alienation. We are environed by a world we cannot control, one that seems to operate behind our backs and without our being able to alter its course—a world of markets whose future no one can predict and whose past no one can really satisfactorily explain; a world of overcrowded cities and impossibly expensive gentrifying neighborhoods and sprawling suburbs meant to be sources of comfort that turn out instead to be sources of ugliness, disaffected young people, unhappy families, and massive traffic jams; a world of pollution and dangerous nuclear power plants and toxic waters and endangered species; and above all nowadays a world whose climate seems to be changing in potentially threatening ways with unpredictable results that no one seems able to prevent. And so of course we think our environment is nature, is beyond our control, is something to which we must submit, something that our failure to obey will cause to take its revenge upon us. Of course we think of it as Gaia, as a living organism to which we stand in the same relation as a cell does to a body, or as a parasite does to a host; of course we think of it as a mother we are unable to fool, a jealous mother who punishes our hubris by repeatedly showing us who is really in charge. *It's the social world that looks to us like nature,* a frightening world we can only observe but can never finally alter. All we can do with such a world is to try to grasp its laws and processes using the methods of science; we feel that we can no more alter the laws of our social environment—the rules of finance, the structure of our political system, the role of the automobile, the workings of gender and the nuclear family—than we can alter the laws of gravity or of thermodynamics.

And so when we say "environment" we mean nature, because we're used to thinking that the world that surrounds us is one we cannot control and cannot change. (Indeed, perhaps we *hope* that it is, because the things we do try to control seem to end up so badly.) To believe that there is a "nature" beyond us and above us, and, most important, more powerful than us—a nature whose rules and strictures we finally just have to obey—is to escape the need for us to figure out what to do, to determine our own values and our own purposes, our own decisions about how to live. If the normative standards for our actions lie in nature, then we're off the hook: if we want to know how to live, we need only consult nature and let it determine for us what we should do. Sometimes presented as a counter to hubristic anthropocentrism, such a view seems to me instead another example of the constant temptation that Kant called heteronomy—allowing something other than oneself to make one's decisions—and thus as an avoidance of responsibility. Our situation is more serious and more difficult than this: we *are* responsible for the environment, which is to say for the world we inhabit. We've built it, and (as everyone really knows) we've built it badly. We have to figure out what we've done wrong, and how to do it better. We have to figure out, that is, how to build a better world, a better environment. This is hard, and there's no way to shortcut the process by attempting to find the answers in something outside of us. To think they can be found in "nature" is to recapitulate our alienation, failing to accept that the world is our doing and hence our responsibility.

In treating the environment as if it were nature, we also reveal ourselves as seeing the world around us in terms of surfaces. We take the things that surround us as what they look like, not as things that had to be produced, had to come into being through processes of labor. We take the present as if it simply *is*, not recognizing its rootedness in the past; our temporality, that is to say, is alienated as well. "Reality is not," wrote Georg Lukács, "it becomes."[34] We take the objects we use and live within and admire or ignore as mere things, not as the product of previous activities of human beings engaged in socially organized practices; we see the chair and not the carpenter or the carpenter's labor (or her tools, or the labor that built her tools, and so on and so on, into the past). To see humans as part of the world, as entwined with the world, would be to see in each object in one's environment a history of human practice, and at the same time to recognize that humans don't think or intend or imagine or perceive or reason or even somehow magically constitute the world but rather *engage in practice within* the world, and use the objects, built by previous practice, that they find around them to do so. To recognize that the environment is not nature, then, would be both to see the origin of what surrounds us in human practices and also to understand that the "built environment" cannot be separated from the so-called "natural" one. There is only one environment, not two, and it comes to be what it is through the actions of those (natural!) beings who live within it: it's always built and it's always natural, both at once.

4

The Nature of Artifacts

On Building and Builtness

One danger often mentioned in connection with the idea that the environment is socially constructed is that it seems to suggest that "society" could legitimately "construct" the environment *any way it wishes*, thereby denying that there could be any constraints, empirical or normative, on the practices humans might choose to engage in to transform the environment they inhabit. The worry here takes two related forms, which might be called the problem of idealism and the problem of relativism. Social constructionism, first of all, seems open to the charge that it sees the environment as infinitely malleable, and thereby ignores the hardness and reality of the world, its resistance to our wishes and our plans, and the limits it places on the sorts of practices in which we may successfully engage. Not everything a society wants can be constructed, after all: some constructions simply fail, and do so because of certain facts of nature. (Further, it is often suggested, this is precisely what is happening today with technologies that are leading to global warming, species destruction, and ecological collapse.) There is something independent of our constructive practices against which those practices are constantly bumping up, and that independent something, it might be argued, is nature. In this sense, Bill McKibben is wrong, and nature will always be with us. If one accepts the view just outlined, social constructionism seems guilty of a kind of idealism, denying the material hardness and recalcitrance of nature, imagining that whatever environment a social order dreams up might magically be constructed, and thus showing itself to be tied to the hubris of an anthropocentrism that recognizes no limits to what human beings can do with and to the world. This is the question I focus on in this chapter.

In later chapters I will turn to the second problem, the problem of relativism. For a postnaturalist social constructionism also seems liable to the charge that in the absence of something like nature as independent of our practices, it becomes impossible to distinguish those practices that are environmentally progressive and beneficial from those that are environmentally harmful: the trouble is, one might say, that without nature everything is permitted. No matter how technologized, polluted, ecologically unsustainable, or even biologically toxic a community's environment may be, it seems, it turns out to be no more and no less socially constructed than any other environment, and so it's not clear on what basis one can be called better or more environmentally appropriate than another. Without the possibility of appealing to nature as an independent standard for judging environmentally consequential actions, whatever standard a particular society comes up with has to be taken as valid. Again, an anthropocentric hubris seems to be revealed here: we humans can do whatever we want, limited in our practices by nothing except our own desires.[1]

I think that these two apparent problems with postnaturalism—the seeming lack of any *empirical* constraint on our practices of construction, on the one hand, and the seemingly equal lack of any *normative* constraint on those practices on the other—are connected, as are the answers to these problems, and I want to show this in what follows. I said above that the two characteristics of the environment we fail to notice under contemporary conditions of alienation are its builtness and its sociality. Understanding builtness, I argue in this chapter, helps resolve the worry about idealism; understanding sociality, I argue later, helps resolve the one about relativism. But it is also the case that neither of these problems can be understood without also thinking about the other, because building is always social and because sociality always expresses itself in building. And both problems, I suggest, find their real solution in the notion of practice.

If "nature" means Nature, or everything that exists, then everything we build and all our acts of building are (of course) natural. But if "nature" means nature, the world independent of us, then the things we build are not natural at all; they're artificial. The question about building is a question about artifice, about the processes through which humans transform their environment. I want to ask in what follows about the nature of artifacts, deliberately using this phrase ambiguously to mean both the question of what an artifact is (and how it is built or constructed, what artifice is employed to produce it) and also the question of the extent to which something like "nature" might be found within artifacts themselves, and within the processes through which they come to be built. I have emphasized in the first three chapters what might be called the *artifactuality of nature*: the way in which the environment we think of as natural turns out to be something that humans have always transformed. But in this chapter I want to speak about the *nature of artifacts*, and in so doing to respond to the objection that the sort of social constructionism I am proposing fails to acknowledge the existence of something like a nature independent of human practices that is the source of the ineliminable recalcitrance those practices seem always to encounter. The alienated and ideological error that leads us to fail to see the environment (which we call "nature") as built has its converse in an equally ideological error whereby we fail to notice that that which we build always remains in a certain way "natural" as well.

Environmental Restoration and Plastic Trees

In 1973 Martin Krieger published an article in *Science* with the provocative title "What's Wrong With Plastic Trees?," and argued (or seemed to argue: I've never been convinced that the article isn't a very dark joke) that the answer was, not much. The value of natural environments, he suggested in what was an early version of (traditional) social constructionism, is socially produced—the "natural" is what is *taken* to be natural in a particular society, and therefore "the way in which we experience nature is conditioned by our society."[2] As a result, he argued, rather than working to prevent the destruction of nature we might instead simply try to redefine and recondition our experience of it in a way that eliminates our concern. It might be cheaper and more efficient, he suggested, to produce artificial environments that serve the same purposes as those now served by the ones we call "natural," or even—by employing strategies from advertising and other forms of social engineering—to manipulate public tastes or even memories so that these new environments would be experienced *as* natural ones.[3] Indeed, something like this already takes place, Krieger pointed out, writing that "the phenomena that the public thinks of as 'natural' often require great artifice in their creation." The flow of water over Niagara Falls, for example, is manipulated through complex systems of pipes and sluices for purposes oriented toward both the generation of electricity and the maintenance of the falls as a tourist attraction.[4] There is no reason why this sort of thing could not be extended further, Krieger claimed, or why it should not be. Indeed, *whatever valued function a natural object serves could in principle be served*

by some sufficiently technologically advanced reproduction of that object, and it will in general be an open question whether the natural or the artificial object does a better job of serving that function. Thus there might not be anything wrong with plastic trees—as long as people enjoy, or could be convinced to enjoy, hiking among them.[5]

Whether Krieger meant this argument seriously or not, at one level his article can surely be read, as Mark Sagoff or Eric Katz have read it, as a kind of reductio ad absurdum of anthropocentric and utilitarian forms of ("shallow") environmentalism that focus only on human experiences of nature.[6] If nature's value derives merely from its value for human beings, then it seems plausible to imagine that artificial ("plastic") substitutes for natural objects could in principle be produced that would provide the same kind of value, or if they could not be produced it would be for contingent reasons having to do with the limits of our technologies and not fundamental ones having to do with the difference between the natural and the artificial. But in fact Krieger's line of argument is quite general, and could apply to nonanthropocentric positions as well. Biocentrists, for whom value inheres in the intrinsic goal-directedness of life or its ability to maintain homeostasis, would have difficulty explaining why sufficiently complex self-maintaining robots are not equally morally considerable as animals; ecocentrists, who value the complexity or biodiversity of ecosystems, would have to acknowledge similar value in a terraformed Mars or an "invented" ecosystem consisting of genetically engineered or even plastic creatures whose complexity and diversity were sufficiently great.[7] If the value of "natural" items depends on some particular empirical property P that such items possess, that is, it seems always possible (again, in principle) for artificial objects to be designed that also possess P and that therefore presumably would have the same value: but this means that the claim that certain items are valuable *because they are natural* (rather than *because they possess P*) is false. The difficulty here casts further light on the notion we found in McKibben that the "end of nature" might be a disvalue *beyond* the disvalues produced by pollution and species extinction and ozone depletion and the like.[8] For the only way around Krieger's difficulty would seem to be to posit a value in *naturalness itself*, just as McKibben does: not a value in what a natural object does or provides or allows, but simply in the fact of that object's being natural at all.

Such a value in naturalness itself seems to be key to the arguments of two environmental theorists who think there is something very wrong with plastic trees, Robert Elliot and Eric Katz, both of whom have written influential articles (which both later turned into books) on the idea of "environmental restoration." Each author employs the notion of nature that I have been arguing environmental philosophers ought to reject, which causes them no end of trouble; the difficulties they find themselves in, however, help clarify what I mean by talking about the "nature of artifacts."

Elliot proposes a series of thought experiments designed to show that naturalness is itself a value beyond whatever other values natural objects might possess, beginning by imagining a mining company that offers to "repair" the damage its activities cause to a particular tract of land by afterward restoring the area so that no difference from the original will be noticeable, even by experts. Elliot compares such a case—which he treats as a purely counterfactual possibility, since surely in practice no such restoration could ever be so perfect—with the case of a work of art being destroyed and then replaced by a reproduction that is perceptually indiscernible from the original, the work perhaps of a master forger. The owner of such a work of art would not be satisfied to learn that her Vermeer has been replaced by a perfect reproduction of a Vermeer by Van Meegeren; and even if the replacement were to take place in such a way that she never learned of it, and continued to admire her beloved "Vermeer" as she always had, we would still be inclined to say that she had suffered a harm, although admittedly one of which she was not aware. The value of a work of art, Elliot argues, derives not merely from our experience of it but from its actual properties, which include not merely its present ones (its physical shape and color and structure) but also its history—the causal chain leading from this pigment on this canvas back to that painter at that moment in time. The genesis of an object, that is, can be relevant to its value. If correct, this point explains why environmental restoration of the sort imagined in Elliot's thought experiment fails in one crucial respect to restore the value lost through environmental damage. The landscape restored by the mining company might look the same as the original one, and might indeed be inhabited by the same sorts of animals and plants and even support precisely the same ecosystemic functioning, but its genesis is crucially different, for it is the product of human action. Such a landscape is not *natural*, although in every respect it looks and functions just as the natural one does, and Elliot thinks this shows that naturalness can have a value over and above the value of all those looks and functions.[9]

Elliot's original article, titled "Faking Nature," argued against what he took as the theoretical possibility that companies engaging in environmentally damaging activities might think they could excuse themselves by promising restorations of this sort; his point was that such restorations were more like forgeries or fakes than anything else, and hence would not fully reproduce the lost value, even if they were possible in practice (which he doubted). Almost a decade later, Eric Katz published an equally important essay (discussed earlier) with an even more provocative title, "The Big Lie."[10] Katz—who has described Krieger's article on plastic trees as having had the same kind of effect on him as the reading of Hume did on Kant—was disturbed to realize that an idea that Elliot saw as "purely theoretical, almost fanciful" had in the interim become something taken seriously, and not by those who wanted an excuse to be able to harm nature but rather by those who claimed to want to protect it.[11] "Ecological restoration" had become (and has continued to be) a booming industry, with its own journals and conferences and practical projects. Among the best known of these is the work on restoration of the tallgrass prairie in northern Illinois by volunteers associated with the Nature Conservancy, led by Steve Packard—work that has been quite successful in recreating some of the prairie biomes and oak savannas that once dominated the landscape of the Midwest but that years of European settlement and agriculture seemed quite thoroughly to have destroyed, and in learning important lessons about the ecosystemic functioning of those landscapes.[12] The idea of restoration possesses an obvious ethical appeal: if nature has been harmed through human action, don't humans have a moral responsibility to repair that harm—to return a landscape that has been damaged to the state it was in before the damage occurred? For Katz, however, this idea involves a deep and telling error. Although he says that he has "nothing but admiration for Packard's work," and indeed emphasizes that he has no objections to attempts to repair damaged ecosystems, he insists that to call such restored landscapes "natural" fundamentally misrepresents what is really going on. "Despite his goal of restoring an original natural condition," Katz writes, "Packard is actually creating an artifactual substitute for the real savanna, one based on human technologies and designed for human purposes."[13] A restored landscape is not a part of nature at all: it is an artifact.

Katz rejects Elliot's analogy between environmental restoration and art forgery, however, because he thinks it is a category mistake to compare a natural landscape to a work of art. The concept of forgery implicitly involves appeal to the idea of an artist or creator, Katz argues: to forge something is to produce an object in a way that deceives others about who created it. But natural landscapes don't have creators. The trouble with an "ecologically restored" environment, Katz writes, does not derive from a misunderstanding over the identity of [its] creator.... It derives instead from the misplaced category of "creator"—for natural objects do not have creators as human artworks do. Once we realize that the natural entity we are viewing has been "restored" by a human artisan it ceases to be a natural object. It is not a forgery; it is an artifact.[14]

What makes something an artifact, for Katz, is its connection to human intention: an artifact possesses an internal relation to a human purpose and would not exist without it.[15] Natural entities, by contrast, are not the product of intention. They were not designed for any purpose, and indeed were not designed at all. Thus they possess an entirely different ontological status from that of artifacts. And since ecologically restored landscapes are indeed the result of intentional human action and come into existence because of human purposes, it follows for Katz that they are artifacts, not parts of nature. To treat restored landscapes as identical or even similar to the ones they attempt to reproduce is to fall prey to an ontological confusion: they are not even the same *kind* of thing.[16] For Katz, it is the attempt to pass off what is actually an artifact as if it were natural that turns environmental restoration into a big lie. The very idea that a natural environment *could* be restored, he is convinced, is itself tied to an anthropocentrism that believes humans can and should transform the natural environment for their own purposes. Despite its claim to imitate and honor nature, Katz argues, restoration as a project in fact paradoxically exhibits the same instinct to dominate nature that is responsible for the environmental problems we face. It represents a "technological fix" that attempts to manipulate nature to satisfy human needs.[17]

Here once again, as in McKibben's argument, the naturalness of something, over and above any specific characteristics it might have, is taken as an independent source of value. Katz, who is explicitly and unabashedly a dualist, understands nature in the same way McKibben does: it consists of that part of the world that is separate from and independent of the human.[18] As separate, nature is "autonomous," Katz writes; to dominate nature is to "destroy ... natural autonomy.... The entities and systems that comprise nature are not permitted to be free, to pursue their independent and unplanned courses of development, growth, and change."[19] Ecological restoration, he argues, dominates nature in precisely this sense. A restored environment is the way it is because humans wanted it to be so, and hence it is not a place where nature is free. The disturbed landscape may have been restored so that it looks like the previous, natural one, but the natural *autonomy* of that landscape has not been, and cannot be, restored. Packard and his followers treat objects in the landscapes they "restore" as means to an end that is finally a human one—to produce a perfect simulacrum of what humans have already destroyed. They burn plants, they pull up weeds, they collect seeds and scatter them far from where they were collected. Even if they were fully successful, the resulting simulacrum would still be a cruel hoax, for nature's autonomy would still be missing. It would be like trying to make up for the loss of a loved one by substituting a robot or replicant who looked exactly like the person lost but whose every act had been preprogrammed.

Katz sees a teleological character to artifacts that is not possessed by natural objects. In this sense his account is staunchly (and admirably) Darwinian. Natural objects, he writes, "were not created for a particular purpose; they have no set manner of use. Although we often speak as if natural individuals (for example, predators) have roles to play in ecosystemic well-being (the maintenance of optimum population levels), this kind of talk is either metaphorical or fallacious. No one created or designed the mountain lion as a regulator of the deer population."[20] But there is an ambiguity here, and one has the sense that Katz is equivocating on the meaning of "purpose." For although it is surely true that living things were not created *for* any particular purpose, it still makes sense (even post-Darwin) to talk about them as *having* purposes, and hence to use teleological terms in describing them—they search for food, they attempt to avoid predators, and so on. In that sense, we can talk about their needs and even (if we're very careful) about what is good for them. But this is not the sort of teleology Katz has in mind. We might distinguish here between an external and internal telos—between the purpose *for which* an object was created (which doesn't exist in the case of "natural" entities, according to Katz, but which he says does necessarily exist in the case of every artifact) and the purposes an object may come to be said to *have* by virtue of its internal structure (including, in the case of living creatures, the—in themselves purposeless—evolutionary processes that have produced it). It is the first sort of purpose that concerns Katz in his account of the difference between natural entities and artifacts: since a restored landscape is produced (by humans) *for a purpose*, that of restoration, it cannot be natural.

Katz's view of nature is in this sense antiteleological: it is precisely the (external) purposelessness of natural objects that is central to his argument and that distinguishes it from biocentric ones that tie intrinsic value to the possession of (internal) purposes by living things. For him the crucial distinction isn't between living and nonliving things but between natural and artificial ones. Plenty of nonliving things (rocks, mountains, beaches) are natural, he notes, and these too deserve moral respect for what he calls their "autonomy" from human purposes.[21] On the other hand, he writes, "artifacts stand in a necessary *ontological* relationship with human purpose," and elsewhere he says "it would be impossible to imagine an artifact that is not designed to meet a human purpose."[22] The external human purpose determines what the artifact in fact *is*. Artifacts, Katz writes, "have no nature of their own, merely the purposes given to them by human interests."[23]

Artifacts and Intentions

Yet it is not at all clear that the connection between artifactuality and intention is as straightforward as this account makes it sound. In particular the tight connection between the builder's intention (the purpose *for which* the artifact was produced) and what the artifact *is* may be questionable. One might argue, for example, that the "nature" of an artifact is not determined so much by what its builder intended as it is by the way in which it is used. Indeed, there may not have been any original intention, or any original builder, at all: think of a stick picked up from the ground and used as a weapon. Furthermore, an artifact built for one purpose may turn out not to be useful for that purpose at all but instead be able to serve a quite different and unanticipated one: think of compounds invented by pharmaceutical companies to treat one illness that are later discovered to be useful for other purposes. And, of course, the use of an artifact may change over time in ways unintended by those who first constructed it, and indeed we may even be ignorant of what those original intentions were: think of Stonehenge, now an artifact for tourism, the Indian mounds in the Ohio Valley, some of which have now been turned into bunkers on golf courses. The point of these examples is to show that the "nature" of an artifact may be independent of what the people who built the artifact intended, even of whether they had any intentions at all.[24]

Katz's claim that artifacts have "no nature of their own" becomes particularly problematic when one considers the case of domesticated animals or of genetically modified organisms. Katz is explicit that he views domesticated animals as artifacts; they are certainly produced for human purposes and have (many of) the qualities they have because they satisfy human needs.[25] The same is true of genetically engineered entities as well. Yet to assert that such entities "have no nature of their own" seems to deny what is quite obvious, which is that such entities *do* possess what I have called an internal telos just as much as do creatures that evolved without human intervention; biocentrists are surely right to claim that all living things possess a teleological character in *this* sense. The fact that such internal purposes may (in part) be there because they serve human interests does not make them any less internal, which is to say any less intrinsic to what the animal or plant *is*; and if that is so, it is hard to see in what sense it "has no nature of its own."

Indeed, it is just that nature that we are concerned with when (for instance) we worry about the environmental or health damage that genetically modified foods might produce. Katz's appeal to human intention as ontologically determinative of artifactuality (and in particular as what distinguishes an artifact from a natural entity) ignores the fact that it is often the *unintended* consequences of human actions and of the products those actions create that cause the most significant environmental concerns, and that those consequences follow from the "nature" of those products, even though nobody intended or even anticipated them.[26] Automobiles are surely artifacts, produced intentionally by humans to satisfy human needs, but what about the air pollution, or the global warming, that the manufacture and use of automobiles bring about in turn? Are *those* artifacts? (They're surely not anything Katz would call natural.) Katz writes that it is "impossible to imagine an artifact that is not designed to meet a human purpose," but global warming was not designed to meet a human purpose, and in fact was not designed at all: that's just the problem. These are human-made items, and so seem artifactual, and yet nobody *intended* them.

Perhaps Katz would say that they are in a distinct category, neither artifacts nor natural, although there's something odd about denying that (anthropogenic) global warming is "artificial."[27] But the issue here is a more general one having to do with the artifacts (automobiles, coal-fired electric plants, etc.) that produce these consequences, not simply with the consequences themselves. The truth is that *every* artifact we build produces unanticipated effects, which means that *every artifact has more to it than its producers intended*—but to say this is to see that what an artifact *is*, its "nature," always *exceeds* its relation to human intention. (And so it always does have a "nature of its own.") This is so because every artifact is *real*, and not simply an idea in someone's head. There may be, as Katz insists, some human intention behind the production (or the use) of every artifact, but because it is real, what an artifact *is* always goes beyond that intention—it's the *realization*, the making real, of an intention that makes an artifact, and that's different. To make something real is precisely to see it enter a realm beyond intention: this is something that every engineer, every gardener, and for that matter every person who acts in the world knows full well. This last point is central to what I want to say about the nature of artifacts. For that realm beyond intention, the one in which every artifact resides, might turn out to be the very realm, supposedly independent of the artificial one, that people have in mind when they speak of "nature." And if that's so, then perhaps we ought to stop talking about nature and start talking instead about reality—a reality in which (real) human artifacts are not "ontologically" distinguished from natural entities but rather recognized as continuous with them.

Katz's own account of the role of intention in the formation of artifacts is too narrowly instrumentalist and utilitarian. His paradigm case seems to be the fashioning of a tool to help satisfy human needs for food or shelter, and he interprets the intentions behind the production of other, less obviously "useful" artifacts in essentially the same way, as though committed to a strictly hedonistic psychology according to which all human actions are performed to satisfy some direct human need and are therefore all "anthropocentric." Yet a little thought about the variety of objects human beings produce through their (intentional!) actions reveals how unlikely this is. Such a list might include artworks, babies, wilderness preserves, religious icons, animal rescue leagues, lunar rovers, suicide pacts, drum solos, jokes.... It just isn't true that every object intentionally produced by humans is produced because of its ability to satisfy human desires (and so is "anthropocentric"), at least if one doesn't so expand the category of desire (or of anthropocentrism) in such a way that one simply begs the question. People have lots of different sorts of motivation for producing objects, and to say that because any motivation humans have is a human motivation everything they produce must serve narrowly anthropocentric purposes is to make a logical error.[28]

In particular, one of the motivations that could operate in certain cases might be an interest in allowing unpredictable things to happen. Starting a garden, hosting a party, writing up chord charts for a jazz combo, making a baby: one might want to do such things out of a feeling that the object produced through one's actions might turn out to be remarkable *in its own right* and *for its own sake*, not because of what it will make possible for oneself. Similarly, one can imagine artifacts built simply for the purpose of seeing what will happen when these particular materials are put together in this particular way. (Here we might think of certain artworks in which aleatoric elements predominate, out of the explicit intention to allow the functioning of forces beyond the artist's control.) We can imagine, indeed, an artifact built precisely because it will be useless, will satisfy no need: its purpose, as the Kantian phrase goes, might be purposelessness. Some works of art surely have this character, and perhaps all do. Those that do would serve as counterexamples to Katz's claim that all intentionally produced objects are intrinsically anthropocentric or express an attitude of domination.

These last considerations return us—from a very different angle—to the question of whether ecological restorations might be accurately compared to works of art. For restorations, too, might have the sort of character that puts into question Katz's narrowly instrumentalist view of the kinds of intentions that might be at work in an artifact. Of course, a restored landscape is not an artifact whose purpose is purposelessness in the way that a work of art might be. But it could have a different purpose: to allow the independent working out of so-called "natural" processes, meaning those processes that would have occurred in an area had there been no human habitation there.[29] And so, while Katz is right that there is a human intention behind restoration activity, he doesn't see that that intention might be the coming into being of an area in which *nonintentional processes would be allowed to occur without hindrance*. The intention of such practices, we might say, is to transcend intentionality. Katz calls the notion of such an intention a "paradox," but it's not a vicious one: the idea is that humans might intentionally produce a situation that is out of human control, beyond our ability to plan or to predict, and perhaps one that bears a close resemblance to the one that existed before we set foot in the area.[30] The product in such a case would doubtless be an artifact, in the sense of having been intentionally produced by human beings, but once produced it would nonetheless be operating according to its *own* "nature," not one introduced from outside.

Environmental restoration takes place in landscapes that have already been damaged by human actions—including, typically, actions anthropocentrically oriented toward the direct satisfaction of human needs. The idea is to restore them by more human action, so as to return them to the condition they were in before the harmful actions occurred. The purposes behind such restorations are surely human, but they operate against human interests narrowly (and anthropocentrically) construed. Katz, as we have seen, argues that all artifacts express the intentions of their human producers, that they therefore possess an internal ontological connection to human purposes, and that they thus are intrinsically anthropocentric. But the examples I have provided suggest that this argument fallaciously trades on ambiguities in the notion of human intention, since humans can in fact intend for nonintentional processes to be allowed to operate, and in general can intend for their own narrow intentions not to be satisfied. When they so intend, I would argue, the product they produce—for instance, a restored landscape—is no longer so clearly "anthropocentric," thus vitiating the force of Katz's critique.

Interestingly, Katz at one point concedes that although intention is a necessary condition for something's being an artifact, it is not a sufficient condition. "Some things," he writes, "are the result of human intentions although we would hesitate to call them artifacts. Human infants, for example, may be the result of intention and purpose. Interhuman relationships—for example, my friendship with John—may also be intentional."[31] Still, Katz argues, natural entities are never the product of intention, and so since restorations are intentional, they can never be natural. Yet the concession is damaging. Much of the rhetorical strength of Katz's position, after all, depends not merely on claiming that restorations aren't natural but also on asserting that they *are* artifacts. But now it turns out that there is a third possible category, consisting of objects intentionally produced by human beings that are *neither* natural *nor* artifacts. And the items mentioned as belonging to this category seem attractive ones from the point of view of intrinsic value: friendships, children, and the like. Arguably artworks might belong here too. But then what about environmental restorations? Katz offers no criteria for distinguishing this third sort of object from ordinary artifacts, and so it is not clear why he thinks the intentional character of restorations puts them in the category of artifacts and not of things like friendships or children.

The example of children came up in chapter 1, and it is worth considering further. Katz is of course right that one would not normally call a baby an artifact. But it remains true that a baby is an object produced through human actions that, although they may be engaged in without the intention of producing a child, may also be engaged in with exactly that conscious intention in mind. To make a baby (and to do so intentionally) is to engage in actions that then set into motion processes that go beyond one's control—processes of gestation and birth, in the first place, but then also afterward processes of physical and mental development that ultimately lead to personhood and autonomy. Indeed, engendering such autonomy may be the intention behind the actions that bring the child to life: the intention might be, that is, to produce something—some*one*—with a "nature of its own." Part of the joy of parenthood might well lie in recognizing and appreciating that the child one has produced is *not* there for one's own purposes. That the child's existence was nonetheless something the parents intended, and that they intentionally engaged in actions and put forces into motion precisely so as to cause it to come to be, in no way detracts from the autonomy thereby produced.

Might restoring an ecosystem have more in common with bearing and raising a child than with forging an artwork or otherwise faking nature? There are reasons to believe that it might. Thus Steve Packard has written that "every restorationist knows the ecosystem will respond in unpredictable ways that rise out of itself. That's precisely what we want to liberate.... The goal of restorationists is precisely to set in motion processes we neither fully control nor fully understand.... Similar to good parenting or coaching or teaching, the goal of restoration is to help some life go forward on its own—and in the process become more truly itself."[32] Whatever the value of the analogy, the problem for Katz's argument is clear: if the products of some kinds of intentional human action by his own admission are not artifacts, and if those sorts of actions seem to involve initiating and then allowing the operation of natural (and specifically biological) forces "to go forward on [their] own," then it is no longer clear why environmental restoration might not be one of them. And so his claim that the product of a restoration is inevitably an artifact turns out to fail.[33]

Restorations as Wild Artifacts

Considerations such as these seem to have led Elliot, in his 1997 book, to take a more moderate view of restoration, acknowledging that the intention behind certain sorts of restorations might indeed be to "assist nature to reassert itself," and criticizing Katz's tendency to assimilate all restorations to the category of anthropocentric artifacts.[34] "A restored natural environment," Elliot wrote, "provided it accords with natural designs and is constituted by natural objects, may possess considerable intrinsic value, and certainly much more than the degraded environment which was the object of restoration."[35] Although Elliot continued to insist that an unbroken "natural continuity reaching into the past" plays a significant role in the value of an environment—a continuity that is certainly broken in the case of restorations—still he seemed to assert an independent value in what he called "naturalness," meaning the operation of natural forces without human hindrance. Restored environments, if the restoration is done in the right way, he suggested, may indeed come to possess naturalness in this sense even if they lack natural continuity with the past.[36]

Such a distinction—between "naturalness" in the synchronic sense of contemporary independence from intentional human involvement and "natural continuity" in the diachronic sense of a history in which human action has never appeared—is a useful one. Katz writes movingly about the white-tailed deer that make their homes on Fire Island in New York (where he spends his summers), and sees in them a reminder of "wild nature"; but as he himself concedes, their presence there—certainly their numbers, and their remarkable tameness—is unquestionably the result of human actions, in particular the removal of predators and the provision of plentiful sources of food in the form of friendly handouts and well-tended gardens.[37] They're thus not "natural" in his strong sense. Katz describes them instead as "vestiges of a truly wild natural community," which seems to suggest at least that their ancestors existed on the island before any humans did. But it isn't clear first of all if this is really true, or second, why it's so important: if it turned out that the deer were first brought to the island by early settlers or on a native longboat, so that there never was a "truly wild natural community" for them to be the vestiges of, would that make the deer *now* less wild?[38] To call them wild is rather to say that the biological or metabolic processes at work in them today operate independently of any intentional human actions, although they surely aren't "natural" in the sense that their behaviors or even their metabolisms are exactly the same as they would have been had humans never become entangled with them. It makes much more sense, that is, to identify the deer's wildness with what Elliot calls "naturalness" than with the absence of humans from their history.

But the same sort of thing might well be true of successfully restored landscapes: they too might be wild in the sense that today "natural" forces operate in them independently of human action. In fact, wildness in this sense seems much closer to what people actually value in so-called natural landscapes than the absence of human intervention in those landscapes in the past. Elliot's example of art forgery certainly sustains his point that the history of an object may be relevant to its ontological status and value, but it does not follow from this that the only history that guarantees a landscape to be authentically "natural" (and so not a forgery) is one where human action has *never* appeared. Instead of ruling out all restorations as inauthentic, in fact, the appeal to history here might well make it possible to distinguish environmentally sensitive transformations of a landscape from harmful depredations of it; some transformations, we might say, acknowledge and honor the history of the land—which includes both its prehuman history *and* the history of prior human transformations of it—while others simply ignore that history, blindly imposing new structures with no concern for what this particular place has previously been and has previously meant. But insisting that the ontological status of an area depends so crucially on the question of whether human action has ever played a role in its history seems merely to be a (misanthropic, and in its own way anthropocentric) fetish. Giving up the fetish raises the question of why we value the "naturalness" of certain areas: is it really because no one has ever been there, or is it rather because we seem to see in them the forces of "nonhuman nature" *currently* at work?

Elliot notes that a forgery occurs when someone successfully reproduces the *present* properties of an entity while hiding the fact that the reproduction's *history* differs significantly from that of the original. Yet this point would only be relevant to ecological restoration if somehow the restorers, having worked secretly in the dead of night, afterward falsely claimed to have discovered a "natural" landscape, concealing their own role in its history. But of course, no restorers actually do this. Nor would any serious restorer even be inclined to say that the restored landscape was the same as or had the same value as the "original" one—which is not, however, to say that its value is less. What, after all, would "the same" mean, especially given that environments are always changing, and have no clear "origin"? A restored prairie in the twenty-first century, brought into being by the hard, intentional, and scientifically informed work of volunteer restorers, is obviously not the same as the eighteenth-century prairie found by early European settlers, not even if a catalog of the flora and fauna turned out to be similar. It has a different history. But an eighteenth-century prairie was similarly not the same as a sixteenth-century one, or as one a thousand years before that. Landscapes change over time because of the actions of the animals that inhabit them—and, of course, among those animals we must also count ourselves. One could call landscapes that humans have inhabited "unnatural" ones, of course, using the sort of stipulative definition of nature discussed in chapter 1. Yet even those landscapes might still turn out to be *wild*, like Katz's deer: and isn't it the recreation of that wildness that restoration is really all about?

Thinking this through might lead us to see how an artifact built by humans might nonetheless at the same time still be wild. To call it wild would be to say that in it, forces are currently operating independently of humans, although it will have been human action (and human purpose) in the first place that led to these forces operating. To produce a wild artifact might mean to (intentionally) put natural forces into action and then (intentionally) to *let them go*, in ways that are fundamentally unpredictable and outside one's control. It is this sort of intention, I have been arguing, that Katz fails to see might be at work within the artifact called an environmental restoration. Elliot is more willing to recognize the possibility of this sort of thing, but his acknowledgment of it in his later book remains grudging. The only sorts of restoration projects Elliot seems to countenance are short-term ones, one-shot affairs in which humans remove ecological harm by reproducing the initial conditions for an ecosystem's healthy functioning, after which the restored area is left to its own devices as "nature" is allowed (as Elliot puts it) to "recolonize" the area. The hope in such projects, he writes, is that "human intervention, although initially quite marked, might diminish and disappear."[39] But in truth, as he notes, many restoration projects require a significant degree of ongoing management, which is to say continual human intervention. And that does seem to raise a problem for him: if *continual* human intervention is necessary to manage the area, doesn't that inevitably rob it of its wildness?[40]

It doesn't, it seems to me, any more than the continued role of human gardens on Fire Island as food for the deer robs the deer of their wildness. Once we abandon the fetish that only a landscape that humans have never touched could possibly be wild, we might begin to see that even ongoing human action within a landscape could be consistent with its ongoing wildness, and could indeed help to maintain it. And once we see that a landscape is a dynamic entity, always undergoing transformation through the actions of the various organisms and weather and geological forces that form it, we might come to realize that the point of restoration is not the reproduction of a particular *thing* but rather the putting into play of processes—of wildness—that we then allow to operate unpredictably and unimaginably in ways that are outside our ability to control. To recognize this would in turn be to see that the wildness that we're after is there all the time, throughout the restoration process; it's not something that comes in at the end, not something we *produce*, but rather something that we *use*. The ongoing interventions that worry Elliot may be significant; they may involve digging, planting, weeding, burning, and a whole series of other activities; but nonetheless, looked at carefully, all the processes these actions require *are themselves wild*.

The remark by Steve Packard quoted earlier makes just this point: so much in restoration, even in highly organized and planned restoration, is outside our control, so much is unpredictable, that it is clear that wildness indeed *is there*. To take just one example, the seeds that are painstakingly collected in a prairie restoration project from one area are then transported to another, where they are dispersed, which dispersal works only through the action of wind and gravity and air resistance; the few seeds that grow begin to germinate owing to contingencies of soil and microbes and insect life; the growing plants burst into flower through the action of sun and rain and temperature; the flowers themselves produce new seeds through the acts of air and bee and butterfly. These processes operate outside us and beyond us; we do not fully understand their workings, and we cannot predict their outcome with any precision. It is not correct to say that we "intervene" in them, nor do we even act to modify them. Rather, we set (some) of them in motion, and then find ourselves absolutely at their mercy. In doing so, we find ourselves in the presence of the wild. In restoration, I am arguing, the wild is always there.

The Wildness of Artifacts

But there's one more step to the argument. For if we begin to think even more carefully, we might come to see that the wild is always there in *all* our acts, and in all our artifacts. If the notion of wildness refers to the operation of forces in an object or organism that operate unpredictably and beyond the grasp of any human actor, then this moment of wildness arises in every artifact, not just in restorations. To construct an artifact is *always* to put processes into motion whose workings we do not fully understand and whose consequences we do not fully foresee. Gardeners and bakers, like parents and jazz musicians, know the feeling of insecurity, the sense that the outcome of one's actions is never what one expects and depends on forces beyond one; but so too, after all, do engineers. To build an object—*any* object—is to build something that always exceeds one's intentions, that always possesses something of the unpredictable and unknown about it. As soon as it's built (and indeed, even before), it starts to crumble, as forces operate on it—forces of air and gravity, of heat and light, of decay and oxidation and time—whose total effects can never be grasped at once: which means that from the very beginning the object has already escaped the builder's control, and so is something other than what she had in mind when she started to build.

And this escaping, this moment of wildness, takes place not merely after the building but is rather the condition of the possibility of building itself. Here the discussion returns, finally, to the question of what building is. We cannot build without the employment of processes whose fundamental character—whose *nature*, I might even be willing to say —is not and cannot be fully known to us. This is a point on which Heidegger insists, noting the blindness—which is no blindness at all but rather, as he puts it, a different sort of sight—with which we use tools, the hammer as "invisible" to one's experience of hammering as any part of one's body is.[41] But more than the tool, I want to emphasize here the processes themselves that are at work in those practices through which I construct new objects in the world: for I could not hammer without the force of gravity, not to speak of the metabolic processes taking place within my muscles and my brain. And as the nail goes deeper into the wood, the chemical structure of the former encounters the biological structure of the latter in a way that produces complex reactions on each side that none of us could hope to grasp or even really fully to imagine, all of these subject ultimately to Newtonian laws of motion, or at different levels to relativistic and quantum mechanical effects as well. Without these processes there would be no hammering; yet the hammering goes on, and indeed can only go on, in a kind of deep ignorance of their details. I depend upon them, and depend indeed upon the fact that I need not worry about them. One cannot bake bread without relying on complex biochemical processes taking place within millions of yeast cells, processes one cannot hope fully to understand or predict; one cannot write a software program either without relying on a compiler and an assembler, and on the firmware underneath them and the logic gates and flows of electrons underneath *them,* which again cannot fully be grasped at once, and in any case needn't be; and, of course, one cannot build a nuclear reactor without relying on processes of radioactive decay whose essential unpredictability is quite explicitly a precondition for its ability to function at all. Building an artifact requires black boxes all the way down: *to design and build anything requires presupposing a whole set of processes that one does not design*, and whose operation beyond one's understanding and intention is necessary for the building to take place.

There is a *gap*, in the construction of every artifact, between the intention with which the builder acts and the consequences of her acts, a gap that is ineliminable and indeed constitutive of what it is to construct something; and in this gap resides something like what I earlier called wildness. And that gap, as I have just been suggesting, is not only the one between what we intend in our actions and the unintended consequences those actions nonetheless inevitably bring about but rather, and perhaps more important, it is there between our actions and their *intended* consequences, too, arising even when the object produced seems to turn out in just the way we had planned. It is a *temporal* gap, what Derrida would call a deferral, for even the successful execution of a plan requires, indeed depends upon, *waiting* for something that goes beyond the planning and beyond even the acts that put the plan into motion. The thought and even the act are never the same as the effect: something *else* must first happen, which takes time. This is clear enough in the work of the gardener (or the ecological restorer), who lays the seed in the ground and then must patiently wait, sometimes for years, for a series of unimaginable processes to operate so as to bring forth the hoped-for plant. But it's there too (and perhaps it's only the arrogant triumphalism of technology that blinds us to this) in the work of the engineer, who also must start processes on their way—whether these be chemical, gravitational, thermodynamic, or whatever—and then must wait for them to act before her intended goal is achieved, though that goal is never fully achieved, and never fully predictable, any more than that of the gardener.[42] Not even science or technology is self-sufficient; even the engineer must wait for something to happen, and that happening occurs somewhere beyond her own act. No artifact can be produced without this moment of waiting, for the thought is never identical to the deed, and the deed itself is never identical to what it does.[43]

When humans produce an artifact, I am suggesting, no matter what it may be, they do so by allowing processes to come into play that then operate *independently* to bring about a result—which result may bear a greater or lesser resemblance to what the producers originally had in mind. And this is true whether what is being produced is an oak savanna or a tomato patch or a nuclear reactor or a baby. In each case we allow forces to operate that are not our own, and so find ourselves facing an inevitable gap. In chapter 2 I argued that there is no way for a human being to be in an environment that does not involve being *active* in that environment and so changing it. What I am arguing here is the converse of this: that there is no way to be active in an environment—that is, to build something—without depending on the operation of forces that *escape* one, that go beyond one's intentions and one's understanding. The distinction between the natural and the artificial on which Katz's and Elliot's arguments depend makes no sense, not merely because we cannot be in the world of "nature" without changing it and thereby turning it into an artifact but also because we cannot produce an artifact without depending crucially and ineliminably on the forces of what Katz and Elliot would call "nature." This is the "nature of artifacts": *every artifact is "natural,"* or, better put, *is wild*, not (only) because we ourselves are wild but because no artifact could come to be without wildness, which is to say without that gap between what we intend and what we actually do. That gap, that wildness, is part of what it is for something to be an action in the world at all; without the twin temporal gaps between the thought and the deed on the one hand and between the deed and what it does on the other, the very idea of an action as something *done* by someone would be meaningless. There could be no practices at all without the operation of forces that are beyond the ken of those who engage in them. In that sense, *nothing we do could be done without* (what here might be called) "*nature.*"

But this last sentence must not be misunderstood. One might interpret what I'm saying here as meaning that there is an irreducible element of "otherness" to the world and our actions in it, and then identifying that otherness with nature in Mill's second sense. Yet this threatens a return to the very dichotomy between humans and nature that I think needs to be overcome, ontologizing it even more radically. To speak of the "otherness of the world" is to suggest that there is something non-other, that is to say something the *same,* over here on the human side; but what I have been suggesting is that the human side, because it is constituted by our practices, and because those practices cannot exist without what I have called the gap, *is itself right out there with and in otherness,* which therefore is not so other at all.[44] There is nothing "other" about the experience of the gardener or the baker or the engineer; when we set processes in motion to produce an artifact, we do so in *utter familiarity* rather than with any sense of otherness, not even noticing the way our every mundane action requires the operation of forces that go (and start) beyond us. Beyond us, but not alien to us. They're beyond our knowledge, perhaps, but not beyond our action, for to experience what I have called the gap, to allow forces to operate and then wait for them to do so, simply *is* what it is to act, and thus as I have argued it is what it is be a human in-the-world. The fact that we employ forces in our actions that are beyond our control or our understanding does not show "nature" to be other than us but rather that humans and what is here called "nature" are *inseparable.* And—to extend an idea from chapter 2—this is not simply because we humans are the passive products of ("natural") evolution but rather because we actively transform the world surrounding us by—passively!—allowing the ("natural") processes within it to operate.[45] We change the world around us with our every act, but in doing so we never leave the single world we inhabit—a world that now can only misleadingly be called the "natural" one, since it includes at the same time all the artifacts that we produce and that we are constantly producing through our actions.

If I am right about the role of "wildness"—which is turning out to mean, simply, *reality*—in all human productive activity, then my suggestion that the landscapes produced by environmental restorations might be *both* artifacts *and* wild now looks like a special case of a more general truth: *all* artifacts are wild. But environmental restoration is indeed a special case, and I do not mean to deny its distinctiveness. What is special about it, obviously, is its intention to recreate a landscape similar to one that existed at the same location at some point in the past (before, typically, some kind of harm to it occurred), and then to allow that landscape to develop as it would have had human beings not appeared on the scene. This is a plausible and often worthy goal, but it needs to be understood in the right way. For once we realize that when human practices transform the world, the artifacts produced by those practices are no less "natural" than any other item in the environment, then the special human practice called environmental restoration reveals itself as merely one such possible transformation, but not one with a privileged or even unique status. It is an option that we might choose to pursue, for social and political reasons, perhaps, or scientific ones, or out of an interest in historical preservation for its own sake—or, of course, out of an admirable desire to fix something that has gone terribly wrong. But it makes no sense to pursue it for what might be called ontological reasons, as though in restoring such a landscape we were somehow magically transforming it, removing the human stain from it and returning it to its original status as part of "nature" (and no longer an artifact). Instead, as I have tried to show, it might be best to think of a restored landscape as more like a work of art—but not as a forgery or a big lie.[46]

But if this is so, then Elliot's concern that restoration projects should minimize ongoing human activity and management seems misplaced. If the role of humans in the environment is, as I have argued, fundamentally a transformative one, then what more appropriate way to interact with the environment is there than through the sort of ongoing, hands-on activity that real restoration projects involve? Precisely in such concrete and sustained action—in clearing of brush, in weeding and burning, in seeding and pruning and cataloging, in coming to know the complexity of the ecosystem being restored and coming to see on the ground the role human action can play in recreating that complexity—people in fact might recapture and appreciate the kind of close, felt connection to their environment that many today are concerned we have lost.[47] Elliot says that the "ultimate aim" of a good restoration project is "to achieve a situation from which humans are absent, except as respectful, careful, and unobtrusive visitors."[48] But such an aim seems to me actually to express a profound estrangement from the environment and a failure to understand the human role in it. We are not visitors on Earth, and indeed we are never absent from it—not, nowadays, from any of it. Restoration's value, I think, would rather come precisely from our experience in it of our involvement in the world, our responsibilities regarding it, the concreteness and the difficulty of the work we have to do in it, and our dependence on forces not our own to make anything we do possible. In the artifact that is a restoration we learn a broader lesson, about the nature of artifacts and at the same time about the artifactuality of what is called nature; we would do better to learn this than to fetishistically pretend that "nature" is something beyond and other from us from which we must (somehow) withdraw.

Two Environmental Virtues

The dualism upon which Katz and Elliot build their arguments against restoration, I have been arguing, is untenable. The world of artifacts cannot be separated from the world of what they call nature. On the one hand, the latter world shows the sign of the human serpent everywhere, and is therefore in that sense itself already an artifact. On the other hand, none of our artifacts could be built without "nature," in the sense that all building practices, and indeed all practices in general, require the operation of processes that we who engage in the practice do not control but on which we depend. The naturalness that Elliot says he values—which I have called instead wildness—is just as much a characteristic of Krieger's imagined plastic forest as it is of the unspoiled wilderness whose loss Katz and McKibben mourn, just as present in a restored prairie as in the one the first European settlers found, just as much a property of the cats and dogs brought out in carriers to Fire Island by the summer residents there—and for that matter of those human residents themselves—as it is a property of the deer that eat those residents' flowers. The two worlds Katz distinguishes so sharply, the natural world and the built one, are really one world, the single world that always already surrounds us and within which we are always already active. And as I have suggested, a good name for this world might be *the environment*.

Learning about the nature of artifacts (and the artifactuality of nature) might lead us to think more carefully about that environment, and about our responsibilities for it and to it. In particular, it might suggest to us two virtues that are central to what could be called environmental responsibility, and might even suggest some ways in which engaging in practices of environmental restoration could encourage the development of those virtues in those who take part in them.[49] The first of these is *knowledge*, or more precisely *self-knowledge*. Elliot's talk about forgeries and Katz's talk about lies raise the specter of restorations as being presented as something that they're not. Elliot is surely right that if somehow an artificial landscape could be built—a plastic one, say, of the sort Krieger imagined—that would fool a lover of wilderness into believing it to have arisen independently of human action, she would be being seriously shortchanged in terms of what she values, and right too that even someone enjoying what she believes to be wilderness but that is really a regrown area on top of an old strip mine would be being shortchanged as well.[50] But whatever reasons there may doubtless be to prefer real trees over plastic ones, what's morally objectionable in such examples is not so much that humans have been involved in the landscape's history as that the viewer has been *misled* about that history. The real problem, that is, has to do with deception, and with ignorance: with a person's experience of a landscape being based on a mistaken understanding of what that landscape *is*.

We might see this more clearly if we shift Elliot's example slightly and imagine someone who visits a Kriegerian plastic landscape now *without* being deceived, and instead quite aware of what it is that she's looking at: might she not find some genuine value in it? No longer a forgery, no longer having been built in order to (falsely) satisfy anyone's desire for wilderness, would not such a landscape, complete with utterly lifelike flora and fauna, at minimum be something *remarkable*? Understanding what I have called the nature of artifacts might allow us to come to see a value even in this sort of landscape—to be amazed and even moved by what humans and "nature" were able together to produce. What marvelous facts about the polymers in the "trees," and the proteins in the brains of those who produced them, made such a landscape possible! What astonishing skills of design and construction were needed to build something that so closely resembled an area from which the human touch was lacking! Why imagine that an undeceived experience of these things would be an experience of *disvalue*, rather than an experience of wonder and pride both in human skill and in the environing world within which (and through which) that skill operates?[51] I don't mean by this to suggest that the value of an artificial landscape would be the same as that of a "natural" one; my point is simply that there might *be* a value to an artificial landscape—and that the disvalue in Elliot's example comes from the deception involved, not the artificiality.

But if there is disvalue in being ignorant of the history of human involvement in a landscape, then conversely there is value in *not* being ignorant of this: in knowing the extent to which the human serpent is everywhere. And a key environmental virtue, it seems to me, consists in just this sort of knowledge: a recognition of our deep and active connection with the world we inhabit, and an acknowledgment of the responsibility that that connection means we have for that world. To possess this virtue is to understand, as I have argued in previous chapters, that the environment is not something separate from us (and so is not "nature," if this word is meant in McKibben's or Katz's or Elliot's sense), and in particular to recognize how much of what we take as natural is already the product of prior human action. Having such knowledge means also no longer thinking that human action represents an alien intervention in natural forces, or that to transform a landscape is to rob it of its authentic character and turn it into something unnatural or fake. To see the extent to which the world we inhabit is always already humanized might be to come to appreciate that world more fully, to see it as *our* environment, with the pronoun expressing not possession but rather entanglement: a world from which the traces of human practices are never entirely missing. But, just as important, to see the extent to which our practices are responsible for the world we inhabit might be to appreciate the world we inhabit today *less*: for as the previous chapter pointed out, there is surely much that humans have done to it that is ugly and ecologically harmful and that ought to be reversed. Understanding the ways in which our practices help to construct our environment, that is, might help us think more carefully and critically about the ways in which we currently organize those practices, and to consider how we might improve them. Thus, part of the environmental virtue of self-knowledge would involve being able to discern, in each landscape we encounter, the consequences it shows of previous human action, and part too would be to acknowledge the imperative to anticipate, before we perform any new action, the consequences for landscapes it will in turn have. And this is surely one of the virtues that practices of environmental restoration help those who engage in them to develop.

But there is another important virtue that engaging in environmental restoration practices might help develop: the virtue of *humility*. The everyday experience of such projects reveals the way in which human actions, consciously planned and intentionally engaged in, can transform environments to improve them and allow them to flourish; but it also reveals the way in which the consequences of those actions always escape the plans and intentions of those who participate in them. To produce an artifact, I have been arguing, no matter what it is, requires that gap, that space between our actions and their consequences (whether intended or unintended) in which the wildness of the world always plays its indispensable part; and those who act to help produce the artifacts that are environmental restorations must surely come to see this, quickly and convincingly, and so must come to understand that our intentions can never fully be achieved, that the full consequences of our actions can never be predicted and indeed can never even be entirely known. Thus to participate in such practices might be to learn important lessons not just about the nature of artifacts but the nature of those humans who produce them and of those practices through which that production occurs. And to speak of the *nature* of humans is to suggest what's most important here: that those who engage in practices of restoration are unlikely to misunderstand "humans" and "nature" as two opposing poles. To build a natural artifact like a restoration is to learn why dualism is false. Practitioners of restoration rapidly come to understand that the environment they inhabit (and that they perhaps once called "nature") has a history in which the transformative actions of many species, including their own, have always played a role, and that it only comes to be the environment it is through and because of such actions, just as (at the same time) the actors whose practices transform that environment have only become who they are through and because of the environment they inhabit. The world comes to be what it is through our actions—and so we had better know what those actions are, and think about what their impact is; but at the same time our actions are absolutely *of the world*—and so our knowledge and our thoughts are not by themselves sufficient to transform it. We need self-knowledge, but we need humility as well.

These lessons, I am suggesting, are easily learned in the practices that produce environmental restorations, practices that is in which humans intentionally work so as to produce an environment that is out of our control. The moment of knowledge, which is to say of self-knowledge, is crucial for such practices, but so too is the moment of humility. And yet I have also argued that *all* environments are finally out of our control, and in particular that *all artifacts are wild*, not just the special ones produced by environmental restorations—and it follows from this that the same lessons could be learned, if only people would be ready to notice them, from the practices of automobile mechanics, nuclear power plant operators, and genetic engineers as well. In all of them the same dialectic is at work: as human beings transform the world through their activity they find on the one hand that the world thereby produced is always and inevitably different from the one they intended to produce, while discovering on the other that their actions themselves require the operation of forces they are entirely unable to master, to predict, or even fully to understand. Those lessons are there to be learned, I am suggesting, in all our practices and all our products: they are the real lessons of building. Yet far too often they are not learned, and indeed are not even noticed, as those who engage in such practices pretend to themselves and to others that humility is not necessary, that to produce a particular result all we need do is imagine it. And too often, too, even those who wish to criticize those practices for what they do to "nature" make the same mistake, too easily believing that *some* practices—"technological" ones—somehow really do escape what I have called the gap, really do domesticate the wild. Fully to pay attention to the nature of artifacts, I want to suggest instead, would lead us rather to acknowledge the unavoidable limitations in our abilities, and in our technologies as well.

To recognize that the products of our practices are indeed *our* products, and so we are responsible for them and for what they do to the world, while acknowledging that at the same time they are fully wild—because they are fully *real*—and so escape our ultimate control, would be to combine the virtues of self-knowledge and of humility. Combining them, it seems to me, might lead one to think about those practices differently, and hence perhaps to begin to engage in different, and better, ones. Indeed, self-knowledge and humility must go together. Either one alone is dangerous: knowledge of one's inevitable impact on the world without the humility of recognizing the limits of one's ability to control that impact results in an arrogance that can lead to disaster, while a humility in the face of "nature" that takes it as distinct from (and superior to) human action and that fails to recognize that the environment is always already the product of such action results in a kind of passivity and caution that lead to misanthropy and disaster too. By itself, each dreams of an escape from reality, dreaming in the first case of a technology that could never fail and would never even require work to produce, and in the second of a Nature radically distinct from human culture that could nonetheless authoritatively answer for us the question of who we humans are and how we ought to act. Combined, though, self-knowledge and humility might be the key environmental virtues, teaching us of our responsibility for the world we inhabit on the one hand but also reminding us not to overestimate our ability to remake it in any way we want on the other. Active transformers of the world, we are yet (or perhaps: therefore) at the same time mortal and fallible too, fully part of the world and in no way capable of a Cartesian transcendence of it. To learn about the nature of artifacts is thus at the same time to learn about *our* nature as well.

Nature, Practice, and Difference

Thinking about the nature of artifacts, and about the building practices through which artifacts come to be, I want to suggest, helps to clarify why the sort of postnaturalist social constructionism I am proposing is not guilty of the charge of idealism discussed in the first section of this chapter. For if "construction" is understood as "building," then as I've already argued calling the environment "socially constructed" doesn't mean that we transform it by thinking about it differently but rather that it is something we build—that it's an artifact. But then since I've been suggesting that *all* artifacts, and therefore all built environments, inevitably exceed our control and planning, and indeed are only built in processes that go beyond our own intentions and even our understanding, it follows that we certainly do *not* have the ability to decide on an "idea" of what the environment should be and then to magically wish that idea into existence. Building, "construction," is a matter of *action in the world,* and not of anything ideal like thought: it is difficult, involves sweat and effort, and is always marked by what I have called the gap between intention and execution.

The charge of idealism, that is, is answered by the appeal to *practice:* we construct the world through our practices, not through our ideas. Practices are not "ideal" but rather are entirely *real.* Engaging in them takes work, meets (indeed, requires) resistance, and frequently leads to failure. What's crucial, however, is to try to think this without rehypostatizing "nature" as some sort of substance that *causes* the difficulty, the resistance, the failure, but rather to see these simply as *characteristics of practice itself.* This moment of resistance is precisely what defines practice and distinguishes it from "theory"; this is why what we produce in our practices always of necessity turns out to be different from what we "thought" we were producing, and it is what distinguishes this kind of social constructionism from one that makes the world somehow the product of thought. But to say it is not the product of thought is not to say it is the product of nature. If the hardness and resistance experienced in building are understood as characteristics of practice itself, this means they are not to be understood as characteristics of some "natural substrate" *on which* the practice is working. To say that all artifacts are wild is not to say that they are really built from pieces of nature: "wild" is an adjective, not a noun. There is no substance or thing called "nature" that *causes* practice to be difficult or lead to unexpected consequences; to think that there is would be to view practice merely as theory faced with obstacles. Such a nature would have to be a noumenal one, since as I have argued we only come to know the world in and through our practices, and talk of a nature that caused the resistance those practices face would be talk of a nature *prior* to them—and the difficulties with the notion of nature as noumena is one we have already examined in chapter 2.

"Idealism" and "materialism," as traditionally conceived, both begin by accepting at least in principle the conceptual distinction between thought and nature, going on, however, to deny that one or the other of the poles is "real" or plays any significant causal or metaphysical role. In this sense both views could be said to remain caught, despite themselves, in a dualist logic. But the position I am defending here, with its emphasis on the concept of practice, rejects dualism more radically. Practice according this view is not something ontologically secondary, not a process in which two preexisting poles—subject and world, actor and nature—are somehow brought into a (difficult) relation. Rather, I am proposing a view that takes practice as *primary*, as that which itself makes those two poles possible: so that both subject and world come to be what they are through practice, not the other way around. The world we inhabit—our environment—is, as I have been arguing, something that has always already been built through our practices; we have no access to some originary world of pure nature on which practice has not yet started to work. And the same is true of the subject. I discover who I am in and through the practices I engage in, and those practices are always ones that I find myself *already* engaged in, ones that have already made me into the person who I am. I have no access to some "true self" that precedes the socially and linguistically organized practices in which I engage. Practices do not arise *after* the world and the self have been given and cannot be explained in terms of a world and a self in which practices have not yet taken place. Neither "nature" nor the "subject" then can serve as foundation for those practices, either in a moral or in a causal sense. I can no longer explain or justify my practices in terms of what the world (or nature) "in itself" requires, any more than I can explain or justify them in terms of my own sovereign desires or thoughts. What I know of nature, and what I know of myself as well, I come to know only through my practices, and thus it makes no sense to appeal to a nature independent of those practices in order to guide them.

One might be tempted at this point to interpret what I have been saying about the inevitable gap between what we intend and what we produce as indicating something like what Adorno talks of as the necessary non-identity between concept and object, and then to suggest that "nature" might be the name we give to that very non-identity.[52] Rather than giving up the concept of nature, perhaps, it could be reinterpreted not as a substantial thing but rather as standing for *difference* itself, for the fact that our every attempt to understand the world or to rebuild it is inevitably infected by failure, by "otherness," by something that escapes our understanding and our control.[53] No longer referring to some impossible world independent of and prior to human experience, "nature" could be retained as a name we give to the otherness of the world, to that which is always left out of any attempt to grasp it as a whole and bring it entirely into the light.

Such a strategy has its basis in some familiar themes in contemporary continental philosophy. The antifoundationalism of thinkers such as Derrida or Heidegger (and surely of Adorno, too) insists on the impossibility of making the world fully transparent and understanding it as a totality. Instead, such a view asserts that all thinking about the world is a partial thinking, and therefore calls on us as a matter of method to attend, in our examination of any linguistic or conceptual scheme, to what that scheme occludes, excludes, inhibits. More to the point, it calls on us to attend to the crucial fact that every such scheme *does* occlude or exclude or inhibit something because doing so is part of what it is to be a scheme of this sort at all. In all understandings of the world—in all interactions with the world—something is left out. But to say this is not to say that there is some particular item or set of items that no scheme can grasp; rather, it is to emphasize (to use Heidegger's terminology) that no revealing of the world is possible without a simultaneous concealing of it as well, and so each scheme conceals *something*, although what it conceals (which is to say, what it fails to grasp) will differ from scheme to scheme. Nor is the idea here that each scheme is "partial," at least not if this is meant to suggest some single world that underlies all the different schemes but is partially obscured by each of them, as if a ("partial") scheme were simply a kind of latticework or set of distorting lenses placed *on* or applied *to* the ("total") world. Instead the claim is that for something to be a "world" at all it must be revealed by what is here being called a scheme; there's nothing hidden by the scheme that could be imagined as unhidden except in the context of another one, and so the notion of the real or total world unobscured by the latticework or undistorted by the lenses is meaningless. The point simply is that there always *is* another scheme, that no worldview or vocabulary can call itself final and complete, that in showing the world to us in some particular way it also at the same time (and necessarily) does *not* show it to us in some other way, and so that all understandings of the world will inevitably be incomplete.

The denial, in this familiar line of thought, that one can meaningfully speak of a world independent of particular social and linguistic frameworks means there is no room in it for traditional conceptions of nature (like those of McKibben or Katz) as that which is independent of, and prior to, such frameworks. And yet "nature" could still have a role here (as suggested) whereby it would stand for something like "difference," which is to say simply for the finitude and limitation of every such framework, without any longer standing for an impossible original and unitary reality before or behind them. Such a view of nature as difference, further, would draw attention to the incompleteness not just of theoretical structures but also, and importantly, of technological practices, emphasizing the very themes I have been developing in this chapter. Thus, while rejecting the naturalistic dream of speaking for and protecting a pure world of nature independent of the human, this kind of "postmodern" environmental theory might nonetheless go on to say that just as no human understanding of the world could ever be complete, neither could any technological remaking of it—and so every humanized world we inhabit will always also already have something of the nonhuman within it. Every making is also an unmaking, which is to say that to build the world in one way is always also *not* to build it in another, and no matter how smart and masterful we are in our building, still those nonbuildings or unmakings are processes over which we have no mastery at all. Thus it is precisely the inescapable moment of resistance, of unexpected consequences and unimagined side effects, in all our practices—the moment of what I have spoken of above in terms of the hardness and realness of the world—to which we might decide to give the name of "nature."

Rather than doing without the concept of nature, as I have been proposing, this alternative strategy would suggest redefining the concept in such a way as to make possible a "postmodern" (but not postnatural!) environmental theory in which "nature" plays a kind of cautionary role, reminding us of the limits of our abilities and the need to be careful and modest about our attempts to transform the world. In this sense it emphasizes what I have called the virtue of humility. (It is less clear, though, that it sufficiently emphasizes the virtue of self-knowledge.) If the move here is understood as purely a nominal one—so that "nature" is stipulatively defined to refer to the moment of hardness or resistance in our practices—I have little reason to quarrel with it. But the trouble, on the one hand, is that it rarely stays nominal, precisely because the word "nature" has a series of other, much more substantive, connotations. And on the other hand, if it does stay nominal it isn't clear what role "nature" as stipulatively defined in this way could possibly play in any contentful and progressive environmental theory. If nature is to stand solely for the inevitable gap between what we intend and what we produce, or between the world and what we think we know of the world, then we have to be careful: nature as so defined *itself cannot be known*, cannot be grasped or understood. Any claims that nature *is* thus-and-such would have to be eschewed. Claims about the holistic character of nature, say, or about its teleological character, or its complexity or tendency toward homeostasis, would all have to be rejected if "nature" is simply defined to mean something like difference. So too would Spinozistic or Gaia-related ideas about nature as a unity or an organism. Nature now would turn out to have no characteristics at all, and certainly none that could be known: indeed, it would no longer be a *thing*, but rather simply a way to refer to the concrete reality of the world that no amount of theorizing or of technologizing could ever overcome. But if it's not a thing, then it's also not some thing we need to "defend"; even talk of "letting nature be" becomes suspect here, because nature in this sense *isn't* anything at all. If nature is *what is left out*, it will be left out too of any attempts we make to protect or support it, or indeed even to talk about it.

But with that the danger arises that the very subject matter of environmental thinking and the concrete motivations that lead people into that thinking start to dissolve. If "nature" simply means "difference," and if difference or nonidentity is characteristic of all human action and all human thought, then it is hard to see how nature could ever be endangered at all. Difference will be just as characteristic of the most anthropocentrically hubristic thought, and of the most technologically hubristic action, as it is of any other sort of thought and action; nuclear power plants, and the scientific theorizing that underlies them, are as marked by difference and nonidentity in this sense as any organic farm, or for that matter any wilderness. Nothing we do could possibly harm this difference, furthermore: if "nature" just means difference, then nature is perfectly safe. And on the other hand, nothing we do could possibly help it either. Indeed, for this sort of view the attempt to "save" or "protect" nature begins to look like the same impossible dream of mastery that underlies the overconfident "identity thinking" characteristic of technology, subject to the same humbling dialectic of unanticipated side effects and inevitable yet also unexpected failures. Thus this view of nature leads to a kind of quietism about the idea of environmental problems as things to be "solved," one that is most explicit in late Heidegger's call for the patient anticipation of a god who may or may not arrive but is implicit too in Nietzschean levity or Derridean irony, not to speak of Adorno and Horkheimer's notion of a fatal "dialectic of enlightenment."[54]

More serious from a philosophical point of view, perhaps, is the logical problem produced when one tries to speak at all about that which by definition cannot be spoken of. The difficulty here is, of course, well known and often acknowledged, and forms a central theme in the work of postmodern lovers of paradox from Adorno to Derrida. If the term "nature" is supposed to remind us of the way our terms never fully capture that which they are intended to describe, then this term too must fail in the same way—which surely means that nature itself must differ from the account of it as difference, and in a way that cannot be said or even thought. "Différance," after all, is neither a thing nor the name of a thing; that's why Derrida so brilliantly uses a name for it that is no name but a simple spelling error. "There is no name for it," he writes, adding that this is "a proposition to be read in its *platitude,*" and not a reference to some "ineffable Being" like God, or, one might, add like the nature that environmentalists typically want to save.[55] But the paradox here—that "nature" is now supposed to be the name of something that cannot be named, and that assertions about it are assertions about something about which nothing can be asserted—*is* a paradox; there's no getting around it, I would suggest, except to take seriously the last sentence of Wittgenstein's *Tractatus*—a sentence, so to speak, to be read in its platitude. If what nature "is"—and it doesn't matter here what techniques one uses to put the "is" under erasure—cannot be said, then the right thing for philosophy to say about nature is *nothing*. And again that doesn't seem to leave much room for environmental theorizing.

The trouble with interpreting nature as difference (or *différance*) is that it falls prey—once again!—to something like Hegel's critique of the Kantian notion of things-in-themselves, to wit that it just isn't clear why it's so important to insist on the existence of something (or worse, some non-thing) about which there is absolutely nothing to be said. What difference does it make, to environmental theorizing or to anything else, whether it exists or not? The only way one can get mileage out of the notion is by playing a kind of shell game, trading on various ambiguities (including, here, various meanings of the word "nature") so as to be able to make assertions about the noumenal realm, on the one hand, while just as quickly taking them back and conceding their meaninglessness on the other. Adorno does this sort of thing all the time, and it is not unknown in Heidegger either. (Derrida is much better at avoiding it, which may be why he actually has very little to say about nature at all.) "Nature"—what is ordinarily called nature, that is: mountains, forests, rural landscapes—thus gets described as somehow "pointing at" or otherwise "indicating" the noumenal world of utter otherness or difference that the term ought in the strict sense to denote, but there's no real account of how this is possible, or of why such landscapes are better able to do this than, say, urban ones, or indeed even of what "indicating" or "pointing" in this sense could possibly mean—or, finally, how any of this could come to be *known*. Better here would be Wittgensteinian reticence, which would direct us back to what we *can* speak about—which is to say, the ordinary world we inhabit, the one in which and on which we work and which we come to know through our practices: not nature, that is, but the world that actually environs us—our environment.

Thus on the one hand defining "nature" as difference makes it too easy to forget that, so defined, "nature" is no *thing* at all, and hence can in no serious sense serve in the role that traditional naturalist environmental philosophy intends for it, while on the other hand it misleadingly suggests the existence of some noumenal world outside the one we actually inhabit which human action is somehow in principle unable to reach (but about which philosophical speculation somehow paradoxically can tell us). The appeal to difference (or to *différance*) is an attempt to get at the hardness or resistance we encounter as we engage in practices; its mistake, though, is to attribute this hardness or resistance to some characteristic of the world outside of us, rather than (as I have suggested) seeing it as a characteristic of practice itself. To pay attention to the real world we inhabit and to the practices through which that world is constructed is to see the extent to which talk of "nature" as standing for "difference" or "otherness," or as a realm that escapes or underlies the realm of human action, is mistaken. To think that the difficulty of our practices, or the wildness of our artifacts, shows there to be some aspect of the world that somehow escapes us only makes sense if "we" and "our practices" are somehow distinct, for after all it is the practices themselves that evince that difficulty and produce that wildness. That which gets called "difference" and "otherness" are not characteristics that escape us at all but rather are familiar and necessary characteristics of those very practices through which we come to be who we are and the environment we inhabit comes to be what it is as well. But to say this, of course, is to say that they are not so "different," or so "other," as they might seem: they are rather the most familiar things in the world.

5

Thinking like a Mall

The She-Wolf and the City

In a famous passage in *A Sand County Almanac*, Aldo Leopold tells of the time he and some others, "young and full of trigger-itch," spotted a wolf and her cubs from a rimrock and shot at them, hitting one of the cubs in the leg and mortally wounding the mother. He writes that he scrambled down to the injured she-wolf in time "to watch a fierce green fire dying in her eyes," and that he saw in that fire something "known only to her and to the mountain" that he had heretofore not understood. This hidden truth, he says, became clear in later years, as wolves were extirpated from many mountains on the theory that "because fewer wolves meant more deer … no wolves would mean hunters' paradise," and the consequence turned out instead to be a population explosion of deer that led in turn to slopes denuded of low-growing brush, and eventually deer herds decimated by starvation. Leopold concludes that we humans must learn to "think like a mountain"—to see that there is more to the world than we understand, and to recognize the dark complexity and depth of the processes of nature that so exceed our limited ability to grasp and to control.[1] This story, and especially its evocative idea of thinking like a mountain, has become a touchstone for much discussion of environmental matters, and has come to symbolize the importance of acknowledging nature's mystery and transcendent power and to caution against a human arrogance that thinks nature could ever be mastered or even fully understood.

My own youth was spent in Manhattan, and was quite different from Leopold's. I had no gun, did no shooting, and saw no wolves. And yet I too experienced the world around me in those days—the honking cars, the hurrying pedestrians, the strutting pigeons, the glimpses of the sun setting over the Hudson as one crossed 14th Street—as something I could surely grasp and master. I spent hours studying the subway map until I knew my way around the underground world of New York perhaps as well as Leopold knew the forests and glens of central Wisconsin. And yet as I grew older I discovered how much I did not know: the forces of gentrification and racism and an economic downturn that were transforming neighborhoods all around the city, the pollution that caused asthma and other breathing difficulties in many of my schoolmates, the plans for urban renewal that destroyed old tenements and replaced them with brutalist high-rise projects, the dependence of the city's health—fiscal and environmental and cultural and human—on much larger forces of finance and geopolitics and energy policy and climate change over which no one, certainly not me, seemed to have any control. Even the subways began to change, with new lines being added and others removed, and the old and familiar trinity of BMT and IRT and IND disappearing.

I have no memory of killing a wolf or anything else (besides cockroaches), though I do have several memories of being mugged, once by a man holding a rusting knife from which I could not tear my terrified eyes, once by a group of teenagers probably my own age who laughed as they told me to empty my pockets, which I did—less scared this time, as we somehow all felt we were actors in some sort of predetermined play—laughing a little bit myself. Once too, when I was thirteen or so, a group of neighborhood kids my own age attacked me by throwing rocks at me, jeering that they couldn't tell, because of my long hair, whether I was a girl or a boy. I tried to run away and begged for help from passersby, who seemed as unsure how to respond as I was. There was a darkness in the city, and in the world, that I had not understood, and my early confidence and feelings of mastery and safety gave way to something different and more uncertain.

Still, the skyline of Manhattan, whether viewed from the Brooklyn Bridge or the Staten Island ferry or an airplane taking off from LaGuardia, remained astonishing in the same way the Alps or the Rockies are: sublime, overpoweringly large, an incomprehensible and yet moving conglomeration not of peaks and valleys but of masses of middle-size buildings mixed with sudden and startlingly tall ones, broken up by vistas of avenues and that great green park in the middle, mixing art deco and modernism, gleaming glass sides and gray granite walls, some lit up at night in varied colors and others simply shadows in the moonlight—an image of energy and beauty and at the same time (and here's the difference from the Alps or the Rockies) of the ungraspable complexity of millions of human lives all going on at once. But even that skyline turned out not to be so easy to understand or master, its changes unpredictable, its meaning always transforming, the Empire State Building—symbol in my childhood of the apparently unlimited power of human ambition, Tallest Building In The World—eclipsed in turn by other buildings that amazingly grew taller (and then by the knowledge that still taller ones had been built elsewhere! Who could have imagined *that*?), and then, of course, that great and terrifying surprise one fall morning when the newly tallest buildings themselves, ugly interlopers originally, became targets of airplanes and, unbelievably, came crashing down, revealing themselves to be parts of *nature*, subject to forces of impact and fire and gravity that somehow one had forgotten had always been in play—and, yes, subject to forces of furious resentment and religious fervor and anti-imperialist anger that one had forgotten as well, or had never imagined could play themselves out *here*—and so showing themselves to be *wild*, just as wild as Leopold's mountain, or as Krieger's plastic forest.

You see, perhaps, what I'm trying to say: if thinking about the artifactuality of what we call nature and then about the nature of our artifacts leads us to see that nature and the artificial aren't so easily distinguished, and that our environment is always already something we have had a hand in creating—and yet something that nonetheless or for that very reason always remains wild—then thinking like a mountain might turn out not to be so different from thinking like a city, or so much more difficult to learn, or so much more unfamiliar. Which isn't to say that either one is so easy or so familiar either but rather simply that cities might have more in common with mountains, or at least with mountain ranges, than one would think. But I'd rather not talk about cities or mountain ranges, because they're too complicated. I'd rather talk about malls.

The City Center Mall

The City Center Mall opened in Columbus, Ohio in 1989. It was a project supported by the City of Columbus in an effort to revitalize a downtown that had been in serious decline for many years by attracting suburban shoppers to an upscale mall anchored by popular retailers such as Marshall Field's and Jacobsen's, neither of which had ever had a store in central Ohio. With 1.3 million square feet of retail space, the mall took up several city blocks in the traditional center of the city and was at the time the largest mall in the region; it included several parking garages, one underneath the mall and another just to its south, that charged only one dollar for a full day's parking, as well as an enclosed pedestrian walkway that connected it to the flagship store of the biggest and most successful local department store chain, Lazarus.[2] The mall was owned by the Taubman Company, and its design was similar to that of several other malls Taubman had developed, including the Beverly Center in Los Angeles. From the street the mall looked like a large white cube, almost windowless. Inside there were three floors, with stores on each level along the sides of the structure fronted by walkways that encircled a large central atrium; one section of the atrium consisted of a kind of amphitheater where one could sit and rest, or eat, while another section included some trees, a small fountain, and a few remarkably lifelike statues of what were apparently supposed to be typical customers (a woman with a small child, a man in business attire holding a newspaper). Two glass elevators rose from the center of the amphitheater. There were also escalators linking the levels, carefully placed at various ends of the mall in such a way that it was quite difficult to get from one floor to another without having to walk all the way around the perimeter, an effect that the designers had doubtless intended so as to maximize the number of stores one would pass on the way. The result was that it was impossible simply to pop into the mall to pick up one item; the organization of pedestrian traffic was such that any trip into the cube was inevitably an extended one. The lack of windows also meant that there was virtually no connection between inside and outside; inside the mall, brightly lit and gleaming with chrome and modernistic fixtures, there was no sense of being in the heart of a gritty and economically depressed downtown, while from the surrounding streets the mall appeared as a contentless white box with only a few signs to indicate what lay within.

City Center was an immediate hit. On its opening day 60,000 people visited, and it quickly became the most successful mall in the area, a "destination" mall that attracted customers from all over central Ohio.[3] By 1995 its sales volume of $400 per square foot placed it among the top 10 percent of all shopping malls in the United States.[4] At its height there were more than 150 shops in the mall, including Henri Bendel, Brooks Brothers, Cinnabon, Waldenbooks, the Body Shop, and many others. The Limited Corporation, whose headquarters are in Columbus and which at the time was in a headlong expansion mode, announced soon after the mall opened that every one of its brands (Victoria's Secret, Limited Inc., Structure, etc.) would have a store there.[5] In those days I lived about eight blocks away, and although I hated the mall I went there much more often than I would have wanted to admit. My kids loved it there; they tell me that their memories are of a glittering place filled with toys and excitement, the first place they saw Santa Claus, the place they learned to toss

Figure 5.1
City Center Mall, exterior

coins in a fountain and make a wish. There were concerts in the atrium (Hanson played there once), parades, parties; there were attractive decorations, nice music, a pleasant atmosphere. It's true that in its fifth year of operation what was described by police as a gang-related shooting took place in the mall in the middle of a busy shopping day, leaving one person dead—but this seemed an anomaly, and barely did anything to damage the mall's reputation as the best place to shop in the central Ohio area.[6]

And yet today, City Center is no more. In 1997 its owner, the Taubman Company, opened a second mall on the northwest side of the city, the Mall at Tuttle Crossing, which was also described as "upscale," also had a Marshall Field's, and so on. The suburbs northwest of Columbus are particularly wealthy ones, and shoppers who lived there now no longer had to drive downtown (and pay for parking) to shop. Taubman, perhaps filled with trigger-itch, apparently thought that if one mall meant profit, a second one meant more profit, and shrugged off concerns that City Center might lose customers.[7] And then a few years later developers associated with The Limited opened a massive new mall northeast of the city (in an area home to a new and even more wealthy suburb) named Easton

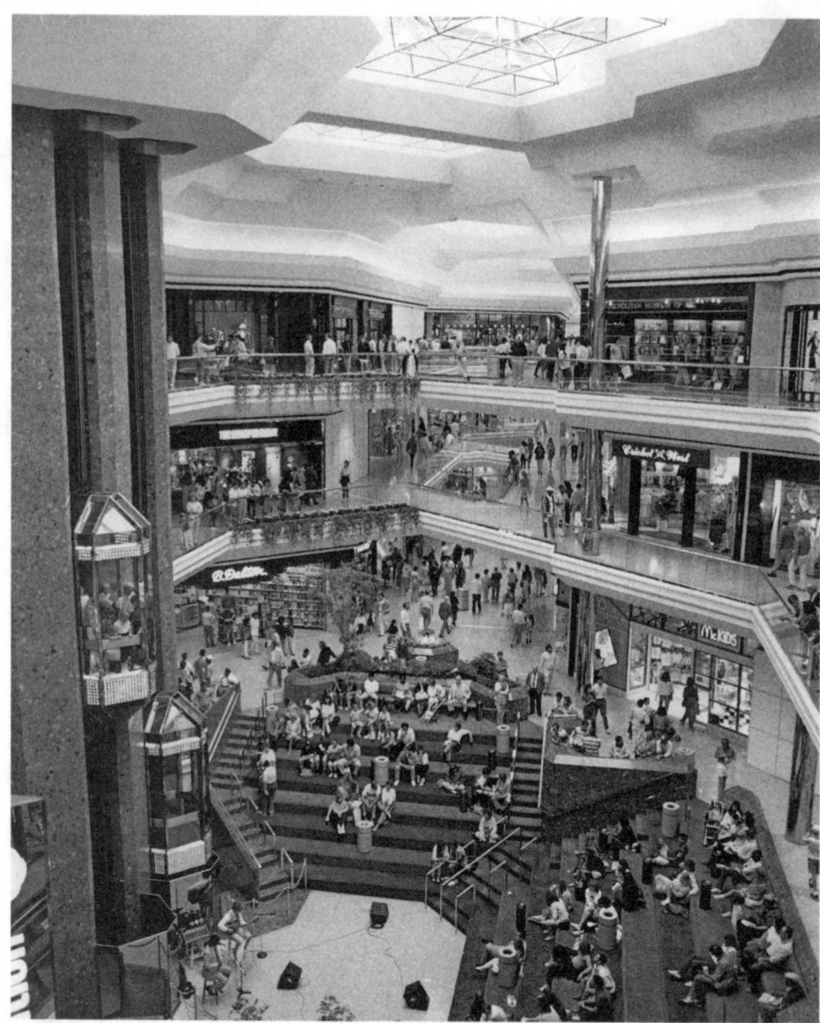

Figure 5.2
City Center Mall, interior

Town Center, while yet another developer opened one on the north side called the Polaris Fashion Center. The consequences of the opening of these three malls—larger, more modern, with free parking—for City Center were fatal.[8] It began to lose customers, and then shops, and then more customers in a death spiral that accelerated remarkably quickly and was not helped by the poor economic environment for big department stores in the late nineties, as Jacobsen's went bankrupt, the flagship Lazarus store closed, and Marshall Field's was sold to Kaufman's, which was then renamed Macy's after being taken over by Federated Department Stores.[9]

Ultimately the loss of tenants was unstoppable, as the mall began more and more to resemble a mountain overgrazed by deer. Upscale stores were replaced by downscale ones; vacant storefronts were rented out for corporate meetings.[10] A big-screen television was placed in the atrium showing soap operas in a desperate attempt to bring in more customers.[11] In 2006 a tattoo parlor moved in (motto: "Put some class on your ass").[12] In 2007 Macy's, the last anchor remaining, announced it was closing.[13] In the summer of that year, the owners (no longer Taubman—the mall by this point had been sold multiple times) stopped paying rent on the land, which was owned by the City of Columbus. A candidate for mayor held a press conference inside the nearly empty mall, criticizing the incumbent for doing nothing about what he called "the world's biggest above-ground cavern" and ending by saying, "Mr. Mayor, tear down this mall!"[14] In 2008 there were no more retail chain tenants, and fewer than twenty tenants altogether; by 2009 that number had dropped to eight.[15] In February 2009 the nonprofit urban development group that had originally planned the mall as a way to revitalize downtown Columbus, and that now had title to it, announced—with the strong encouragement of the (reelected) mayor—that it would be closed, the fixtures sold off at auction, and the building demolished, to be replaced by a new public park.[16] Demolition began in October 2009 and was completed in March 2010. Construction of the park, named the Columbus Commons, started soon afterward. It opened to the public on May 26, 2011.[17]

No one mourns the mall much, though some, like my children, feel nostalgic for it, and presumably there are investors who are sad about the money they lost because of its failure. Many others are glad to be rid of an eyesore, and happy to have a park. But in the pages that follow I want to ask about the difference between the death of a mall and the death of a mountain, or the death of a she-wolf. Leopold's description expresses sadness about the wolf's death, and about the destruction of the mountainside that death portended, and, of course, it expresses as well his own retrospective sense of guilt, and of shame over his youthful naiveté and that of his comrades. But nobody, I suspect, feels similarly about the loss of the Cinnabon at the City Center, tasty though its products were, and although there may be some investors or developers who feel guilt (and maybe even shame) about the failure of the mall, I doubt that those who ordered its demolition feel anything along those lines—nor do the young men of the demolition crews, full of trigger-itch in those days themselves, perhaps, who actually carried it out. Nor will they, I suspect, as they get older. I want to ask quite seriously about the differences here: about why we find the loss of a wolf, or of a mountain, a matter for regret and yet feel nothing similar about the loss of a piece of the built environment. And, more important, I want to ask what it might mean to *think like a mall*, or whether thinking like one might help us better understand our environment, at least as well as thinking like a mountain would. There were no windows at the City Center Mall, as I have noted; and yet I cannot help but wonder whether, as the final walls and girders were smashed by a wrecking ball on the last evening of demolition, one might have been able to see, in the reflection of the suddenly visible setting sun glinting off the debris of sales counters and display cases as they lay on the ground, a fierce green fire dying there in Marshall Field's. Was there something the mall knew that the Taubman Company did not? Is there something we might learn if we tried to think like a mall?

We do mourn buildings, sometimes: the old Pennsylvania Station in New York is a well-known example, designed by the prominent architectural firm McKim, Mead & White and demolished in 1963 in what

Figure 5.3
City Center Mall, demolition

the *New York Times* called a "monumental act of vandalism against one of the largest and finest landmarks of its age."[18] The World Trade Center is another and different sort of example. Large-scale destruction of buildings is deplorable, too: we mourn what happened to Hiroshima, to Dresden, to London during the Blitz. But in these sorts of cases what we mourn has to do with the aesthetic or symbolic value of the buildings, or more directly with the people inside them who died in their collapse. If there is anything like "intrinsic value" to these buildings it might have to do with their beauty or their age or their cultural significance; nothing like a Leopoldian land ethic with its call to value the integrity, beauty, and stability of a biotic community is suggested by our sadness about these particular losses. That's why I choose for my example a building that no one loved (not even the Taubman Company, apparently—they sold it as soon as it started to lose money), that no one found to be beautiful, that had no deep cultural significance (though it had an economic one), that was nobody's home, and whose demolition, as far as I know, caused no injuries or deaths to people.[19] Should we be sad about its loss—not because of how it looked or what it meant or who it was who loved it or how much money they had invested in it, but *for its own sake?* It's hard to imagine that we should. But then why should we be sad about a wolf, or about a mountain?

The Autonomy of Artifacts

And it's really the mountain, not the wolf, that's in question here. Although for many environmental thinkers the wolf might be said to deserve moral consideration because it is alive or because it is sentient—characteristics the mall surely lacked—neither of these is what Leopold appeals to. As is well known, he was and remained a dedicated hunter throughout his life, despite the experience he describes.[20] The "fierce green fire" in the she-wolf's dying eyes is mentioned not to point out that the creature Leopold killed was living and conscious—surely he understood that, even as a young man—but rather to suggest that there was something she *knew*, about the land or more specifically about the mountain, that the young Leopold did not and that he glimpsed only at the moment of her death. The mountain is what's harmed, ultimately, by the loss of the wolves: "just as a deer herd lives in mortal fear of its wolves, so does a mountain live in mortal fear of its deer," he writes, adding, "and perhaps with better cause."[21] But mountains aren't alive, and they aren't sentient.[22] What they are, though, is *natural,* and this does seem to be key to the intuition that their loss has a moral significance that the loss of a piece of the built environment like a mall does not. And so again we've returned to the question of "nature": why does the destruction of a natural entity such as a mountainside raise moral questions while the demolition of a building does not?

It has frequently been noted that proposed criteria for moral considerability such as sentience or life emphasize the commonality between humans and certain nonhumans, and support extending the moral considerability we unquestioningly accord each other to nonhuman entities to which we are significantly *similar*. But when Leopold speaks of "thinking like a mountain" he is invoking a metaphor whose point isn't to indicate how similar mountains are to us but rather to show how *different* they are; one is supposed to think *like a mountain, not like a human*. The mountain's moral status thus stems from its difference from us, from its possession of a perspective nothing like our own. Indeed, one might go further and say that for Leopold, its moral status stems from its *in*difference *to* us, from the fact that to it we are as little significant as the deer are, and less significant than the wolves. To Leopold, that is, the moral significance of the mountain has to do with its distance from human beings and human purposes, its unconnectedness to the realm of human concerns and needs. And this would seem to explain why our intuitions about the moral significance of the City Center Mall are quite different, for the mall does not seem to possess this kind of distance in the slightest. It is an artifact, as Katz would say, which for him means that it is ontologically related from the very start to the human realm. It is what it is *because* humans built it, *because* it serves human purposes, and so it appears merely as an expression of those purposes—a symptom, perhaps, of the hubristic human desire to dominate nature, transforming what was once the frequently flooding east bank of a minor river into a glass-and-steel edifice devoted to commerce.[23] And so it makes no sense to suggest that we learn to "think like a mall" as though this were something new or strange to us: a mall is a human artifact, and so whatever thoughts it might be said to have, even metaphorically, would be human thoughts. Thinking like a mall, one might say, *is* human thinking: it's what we do all the time. To think like a mall is to think like us.

Natural entities, one might argue, exist independently of us; as Katz put it, they have a nature of their own. In this sense our actions can be described as respecting that independence or as violating it.[24] Buildings, on the other hand, have no such independence; they only come to be because humans have chosen to build them, and they have the characteristics they possess because humans have chosen to give them such characteristics.

And thus, one might say, there's nothing we can do to violate that independence—there is nothing in a built object that is *autonomous* of the human, nothing beyond the human, and thus nothing *intrinsic* to it for human action to violate. Such an argument, I suggest, frequently undergirds our sense that harm to a mountain is a more serious moral matter than the demolition of a shopping mall. And yet the considerations of the previous chapter have raised questions about this line of argument, for I suggested that "wildness" is characteristic not just of natural entities but of artifacts as well—and isn't "wildness" associated with what is here being spoken of as autonomy or independence? There's no question, of course, that the mall could not have come to be without humans: humans built it, and they did so for a reason. But does the fact that humans played a significant and intentional role in the genesis of an entity necessarily mean that the entity has no autonomous existence independent of them, no moment of distance from them?

There was, it seems, a human intention behind the mall, in a way that there isn't behind a mountain. Yet talk of "the" intention behind the mall is misleading, since the intentions behind it were surely plural. The city had one intention, which had something to do with revitalizing the downtown; the Taubman Company had another, presumably involving potential profit from leasing stores in the mall to tenants; the engineering firm had a third, concerned as it was to design a safe and sturdy and well-functioning building; the construction company had a fourth, that of actually producing that building on the ground. And each of these intentions could doubtless be subdivided as well. Which of these was *the* human intention behind the building of the mall? And none of these entities, further—"the city," "the Taubman Company," "the engineering firm," and so forth—are themselves *humans*: they're abstractions. The individual humans involved in the design and building of the mall doubtless each had his or her *own* individual reason for engaging in those activities, including (possibly) personal satisfaction, income, career advancement, the good of the community, risk aversion, the admiring glances of passersby, and so forth. The intentions behind the building of the mall were therefore irreducibly plural, complex, confused, doubtless sometimes contradictory, and probably in some cases unconscious. The mall itself was certainly the result of all these intentions at work (and of other things too), but in what sense does that make it reducible to or identical with human intention, or somehow entirely "dependent" on humans in a way that "natural" objects are not? Katz's idea that every artifact is the expression of "a" human intention seems to fail to grasp the real situation here.

And in any case, there were many things about City Center that *no one intended*, things that may have resulted from human actions but were not themselves the goal of those actions: the whining of the escalator on the ground level, the tinklings of the music boxes from a neighboring gift shop that entertained the customers of Godiva Chocolatier, the condensation that fogged the walls of the skywalk to the parking garage on a rainy day, the way the yells of panicked shoppers echoed back and forth after the gang member was shot. A few years after it opened cracks appeared in the concrete beams providing underground support to the mall, and concerns were raised about its structural soundness.[25] Leaks developed sometimes when it rained. One urinal in the men's room on the second level seemed never to work in all the years I went there. It simply was not true that everything about the mall was deliberately created by human beings for human purposes: birds enjoyed nesting on its roof, and sometimes even found their way inside; the shadow of the building's walls meant fewer pedestrians on the west side of 3rd Street; the financial troubles of Lazarus resulted in less foot traffic (and fewer sales) near the upper walkway and therefore less physical wear and tear on the carpeting there; the handrails near the Exploratorium store were polished to a higher sheen than elsewhere in the mall because of the many excited children congregating in the area; unexpected weeds grew in the planters by the Cinnabon. None of these were designed into the structure or were part of the business plan.

And some things about the mall had nothing to do with intention at all—some things just *happened*, foreseeably, maybe, but not intentionally. Its exterior walls were heated and bleached by the sun; rain and snow and sometimes hail fell on and weathered its roof. It was subject to the same "natural" physical forces as a mountain, including wind, temperature, gravity, and for that matter inertia and entropy as well. Gamma rays pierced it, and an earthquake (had a sufficiently strong one occurred) would have caused it to collapse. Indeed, the mall began slowly to crumble—as all buildings do, as all living things do—from the moment of its construction, and although the designers and builders knew this, of course they certainly had not intended it, nor for that matter did they want it. In what sense, then, was it not "independent" of them?

Why, I am asking, does the role of human agency or intention in the genesis of something *real* mean that that thing lacks independence from humans? The real *is* independent (unlike the ideal, or the thought, or the intention): that's what reality *is*. There were some things about the mall that were intended by its designers, while there were other things about it that no one intended, and still other things about it that some people intended but weren't themselves part of the "official" intentions of those who planned it: mall-walkers used it as a way to get exercise, while the gang members apparently used it as a meeting place or perhaps a turf to be fought over. I hear it was a good place for mid-afternoon assignations as well. Late in its life the mall was used to house several charter schools, which was surely not part of what the original architects had planned for.[26] Each of these uses changed the character of the place, changed the mix of people there and their behaviors, even changed its physical structure. And the effects of all these intentions—the developers', the customers', the shop owners', the gangs'—presumably combined with each other in unexpected ways to produce results that weren't planned or predictable by anyone, and so were independent of everyone. Isn't this a kind of autonomy, a kind of distance from human action and intention, even if produced *through* human action and intention?

Indeed, sometimes—paradoxically—this "autonomy" itself was actually part of the intention. The fact that one could not get from the first level to the third by escalator without walking all the way around the mall was a source of constant frustration but was also presumably a deliberate part of the design, intended by the architects to maximize the number of storefronts one would pass and therefore the chance that one would be tempted to make a purchase. Knowing this did nothing to decrease the frustration, the annoyed sense that once again one's trip to the mall was being extended beyond what one wanted, meaning that one's intentions when entering the mall could *not* be straightforwardly satisfied but rather were being blocked by something *independent*. (Nor did it decrease the frequency with which one was sucked in, despite one's firm resolution to buy just that one thing, by an attractive window display or a sign advertising a sale.) And it is important to note that this was not just a matter of one set of humans (the designers, say) imposing their intentions on another but rather of an artifact independent of *any* human. For I assume that even if Mr. Taubman himself had tried to get from the first level to the third—perhaps having found himself, on the way to a board meeting, in need of a Cinnabon to tide him over—he too would have been struck (although maybe not surprised) by the difficulty in getting there, frustrated by how long it took, and perhaps even persuaded by the odors wafting from the White Barn Candle Co. also to pick up a scented candle or a sachet for a friend. An artifact's independence from us, that is, may be designed into it, with the intention of causing us difficulty and frustration, but that does not make it any less independent, even from those whose intention that was.[27]

The point I am making here is not really a deep or surprising one, but perhaps its implications are. *The mall was a physical object.* Yes, it was the result (in part) of human intention, but being physical meant it was subject to physical forces and had physical properties, just like Leopold's mountain and she-wolf.[28] Such forces and properties are characteristic of all physical objects, whether built by humans or not, and they operate independently of human intention. No doubt humans sometimes make predictions about those forces and properties and use those predictions to try to get certain things to happen: using inertial forces to shoot an animal with an arrow, using tensile forces to weave a blanket with a loom, using microbiological forces to cure an infection with an antibiotic, using marketing forces to sell scented candles with a mall. But the artifacts that are built and used by humans for these purposes (the arrow, the loom, the antibiotic, the mall) remain nonetheless physical through and through, and in that sense they are "independent" of the humans who built them, no matter why or how they came to be (and note that "how they come to be" is itself always a physical process, a process of building).

But it was not just City Center's physicalness that assured it an independence from the humans who built or owned or used it. Ultimately the clearest indication of the fact that the mall was independent of humans, subject to its own developmental processes in ways that that no humans could ever fully grasp or predict, lies in the fundamental fact about City Center: it failed. Its physical demolition was the consequence of its commercial failure. The Taubman Company planned it, but surely did not plan for it to fail. The firm *intended* a successful mall. But the mall it *built* failed, which is to say it did not have the characteristics the company intended it to have. As I argued in the previous chapter, to build something (anything!) is to set forces into motion—the physical forces of construction, first of all, but second also social forces, of commerce, of human sociability, of urbanization and suburbanization—and then to *see what happens*. For what happens when one sets forces into motion is never entirely knowable, never predictable, never fully graspable, because those forces are always beyond the control of the builder. They are forces he or she tries to *use* but is never fully able to master. And so the building is always beyond the builder, too, always something with its own "autonomy"—a fact that the builder, and later the owner, frequently come to rue. *No one could have predicted* exactly what the future of the City Center Mall would be, on that first happy day in 1989 when it opened—surely not the executives of the Taubman Company, who had planned it so carefully but who doubtless knew, as it opened, that they were opening it up to a world of commerce that was in its very essence unpredictable, and who later must have agonizingly realized, like the heroes of a Greek tragedy, that it was their own hubristic act, the opening of the Mall at Tuttle Crossing, that set in motion City Center's demise.

The fate of the City Center Mall was the product, in fact, of the billions of individual decisions of hundreds of thousands of consumers and store owners and highway designers and government officeholders, each one of which was made on the basis of each individual's limited and inevitably partial view of his or her own needs, wealth, responsibility, and the world itself. That product was not knowable or predictable by anyone ahead of time: it occurred autonomously, independently of the choices and desires of any person or any corporation. This is the essence of a capitalist economy, and it even has a name in the history of economic theory: the invisible hand. If anything controlled the mall's fate, it was that hand—but that hand is not the hand of any one of us, and so the mall's fate was not in *our* hands. There is an ecology of the market, too, just as there is of the biotic community, and the Taubman Company failed to grasp it. Like Leopold and his comrades, the Taubmans lacked a sufficiently adequate understanding of the environment they confronted—an environment of which they believed themselves to be the master. If thinking like a mountain means recognizing the complexity of nature, and the way in which a single action (like the killing of a wolf) has so many interlacing and unpredictable consequences that its ultimate impact is impossible to grasp, then thinking like a mall might mean recognizing the complexity of the capitalist social order and recognizing that it too will always escape our attempts at prediction and control—and that it therefore functions *like a kind of nature* (Hegel called it a "second nature") just as capable of autonomy with respect to human wishes as a mountain. To add *this* ecology to the (first) "natural" one that environmentalism has always emphasized, recognizing that the two are not distinct from but rather entirely entwined with each other, would perhaps be to begin to develop an *environmental philosophy after the end of nature*.

The tens of thousands of customers traveling daily through the mall in its heyday, each concerned with his or her own needs and responding almost unconsciously to the environment around him or her, *together* set forces in motion that caused its failure. No one intended that, or planned it, or was able to predict it. Neither natural objects nor social ones are ultimately subject to human control. Everything that is escapes us. The problem isn't that we try to impose on nature the kind of control we exhibit in the social world; the problem is that control of this sort is impossible *anywhere*. It is not the "autonomy of nature" that is revealed to us when a tsunami destroys a set of nuclear reactors and threatens massive poisoning of a landscape, it is the autonomy of the *built environment*—which is the same autonomy revealed when a real estate bubble bursts and the financial companies that thought they had "managed" their "risks" realize that the real world (which includes earthquakes and reactors and collateralized debt obligations as well) is always capable of surprising us, sometimes with catastrophic consequences. The question is not, then, how to learn to respect nature's autonomy, any more than it is how to learn to respect the autonomy of the reactors, or of the market, or of the mall. The question is how to think about how our practices affect and are affected by our environment, the built one *and* the natural one, in a way that takes account of the autonomy it always possesses, an autonomy we have no ability to remove but rather must learn how to accept and acknowledge.

The Moral Considerability of Artifacts

Environmental ethicists often use the term "moral considerability" to talk about the difference between those items in the world to which we owe some sort of moral concern and those to which we don't. Is it impossible to imagine that the City Center Mall was morally considerable in this sense? Murray Hunt published an article in *Environmental Ethics* in 1981 that asked, "Are *Mere Things* Morally Considerable?" In it he questioned why moral considerability shouldn't be extended to *everything*. Kenneth Goodpaster in his classic 1978 essay on the topic of moral considerability had argued that drawing the line of our moral concern at rationality or sentience was fundamentally arbitrary, and that the line ought rather to be drawn at *life*: all living things (including plants and insects) deserve moral consideration, he claimed, not merely animals or humans. But Hunt asked why the criterion of life isn't itself just as arbitrary as sentience or rationality, and suggested that no criterion short simply of *being in existence* could avoid the same criticism. Hunt seemed to intend his article as a kind of reductio of Goodpaster's line of argument, but the position isn't as absurd as he apparently thought.[29] The idea that (some) nonliving items deserve our moral respect and consideration is perfectly coherent, and indeed, as noted, is one way of understanding what Leopold was suggesting with respect to the mountain itself. Keekok Lee has argued strongly for this kind of view, discussing, for instance, the moral status of extraterrestrial planets and arguing with some plausibility that the terraforming of Mars might well be thought of as a violation of that planet's autonomy and yet another example of the insatiable human desire to dominate and remake all of nature into our own image.[30]

We saw in the previous chapter that Eric Katz is explicit that for him, the key moral distinction is the one between the natural and the artificial, which he notes does not coincide with the one between the living and the nonliving; there are plenty of natural entities that are not alive, he points out, and they too deserve a certain sort of respect.[31] Elsewhere Katz uses the example of debates about the use of metal bolts in rock climbing to make this point. It has been argued that the practice of hammering such bolts into rock faces to assist in climbing, and especially of leaving the bolts in place to assist future climbers, can be viewed as a violation of the rocks' "autonomy" and even "freedom," and although Katz concedes there is something unusual about such locutions, he argues that it makes sense to use them in this sort of case.[32] As in Lee's example of terraforming Mars, the idea is that even nonliving entities have a prima facie right to be left alone, not to be modified by human actions. Katz quotes Herbert Marcuse's remark that "nature, too, awaits the revolution!" and suggests that there is a moral imperative to assist in the "liberation" of *all* natural entities, living and nonliving, from human domination.[33]

Still, neither Katz nor Lee (nor, of course, Leopold) really goes as far as Hunt's title taken literally would suggest, to the idea that all things, living and nonliving, *including artifacts*, might turn out to be morally considerable. That the "mere things" to which we might decide we owe moral consideration could include things such as automobiles, toasters, or shopping malls seems much harder to imagine, and it is striking how infrequently that possibility comes up even in discussions of the moral status of nonliving entities. Thus, for example, Robert Elliot writes in a survey of environmental ethics about what he calls an "everything ethic" that would extend moral considerability beyond humans and animals and plants to nonliving things, but in his discussion of this ethic the only examples given are rocks, dunes, icebergs, and the like; he never raises the question of whether other things commonly encountered in the world—key chains, mailboxes, airplanes—might also deserve moral consideration.[34] The extension of moral considerability is often described in terms of a process of moral learning or development, moving from a primitive concern limited to the family or tribe to the nation and then to humanity as a whole, and next in turn from humans to animals and then to living things in general; those who want to extend considerability further, however (that is, beyond the biotic), typically only extend it to *natural* things, as Katz and Leopold and Elliot do, not noticing that there's one more step possible in the extension—the move to artifacts, to the human-made things of this world, and to the question of *their* moral status.

(Lee's book *The Natural and the Artefactual* cannot be said to miss this question, it's true. One of its central points is that artifacts possess a fundamentally different ontological character from "natural" items and that the latter deserve our moral concern because nowadays our destruction of them threatens the elimination of an entire ontological realm. Yet one is hard put to find an actual argument in her book for this claim of a "primary" ontological difference between the natural and the artifactual. The closest thing one comes across is this: "As artefacts are the deliberate products of human intelligence to serve human ends, having been engineered with features and mechanisms which are not the outcome of the processes of natural evolution, they belong to a distinctly different ontological level from that of naturally-occurring beings or things."[35] But to see how unconvincing this is, compare it to the following: "As webs are the silken products of spider spinnerets to serve spider ends, having been spun with features and mechanisms which are not the outcome of the processes of natural evolution, they belong to a distinctly different ontological level from that of non-webs." The idea that "human intelligence" and its products are somehow on a "distinctly different ontological level" from nature, and that the "features and mechanisms" of those products are not the outcome of "processes of natural evolution," is *presupposed* by this argument, it isn't justified by it.[36])

When Katz and Lee, and those with similar views, talk about the "autonomy" of natural objects as something to be respected, they mean that such objects possess a kind of *independence* from human beings, and that therefore we ought not to modify or interfere in the processes those objects would undergo if they were left alone. But I have been arguing that in fact the very same thing might be true of the City Center Mall. Nature can be said to be "free" and "liberated," Katz writes, "as long as it is not being molded and transformed by human impacts."[37] But why can't artifacts be liberated in this way as well? The fact that human beings played a significant role in helping to bring the mall into existence (although again, not the only role: gravity helped, and rainfall, and birds, and sunlight, and so forth) doesn't mean we couldn't decide to stop "molding" and "transforming" it *now*: why not treat it as Elliot suggests restored environments should be treated, acknowledging the role of human action and intention in its history but committing ourselves to leave it alone, to "liberate" it from our "domination" *from now on?*

Katz makes clear that what he describes as "hybrid" environments like Fire Island also deserve a kind of hands-off respect: even there, he writes, where there have been years of human habitation and development, "we should choose the least intrusive policy."[38] Yet in what sense is the mall too not a "hybrid" environment (built, after all, of iron and sand and clay and wood that were modified in various ways) that we ought now to allow its own independence, its own freedom?

The Good of the Mall

Goodpaster had argued—following some ideas raised by Joel Feinberg and G. J. Warnock—that a necessary condition for being morally considerable was the possession of "interests," or of what Feinberg spoke of originally as "a good of one's own."[39] Although Feinberg had taken this idea only to suggest that animals might be morally considerable, explicitly denying that plants ("mindless creatures") could be said to have interests, Goodpaster argued instead for the moral considerability of living things in general. Feinberg had talked of interests as being essentially tied up with desires and beliefs, which plants surely lack, but elsewhere in the same article (Goodpaster noted) he had connected them with the possibility of being "represented" as in a court, and had admitted that "we do say that certain conditions are 'good' or 'bad' for plants, thereby suggesting that plants, unlike rocks, are capable of having a 'good."[40] Goodpaster's claim was that an entity need not be consciously *interested in* something in order to *have an interest* in it: the idea that a tree has an interest in receiving sufficient sunlight and water to grow is certainly not incoherent, nor does it involve imposing on the tree what is really a human interest. And human advocates might well be employed to "represent" those interests in a legal case. Goodpaster quoted a well-known passage from Christopher Stone's essay "Do Trees Have Standing?": "I am sure I can judge with more certainty and meaningfulness whether and when my lawn wants (needs) water than the Attorney General can judge whether and when the United States wants (needs) to take an appeal from an adverse judgment by a lower court."[41]

Hunt in his article takes the next step: if it is meaningful, he writes, for Goodpaster or Stone "to assert that one can know when his lawn needs watering, then it is no giant step to assuming that it is meaningful, also, to assert that one knows when his porch needs painting," and from there presumably to talk of the porch's interest in being painted, and of failure to paint it as a harm to the porch.[42] But that's about as far as Hunt goes in offering an argument, and as a result, his discussion (which mostly seems sarcastic) doesn't provide much in the way of serious examination of the idea that "mere things," including artifacts, might deserve more moral consideration than they are normally given. His article simply asserts that life as a criterion for moral considerability is just as arbitrary as the criteria Goodpaster criticizes, such as rationality or sentience, and therefore that a criterion of (mere) existence makes more sense, but he doesn't do much to examine the sorts of arguments that could be offered to show why life might indeed be a morally relevant property. It just seems false to say that the choice of life as the criterion is arbitrary; surely there have been some strong and intuitively persuasive justifications that have been offered by biocentrists in its favor. The problem is that if one tries to consider such justifications carefully, one discovers that the characteristics of living things on which they depend are possessed by some nonliving things, including some artifacts, as well. They're possessed, in fact, by things like malls.

Paul Taylor in his 1986 book, *Respect for Nature: A Theory of Environmental Ethics*, offers a series of carefully worked-out arguments for a position similar to Goodpaster's, defending the claim that all living things deserve moral considerability, not just humans and not just animals. To be a moral subject, he says (that is, to be morally considerable), requires being an entity with a "good of its own," or, to put it another way, being the sort of thing that can be "harmed or benefited." All living organisms have goods of their own in this sense, he claims, while inanimate objects do not, and so are not moral subjects.[43] Unlike Goodpaster, Taylor is prepared to reserve the concept of "interest" to beings for whom the satisfaction of their goals can be said to *matter* in the sense of being something of which they are aware (or in which they are "interested"), a class that seems to consist only of sentient animals; his point, however, is that a living but nonsentient creature (for example, a plant) that does not possess interests in this sense may still nonetheless have a good of its own, be capable of being harmed or benefited, and therefore be morally considerable.[44] Certain things are good for plants and others are bad for them; certain behaviors toward them help them grow and flourish while others damage and stunt them. It is possible, he says, to "take the standpoint of a plant and judge what happens to it as being good or bad from its standpoint."[45] We can act out of concern for a plant, and try to do what we can to help it thrive; we can feel morally obligated not to injure it. These characteristics, and not its possession of a conscious interest in being well treated, are what make it an appropriate "moral subject," Taylor claims.

But at first sight it seems that the same characteristics were possessed by the City Center Mall. A healthy customer base was good for it, the gunfight in the atrium was bad for it; the city's encouragement and tax subsidies encouraged it to grow, and the Taubman Company's investments helped it to flourish; construction of newer malls at Tuttle Crossing and later Polaris and Easton harmed it, and the wrecking ball, of course, damaged it quite directly. We can take the standpoint of the mall, thinking of the implications for it of continued middle-class flight away from downtown or wondering whether the decision to make it mostly windowless was beneficial for it or not, and recognizing that even if the new park is much more attractive and pleasant to visit—better, maybe, for humans—still, from City Center's point of view, the story of its short life and ultimate demolition is an unhappy one. The Taubmans, perhaps, acted out of genuine concern for it in their attempts to help it succeed, or maybe they didn't—maybe they were merely money-grubbers—but even in this case it would be nice to think at least that some of the artisans who maintained the floral arrangements in the atrium did so out of a real desire to improve the mall, or that a few of the workers who constructed it felt a pride in accomplishment for having helped build such an excellent mall.

Taylor is quite explicit, however, that for him, nothing like this even begins to entail that the mall had a good of its own, and therefore might have been a moral subject. Nonliving things, he says repeatedly, have no such goods. It's worth examining his arguments closely. He begins by considering as an example a pile of sand. If someone were to suggest that it ought to be protected from the rain because it would be harmed by getting wet, we would have trouble understanding what was meant, Taylor says. Perhaps the sand is going to be used for some (human) purpose that requires it to be dry—but in that case, wetting the sand is harmful to the humans whose purpose that is, not to the pile itself. This seems right, but it also seems more or less irrelevant to the case of the mall, first of all because a mall is a considerably more complex and internally articulated object than a pile of sand, but second, and more important, because while it's quite correct that there's no "purpose" to a pile of sand that moisture could be said to damage, there *is* a purpose to a mall: it's a commercial establishment whose goal is the selling of consumer goods at an operating profit. The purpose is intrinsic to what a mall *is*.

It's true, of course, that that purpose is in a certain sense (but only in a certain sense!) a human one: humans wanted there to be a mall in downtown Columbus in the late 1980s, and they wanted it (in part) because its goal was going to be to make a profit and they hoped to keep that profit, and so they put forces into motion that helped cause the mall to come into existence (though remember there were other reasons too).[46] Yet it isn't clear why this makes a difference with respect to the question of whether something could be good *for* the mall itself. Taylor tries to explain why in his next example, which more clearly describes an artifact and jumps up several levels of complexity from the sandpile:

> If we can say, truly or falsely, that something is good for an entity or bad for it, without reference to any *other* entity, then the entity has a good of its own. Thus we speak of someone's doing physical exercise daily as being good for him or her. There is no need to refer to any other person or thing to understand our meaning. On the other hand, if we say that keeping a machine well-oiled is good for it we must refer to the purpose for which the machine is used in order to support our claim. As was the case with the pile of sand, this purpose is not attributable to the machine itself, but to those who made it or who now use it.[47]

The notion that it should be possible to specify an entity's good independently of any other entity in order for that first entity's good to be its own isn't completely clear. Photosynthesis presumably is good for plants, but there can be no photosynthesis without the sun, and so talk of a plant's good requires reference to "another entity." Or does Taylor mean to say that there need be no reference to the *good* or *purposes* of another entity? But this doesn't seem right either: I might feed my oxen well in order to make them better able to pull my plow, and perhaps in a situation where without me they would have no source of nutrition, so their good will be achieved only if I feed them; does that mean their good is not their own? (Or for that matter, I might selfishly encourage my athletically talented but rather lazy child to exercise in the hope she will become a highly paid sports star and take care of me in my old age: again, the exercise, and the stardom, could still be good for *her*.) Or is the idea that in these sorts of cases it's still possible to talk of the oxen's or the child's good independently of any concern for the uses to which I might intend to put them, while this isn't true of the machine? But then Taylor hasn't gone much beyond where he started because we still need to know whether it is possible to attribute a good to a machine without concern for my use of it—and he's simply asserting that it isn't. The examples of the oxen or the athlete show already that the mere fact that a human has an interest in (is benefited by) an entity's achieving a good doesn't mean that the good isn't *its own,* and there's no argument here that this isn't the case with the machine. Without oil the machine breaks down, ceases to function, doesn't perform according to a norm that is built into it and therefore intrinsic to it. Indeed, eventually it ceases to exist, which is to say that it is no longer the particular machine that it was—it turns into something else, a rusting hulk of metal perhaps, and no longer a die-cutter (or whatever) at all. Why not say, then, that a lack of oil harms *it* and therefore that keeping it well oiled is *good for it*? It may well be that we can't specify the good without talking of the "purpose for which it is used," but why can't that purpose be *its own*, as in the case of the oxen or the child athlete?[48] (And to say that, well, inanimate objects don't have their "own" purposes is simply to beg the question—isn't that precisely what's under debate?)

Dogs bark at other animals in order to protect themselves, presumably as a way of frightening off potential predators and possibly to warn other members of the pack of danger. In this sense one might say that barking is good for the dog, and that doing so is in the dog's interest. But this characteristic may be noticed by humans and taken advantage of by them in order to extend the protection to themselves; they bring dogs into their homes in order to be warned about, and to frighten off, intruders. (They may even breed dogs to encourage this or similar traits.) The dog's good is surely still *its own* in this case. One could talk in similar ways about the use by humans of sheep growing wool, or of bees producing honey or pollinating plants. Now imagine a more complicated case, where the humans *construct* an object—such as a machine—instead of using a preexisting one, knowing (or at least hoping) that the entity that results from their construction will have certain characteristics that will turn out to be helpful for particular human purposes, at least as long as it is functioning well: it will help transport materials, perhaps, or will make possible the cheap production of textiles. Is this case really different? Unlike the case of the dog, it is true, humans have deliberately built the machine to have certain properties, because they find objects with those properties to be useful—but does this mean that the properties are not those *of the machine*? (They're surely not properties of the humans!) And certain ways of acting toward the machine (such as oiling it) may encourage the development and flourishing of those properties, just as feeding the oxen does, while others may harm them—again, why should we not talk here of these ways of acting as good or bad *for the machine*? (And before answering, we should consider the case in which the "machine" being "constructed" by humans is a baby. It is surely possible to specify a baby's good without referring to the purposes its parents might have had in creating it.)

And indeed, the fact that dogs are themselves domesticated animals, often specifically bred by humans for certain purposes (as are sheep, and some bees), suggests that the difference between the two kinds of case is not so large. Many key agricultural crops—corn, for instance—have been bred so that they cannot reproduce without human assistance; what makes the kernels edible and suitable for human cultivation also makes it impossible for reproduction to take place "naturally." Wouldn't it be correct here to say that the good of the plant—its ability to reproduce—cannot be specified without reference to humans, and even precisely to the purposes for which the plant has been bred? And yet it would seem curious indeed to claim that the plant had no good of its own: reproduction is typically one of the standard examples of the sort of internal teleology associated with the notion of an organism's "own" good. (Although it is worth noting that there would seem to be some difficulty, in the face of Taylor's argument, explaining why reproduction is a good or an interest of any organism, since in fact it can never be specified without reference to something other than the organism!)

Taylor (like Katz) seems to think that if an object is produced to serve a human purpose, then it cannot have a purpose of its own. And he seems to say that this remains true even if the object behaves in what are apparently intelligent or teleologically structured ways. Thus, later in the book he writes of "complex mechanisms" that "have been constructed by humans to function in a quasi-autonomous, self-regulating manner in the process of accomplishing certain purposes," mentioning as examples "self-monitoring space satellites, chess-playing computers, and assembly-line 'robots.'" (But again, wouldn't babies satisfy this description too?) Although admittedly such machines "are understandable as teleological systems," he says, "they remain in actual fact inanimate objects." This seems like a non sequitur—are these two categories mutually exclusive?—but then he explains the real point: "the ends they are programmed to accomplish are not purposes of their own, independent of the human purposes for which they were made."[49] It may be true, in these sorts of cases, that the purposes the machines attempt to attain are not *independent* of the human purposes for which they were made, but why does that mean they are not their own? Suppose the chess-playing computer in a given situation initiates a series of moves directed toward a queen sacrifice: was that sacrifice itself one of the "purposes" for which the computer was programmed? The programmer may never have even considered it! (And suppose the child whose athletic ability is honed and developed by the selfish parent goes on to form the desire to become an Olympic champion, which the parent had never dared even to imagine? Is that desire not the child's own?) Can't an entity, for that matter, have a purpose of its own, *as well as* a purpose programmed into it by humans? Or, more strongly, why can't those two be identical? Indeed, why is it conceptually impossible for humans to program into an entity *a purpose of its own*? Isn't this exactly what has happened in the case of dogs, or of corn, or of the myriad other living things we have come not only to use but through our behaviors to help shape so that their own purposes are useful to us?

The existence of living artifacts—of domesticated animals, hybridized plants, and in particular organisms produced by genetic modification—is a serious problem for the sort of biocentrism Taylor defends, which wants to assert the moral considerability of living things, on the one hand, while denying it to artifacts on the other. In his discussion of what he calls the "bioculture"—the world in which humans "control" and "regulate" the environment, and which he contrasts to the "natural world" that is his main concern—Taylor claims that "by means of hybridization, breeding programs, and other methods of genetic control, *humans produce the kind of animals and plants that will best serve human purposes,*" which would seem to make their "ends" dependent on those purposes, just as in the case of the robots, and hence to suggest that no more than these latter can they have a good of their own.[50] But then two pages later he explicitly asserts that "it is a truth of fact and *not* a value judgment that *all the living organisms being used in any society's bioculture are entities that have a good of their own.* They can be benefited or harmed. In this matter they are exactly like wild animals and plants in natural ecosystems."[51] If both of these are true, then it is possible for something both to be produced for human purposes *and* to have a good of its own: and now it just isn't clear what the arguments about the oil-needing machine or the robots were supposed to show. Why can't other, nonliving artifacts fall into the same category?[52]

One way to explain why they can't would be to show that there's something inherent in all living things—including "living artifacts"—that is simply lacking from merely mechanical ones like the oil-needing machine or the robot. This appears to be Taylor's view, although he never says it directly. I'm not aware of any place where he explicitly defines life, but it also seems clear that he thinks there is a fundamentally teleological character to living things that no abiotic artifact could ever possess. Here's his account of why a butterfly, even though it doesn't seem likely to have "interests" in the conscious sense, still ought to be understood as having a good of its own:

> Once we come to understand its life cycle and know the environmental conditions it needs to survive in a healthy state, we have no difficulty in speaking about what is beneficial to it and what might be harmful to it. A butterfly that develops

through the egg, larva, and pupa stages of its life in a normal manner, and then emerges as a healthy adult that carries on its existence under favorable conditions, might well be said to thrive and prosper. It fares well, successfully adapting to its physical surroundings and maintaining the normal biological functions of its species throughout its entire span of life. When all these things are true of it, we are warranted in concluding that the good of this particular insect has been fully realized. It has lived at a high level of well-being. From the perspective of the butterfly's world, it has had a good life.[53]

Taylor goes on to consider the example of simpler life forms, too, saying that even with respect to one-celled protozoa, "it makes perfectly good sense to a biologically informed person to speak of what benefits or harms them, what environmental changes are to their advantage or disadvantage, and what physical circumstances are favorable or unfavorable to them." The more we gain knowledge about such organisms, he adds, "the better we are able to make sound judgments about what is in their interest or contrary to their interest, what promotes their welfare or what is detrimental to their welfare." Recognizing this shows how it is possible to "*take an animal's standpoint*" and thus be able to decide "without a trace of anthropocentrism" what is good or bad for the animal from its *own* standpoint—and so recognize its moral considerability.[54]

But if we return to the City Center Mall and its sad fate, we might ask whether it too might have satisfied this description, and thus whether it might have had the sort of teleological character that would suggest it had a welfare or good of its own. Like the butterfly, it developed through several stages: design, construction, the initial leasing of retail spaces, the transformation of the interior in preparation for the public opening, and then something like a "healthy adulthood" as it came into full operation. For the first decade or so of its life it certainly thrived and prospered—as noted, it was one of the most successful malls in the nation. It adapted to its surroundings: as tastes in fashion changed, for instance, so did the sorts of clothing that appeared in the mall's stores; had they not, the mall would no doubt have died sooner. Similarly as more sophisticated appreciation and interest in gourmet coffee began to develop throughout central Ohio, the coffee served in City Center establishments began to improve, and new stores devoted only to coffee began to sprout up in the mall. The same was true as a "green consciousness" began to develop in the area, leading to the appearance in the mall of businesses such as The Nature Company, oriented toward providing consumers with bits of nature that they could purchase and bring home, or use as gifts.[55]

Like the butterfly, that is, the mall grew and developed, and it responded to its environment. Now, it's true that Taylor writes of the butterfly "maintaining the normal biological functions of its species," and doubtless the mall did not do this, since of course it had no "normal biological functions." But if Taylor meant by this remark that only biological functions count in determining whether something has a good of its own, he would be begging the question of whether abiotic things could be morally considerable, presupposing a biocentric answer where the passage about the butterfly seemed to be trying to argue for it. A more charitable reading would take the passage as suggesting that *for a biological entity* like a butterfly it is the maintenance of normal biological functions that matters; but then for a commercial entity like a mall one would expect the key question to involve the maintenance of *commercial* functions—generating revenue, producing profit, increasing foot traffic, and the like. Using Taylor's own language, it seems to me to make perfectly good sense, given a certain amount of information about retail businesses, to speak about what benefits or harms malls (strong anchor stores, on the one hand; concerns about safety, on the other), what environmental changes are to their advantage or disadvantage (booming economic conditions, on the one hand; the building elsewhere of more modern and better-located malls, on the other), and what physical circumstances are favorable or unfavorable to them (convenient parking, on the one hand; distance from the customer base, on the other). Learning these sorts of things about a mall, it would seem, would just as in the case of the butterfly permit us to make better judgments about what is in the mall's interest or what is contrary to it, what promotes its welfare or is detrimental to it. Thus again it should be possible to *take the mall's standpoint* and, "without a trace of anthropocentrism," see what sorts of actions are good for the mall (the hundreds of thousands of customers who patronized it during the first heady years of its success, say) and what sort are bad for it (the smashing of it by a wrecking ball, say).

The mall, I'm suggesting, had a teleological structure, much more like a butterfly than like a rock or a pile of sand, and even more so than a simple machine. It grew, first of all—beginning as a hole in the ground and then slowly developing both upward as it was built and also outward as connections (a skywalk, an underground passageway) developed between it and the surrounding buildings. It responded to changes in its physical environment in a way oriented toward homeostasis—its internal temperature, for example, was regulated in accordance with changes in the weather outside, as the heating and air-conditioning systems cycled on and off via thermostats. It underwent repetitive transformation in accordance with diurnal, annual, and other cycles. The lights inside the mall went on in the morning and went off at night, while external lighting came on toward evening and stayed on until daybreak. The music that played in the mall changed according to a regular schedule, depending both on time of day and time of year. Christmas decorations appeared throughout the mall after Thanksgiving and disappeared following New Year's; Easter eggs and bunnies showed up in store windows a few months later, and later still the windows of the clothing stores displayed bikinis and Bermuda shorts, in a pattern that repeated itself in accordance with the motion of the Earth around the sun. As the mall began to fail, of course, its ability to maintain homeostasis faltered as well: the decorations lost their vitality and the regularity of their changes, the intervals of light and darkness shifted as the opening and closing hours altered, eventually the HVAC ceased to function and differentials in internal temperature began to increase chaotically. The signs that the mall was in trouble, that it was failing to thrive and prosper, were clear to everyone. Ultimately the end was swift, though, and not due to homeostatic failures at all: the demolition was violent and destructive, as City Center's human owners, unwilling to "let the mall be" and intent on destroying it because it no longer served their own purposes, insisted instead upon the sudden and cataclysmic termination of all the processes that had helped maintain it in existence for twenty years.

I know, I know: the construction of the mall, the changing of the decorations at Christmastime, the setting of the thermostats—all of these were the work of *people*, and so the "teleology" I'm claiming to find in it isn't "real" teleology. But why not? Why does the role of human action in producing something mean it cannot have its *own* teleological character? Anthills have a teleological character, even though they're built by ants. The idea that *human*-produced entities can't produce a "real" (that is, a "natural") teleology is simply another version of the kind of reverse anthropocentrism we've considered repeatedly. And the argument, if put this way, seems entirely ad hoc: Taylor and similar biocentrists are claiming that possession of a teleological character (e.g., by the butterfly) itself grounds moral considerability, and that claim seems not to depend at all on how that teleological character comes into being, but then suddenly when cases like the mall are considered one learns that human-produced teleology for some reason doesn't count.[56]

If the idea is that a teleology that is "consciously intended" by those who create the system cannot be intrinsic to the system itself and so has a different status, we're back to the problem of intention, and of why a teleology can't be both intended and intrinsic. But we're also back at the problem that this way of putting it mistakenly imagines that what humans intend to build is the same as what they actually build, a mistake that depends on anthropocentrically viewing humans as omnipotent and as magically able to impose their will on the world without resistance or failure. It was not the intentions or desires of humans, after all, that determined the mall's teleological structure, it was their *actions*. If a janitor had mistakenly set the thermostat for 62 degrees instead of 72 degrees the homeostatic processes at work in the mall would have directed themselves toward that lower temperature, although no one would have *intended* that. Similarly, no one intended that the unattractive walkway from the main mall to the older Lazarus store would lead to the latter's demise, but that's what happened.[57] And more broadly, as I've already suggested: at the end of its lifetime the mall's goal was to *continue* (and better stores, more customers, higher sales, would all have helped achieve that goal), even at a moment when every human involved in managing it had turned against that goal—the mayor wanting it off his back, the owners wanting to get rid of it, and finally the demolition company wanting it destroyed as quickly and as cheaply as possible.

Earlier I wrote that there is an ecology of the market, an ecology of commerce, as well as the biotic ecologies that environmental thinkers emphasize. The mall, in a way, was an ecosystem—indeed, was something like the "land" that Leopold talks of when he presents his land ethic, a "biotic community" like the mountain he wants to learn to think like. Animals and other living things had their place in the mall: human animals, primarily, but insects, rodents, plants, and domesticated animals too could be found there, and all of these played a role in making it the place it was. Those living creatures (again, especially the human ones) interacted with each other, with individual stores, and with the mall as a physical structure in complex and unpredictable ways that nonetheless for two decades allowed City Center to continue to thrive and to grow, a healthy and stable ecosystem, functioning well, maintaining itself in existence. Leopold talks of an "energy circuit" operative within his biotic community; I'm tempted to say that rather than energy what circulates within something like a mall is money, but this seems oversimplified. In any case, while the circuit at work in the mall is clearly different from the one Leopold describes, still the analogies to the workings of what he calls "land" remain striking. He writes at one point that "when a change occurs in one part of the circuit, many other parts must adjust themselves to it. Change does not necessarily obstruct or divert the flow of energy ... [but] man's invention of tools has made it possible for him to make changes of unprecedented violence, rapidity, and scope."[58] The Taubmans, poor ecologists as they turned out to be, ought perhaps to have paid more attention to this, and to Leopold's discussion of the sorts of damage such violent and rapid changes can produce.

The Last Person at the Mall

I am suggesting, with a certain amount of seriousness, that malls might possess a similar sort of complexity and teleology as butterflies (although the *degree* of complexity may not be the same), and hence by Taylor's own argument might be said to possess something like interests and a good. Aristotle, writing before Darwin, can be excused for believing there was something metaphysically unique about living things that nonliving ones (especially artifacts) simply lacked. But neo-Aristotelians cannot hide behind this excuse. It's striking how frequently biocentric arguments for the intelligibility of the idea that a plant possesses a good of its own simply assert that artifacts, despite their admittedly possessing a teleological character too, nonetheless just don't possess such a good. Thus (to choose one more example) Robin Attfield in his essay "The Good of Trees" rejects Feinberg's claims that nonsentient creatures can't have a good of their own, pointing out how even Feinberg suggests at one point that possessing "latent tendencies, direction of growth and natural fulfillment do jointly seem ... sufficient conditions of having interests." But Attfield immediately hastens to add that "this is not to endow machines or cities ... with interests, as they lack *natural* fulfillment even when built according to a plan," and that even things like forests or swamps are excluded because they lack "inherited capacities."[59] Absolutely no argument is given, however, for the limitation of the sorts of "fulfillments" permissible to "natural" ones, or for the claim that the capacities involved have to be inheritable: again, these seem like completely ad hoc additions to the theory, with no basis in the teleological account.

Attfield, like Taylor and Goodpaster, is concerned to block the argument that what we take as the interest or the good of a plant is really only *our* interest, something that humans appreciate or value in the plant. He takes for granted as uncontroversial that this argument *does* apply to what we might otherwise call the interests of artifacts—of a building in remaining standing, of an automobile in running smoothly, or of a mall in expanding its customer base. Again, however, if we are Darwinians (and naturalists), and no longer believe living things to possess some sort of special spark or entelechy that would render them metaphysically unique, it isn't clear what the principle is on the basis of which the desired distinction could be drawn here. Attfield acknowledges that sometimes the interests of a plant and those of humans *in* the plant might coincide, as when we grow the plant in a garden because we appreciate the beauty of its blossoms, but he points out that such a coincidence is contingent, and that, for example, "if it were our purpose to hang plastic lanterns on [plants], we could not claim that their bedecked condition was *ipso facto* one of flourishing: flourishing states have to be states in keeping with a plant's nature."[60] But after Darwin the reference to "nature" here can't be taken in any metaphysical or vitalist sense as opposed to a sense in which malls too might have a "nature." And then just as with the plant, there are plenty of things we might decide it to be in our interest to do *to* the mall—turn it into a museum, use it as storage for toxic waste, or for that matter demolish it—that it wouldn't make sense to say were in the interest *of* the mall, because to do them would cause it to cease to exist as a mall, and so would certainly not be in keeping with its "nature."[61] Malls can flourish, and they can fail to flourish; it may well be true that developers usually build malls in the hope that they will flourish, but nonetheless there could be occasions where they have other ends in view. City Center was built in the hope that it would revitalize downtown Columbus, but I would be hard put to argue that doing so was part of what it would have meant for the mall *itself* to flourish. And note that Attfield's other example of the noncoincidence of human interests with those of plants is what he calls "the common and garden experience of unwanted flourishing"—the growth of weeds, the overgrowth of even desired plants, the harm done to sidewalks and foundations by unchecked tree root development, and so on.[62] Sometimes in gardens, but elsewhere too, we help cause something to come into existence whose later flourishing we discover we really do not want—that is, it is really not in *our* interest. That this can happen surely shows that the entity thus produced had its *own* interest, resulting, one might say, from its own "nature." But isn't this what happened as things like tattoo parlors began to replace the genteel Henri Bendels and Limited Toos that the Taubmans had originally hoped to see populating the mall? It was, indeed, out of fear of what the unchecked mall could become that the decision was made to destroy it: like the sorcerer's apprentice, the developers and city officials who brought the mall into existence were now unhappy and even frightened about what they had wrought, and so brought their power to bear to kill it, choking off its flourishing and violating its interest just as a gardener does to an unruly and invasive weed.

A standard move in the literature on the moral considerability of nonhumans is the "last person" intuition pump, in which one imagines the last human being on Earth—following a nuclear catastrophe or something similar—facing his or her imminent demise and deciding whether to destroy some object.[63] (In Mary Midgeley's version of the example, it's Robinson Crusoe about to be rescued, considering whether to burn down everything on his island.[64]) The question is then whether the imagined act of destruction would be morally wrong or not, given that ex hypothesi no "human purposes" will be frustrated because all human purposes are about to disappear. Finding the act to be wrong suggests that one thinks that the threatened object is morally considerable in itself, which is to say independently of its role in human projects. To Leopold, if the last act were something like his youthful shooting of the she-wolf, presumably a wrong would have been done, and not just to the wolf but also to the mountain and the land. Taylor, Goodpaster, and Attfield would all seem to agree that uprooting a tree purely out of random wanton anger or despair would be wrong as well. Katz and Lee would apparently go further and say the same about arbitrarily smashing a rock or damaging a cliff. What's curious is that in various discussions of this sort of case there's rarely any consideration of artifacts: it seems to be taken for granted that *they* have no moral standing, and that the last person would do nothing wrong in, say, smashing a window or even blowing up a building. Yet it isn't clear why this is so. Would the destruction by the last person of something produced by another species—an anthill (even an abandoned one), a beehive, a beaver dam, or a spiderweb—be so easily treated as morally neutral? Shouldn't biocentrists find some value in the things that living organisms have produced themselves, things the production of which must surely be counted as an element of their *own* good, their *own* flourishing, things they produce for their *own* purposes? And if this is so, why not find value in the perhaps poor but sometimes well-meaning creations of that species of which we are ourselves members?

So imagine an enormously complex machine, powered, let us say, by artificial photosynthesis, fully automated so that under normal conditions it can run by itself for long periods. It has a Rube Goldberg structure, where one complicated mechanism generates as output a movement or electrical impulse or chemical reaction that starts the next one, which in turn helps cause the next, and so on and so on, through myriad different processes, so that the whole machine is really a linking of hundreds or maybe thousands of smaller ones. The input material to the machine perhaps is sea water, or maybe it's an enormous sandpile of the sort that

Taylor wrote so dismissively about, or maybe it's the excess carbon from an atmosphere that has been heated up by years of human use of fossil fuels. The output is something magnificent, enormous, gorgeous: a structure of the size and majesty of a Gothic cathedral, perhaps, or a tiny artificial jewel on which has been etched the faces of all the people living on Earth when the machine was first built. Or perhaps it simply plays aloud the Deutsche Grammaphon recording of Mozart's Sinfonia concertante K.364 with Pinchas Zukerman and Itzhak Perlman. The machine is constantly monitored by sophisticated electronics under the control of a set of computers that maintain an appropriate temperature while also making sure that each individual mechanism is working correctly, and that also arrange for (automated) repairs of any damage that occurs owing to parts wearing out or the effects of weather or seismic activity or curious animals or overgrowing plants that might happen to infringe on its actions; the computers also monitor themselves, of course, and take themselves out of operation and turn on backups if any anomalies are detected. An entire subsystem is devoted toward making sure the various mechanisms are kept well oiled; a failure of that subsystem would be fatal to the entire machine.

And now comes the catastrophe in which humankind is destroyed. The last person on Earth turns out to be one of the designers of the machine—the one who designed the subsystem that controls the oiling of the mechanisms. Her own death is imminent. Filled with resentment and rancor, and perhaps a sense that it was the growth of human technology itself that was ultimately responsible for the catastrophe, she turns to the machine, which she knows full well will continue humming away for years and maybe decades after her death, but which she also knows how to destroy by disabling the oiling subsystem. Would it be wrong of her to do so? If she did, the machine would attempt valiantly to continue, would even try to repair itself, but (since the repair mechanism itself requires oil) would ultimately fail. It might last a while, might even (depending on the sophistication of the programs controlling it) be able to make some changes to itself to allow it to bypass various individual mechanisms as they begin to falter and go offline. But at last it would succumb, no longer able to function, no longer capable of generating that cathedral, that jewel, that music, and turn finally into a motionless and inert collection of pieces of metal and silicon and plastic subject to the same rust and decay that all other human artifacts would be undergoing.[65] Would something bad have happened here? Did the designer do something wrong? Would something valuable here have been prevented from achieving its (own) purpose, its (own) good, its (own) flourishing?

I grant that there probably are many who would answer these questions with no.[66] But I cannot help but think that such an answer, if combined with an answer of yes to similar questions about a tree, a spiderweb, or a rock, requires a sort of misanthropy that I find difficult to justify no matter how ugly, poorly designed, and ecologically dangerous most human artifacts unquestionably are. The machine I've described seems to me to have as much of a telos as many living things, and perhaps more than some; it acts as if it "wants" something to happen, responds to changes in its environment to ensure that that thing happens, and seems to be flourishing as the thing it is until the last person damages it and keeps it from achieving its goal. (And that goal, furthermore, is pretty impressive itself.) But that's not actually why I think it would be wrong to destroy it – because I don't, in fact, accept the view about the value of teleology that one finds in Attfield or Goodpaster or Taylor. Rather, I think it would be wrong to destroy it because such a machine would be a remarkable example of what human beings can accomplish, because the development of creatures with the ability to imagine and then build such a thing would have been a stupendous achievement in the history of the universe, just like the ability of early eukaryotes to photosynthesize, of the first amphibians to leave the water, of the first mammals to bear their young live. Human products—or rather, some human products—are amazing, and deserve to be preserved. They're also, I've been arguing all along, natural, or at least as natural as anything else. And I hope that after we're gone they will still exist.

But if the answer as to whether the machine's destruction would be wrong is yes, as I think it is, then it is not ridiculous to ask about the moral considerability of the City Center Mall, and to wonder about the thoughtlessness with which we use, interact with, and often destroy the artifacts we (help to) produce. I hope it's clear that my argument here is meant, like Hunt's, as a kind of reductio: I'm not suggesting that City Center ought not to have been demolished, or that the mayor who ordered its destruction or the workers who carried it out did anything wrong. I didn't much like the mall, as I've said, and I rather enjoy the park that has replaced it. But if living things deserve moral consideration because of their teleological character, or if abiotic natural entities such as rocks deserve protection from human interference because they possess what Lee calls "trajectories" independent of us, or if biotic communities should be respected and preserved because of their unimaginable complexity and the difficulty we face in "thinking like" their members, then it seems to me that something similar would have to be said about City Center as well.

And so modus tollens would suggest that if we don't think City Center deserves moral consideration, then we need to reconsider the grounds for Taylor's biocentrism or Leopold's ecocentrism or Lee or Katz's desire to protect nature against human transformations of it. And what we need to ask, as I have been suggesting, is whether these views depend on an unsupported vitalism, or a (non-naturalistic!) human exceptionalism, that seems significantly inconsistent with the modern post-Darwinianism that most environmental philosophers typically defend.

Responsibility for Things

We are thoughtless about our artifacts. We treat them as morally insignificant, and, more to the point, we treat them as ontologically insignificant—less important not only than living things but also than "natural" abiotic things like rocks or piles of sand. We use them, and use them up, and then we discard or destroy them without a second thought. The considerations of chapter 3 return here: we have built those artifacts, through socially organized practices of labor, and they play a central role in the social practices in which we are constantly engaged, and yet that builtness and that sociality remain almost entirely hidden from our attention. We use artifacts, inhabit them, wear them, eat them, sit on them, watch them, depend on them, without giving them a second thought. It's characteristic of our thoughtlessness that we worry more about harms to "nature"—to rocks, to mountains, to the atmosphere—than we do about harms to the buildings and communities in which we live, and that we care more about the beauty of nature than we do about the beauty of the objects that we have built and that surround us all the time. (And characteristic, too, that we find more awe at the thought of Nature, or nature, than we do at the capacities of humans to help build those objects.)

I do mean what I have been arguing here as a reductio: I don't want to suggest for a moment that failing to change the oil in one's car is immoral in the way that failing to feed one's child would be, or even failing to feed one's cat. But an automobile is not nothing, I want to say; it's more, in a certain sense, than a rock is, and if not more than a cat then at least also something quite remarkable. That people have been able to combine parts of the world and take advantage of forces within it—forces they do not fully understand and can never fully predict the operation of—to produce a new entity capable of traveling under their control at speeds their legs alone could never make possible and filled with other teleologically structured systems (for braking, for temperature control, for indicating direction, for choosing gears) is astonishing. And that millions of these entities exist, as a result of the labor of tens of millions of human beings working in enormously complex ways that are themselves not fully knowable or predictable by anyone, through processes of cooperation that are coordinated by international market mechanisms that are themselves enormously and almost incomprehensibly complex, is perhaps even more astonishing. And more astonishing still is the way in which those entities have literally transformed the entire Earth, causing the building of roads and suburbs and shopping malls, helping to create an entire global industry based on oil production that in turn has had had immeasurable social, economic, geopolitical, and other effects throughout the world, changing humans' experience of time, space, family, sex, and leisure, spewing pollution worldwide in unimaginable quantities, and finally, playing a profoundly significant role in causing the very atmosphere of Earth to change in ways whose consequences we do not yet know. Not all these things are good, it is clear, and some of them may be horrific and tragic in their implications. But they are things that *we have done*, and we ought to recognize that fact and acknowledge its immensity, as both a moral and an ontological matter.

To see that the world of artifacts that surrounds us—what I have been calling our environment—is something we have built, and that we have built it together (socially), is not to find it intrinsically valuable or even morally considerable. I would not make either of those claims. It is, however, to see ourselves as *responsible* for it. Responsibility is the key concept here, I think, and as I've already said in chapter 3, it has two separate meanings in this context, one causal and one moral. We are responsible for the artifacts that surround us in that we made them, or helped make them: they are part of a world that we have worked through our labor to bring into existence. And we need to come to recognize this, as I have said, more clearly than we do. But to be responsible for them in that way is also, I think, to see that we *ought* to be responsible for them in the sense that it should *matter* to us what happens to them—how they are used, how they are destroyed, and, most important, simply what they are. *We are responsible for the environment*: this seems to me the central conclusion of what I am calling postnaturalism in environmental philosophy. The environment itself is an artifact that we make through our practices, and hence one for which we are responsible and about which we ought to care. If the artifacts that surround us are ugly, if they work poorly, if they generate poisons and other toxic waste, if they make life worse for us and for the other creatures that inhabit the world with us—and for that matter if they make things worse for themselves and their fellow artifacts as well!—this is (in part) our doing, and our fault. And so it is also our responsibility to fix.

That we are responsible for the environment means both that what we find ourselves surrounded by today is (already) our own doing, and also that we must take responsibility for it. The environment today is pretty terrible: it's ugly, it's dangerous, it's deadening, in many ways it encourages people's worst instincts and prevents them from developing their best ones, and worst of all, it seems as though it may be on the verge of a cataclysmic collapse. *We have done this*: we have created it through our practices. What we have to do now is to figure out ways to change our practices, both to prevent any further deterioration and to reverse what has already occurred. We built the environment, through our social practices: the problem is to find new ways of building it that will make it a *good* environment, one that fosters good human life in community and that is filled with beauty, with pleasure, with freedom, and with happiness for all the beings inhabiting it. To do that would be to overcome alienation. It is also what it might mean finally to think like a mall—to recognize, as the mall might, if it could think, that it too is part of the environment, not some piece of disposable human detritus with no moral or political significance but rather something that humans have (helped) bring into existence and for which they ought to claim responsibility—and for which they might have reason to feel pride. City Center was nothing to be proud of, though—it was pretty awful. If we had acknowledged our responsibility for it, rather than pretending either that it had no moral relevance or treating it as something beyond us, simply a fact of downtown Columbus, or a piece of the Taubmans' private property that wasn't our concern, or the quasi-"natural" product of independent market forces whose construction and demolition were out of our control, then perhaps what we would have built in downtown Columbus would have been quite different, and much better. But none of us had any chance to do that: all any of us could do was to choose to patronize it or not, a choice that was hardly a choice at all.

One might object here that saying that the environment is our responsibility and that we are therefore responsible for fixing it sounds dangerously like the sort of hubris that sees us as masters of the world and takes the world around us ("nature"?) as meaningless matter we should feel free to mold in anthropocentrically arbitrary ways. I understand this objection but do not think it is valid. As I have written above, it is our *practices* that (help) produce the environment, not, ultimately, our *ideas*.

We may be master of our ideas, but we are surely not master of our practices. The recognition of our responsibility for the environment requires as a crucial element the humility I wrote about in the last chapter—the humility that comes from recognizing that our practices always escape us and that the artifacts we produce always have more to them than we can ever understand or predict. No human transformation of the world ever fully produces the exact results those humans who undertake that transformation intended; in part that is because there is no such thing as a *merely* human transformation of the world. All transformations involve the interaction of all sorts of forces, and only some of them are human forces: gravity plays a role, as do heat and cold and sunlight, as do—always—other living organisms as well. (That's part of what Leopold meant by thinking like a mountain, and it's what I have tried to emphasize in suggesting that we expand such thinking to artifacts like malls as well.) And so if we were, as I suggested earlier, to work to fix the awful environment that surrounds so many of us nowadays—by engaging in different sorts of practices, differently organized, oriented toward producing a more beautiful, more sustainable, more marvelous world—we would have to do so in full knowledge that our attempts will often fail, will often be stymied, and even at their most successful will end up differently than we expected. We can only do the best we can, perhaps making use of the unanticipated outcomes (which may also be better than we had hoped for, as well as worse!) to serve as inspirations for corrections, for new ideas, for new forms of practice, but with the ever humble recognition that what we do will never quite match our intentions and that the world will always escape our ability to predict it.

Thus our practices would have to be marked by a spirit of tentativeness and fallibilism, not by hubris. The kind of hubris this objection worries about is a hubris that does not think like a mountain or a mall but rather believes that whatever humans dream up they can immediately and unfailingly make, without unexpected consequences or undesired side effects. Such a hubris feels no responsibility for its artifacts themselves, believing (without even looking at them) that they will turn out identical to the blueprints that preceded them, and that they will always do exactly what they were "intended" to do. But that same hubris, I've been trying to suggest, lies behind the way Katz or Lee or Goodpaster or Taylor write about artifacts too—as though again they were always successful, as though they always achieved the goals of the humans who built them and thus had no good of their own. Artifacts are real, just like mountains, and so they both do and do not escape us, just as mountains do. And the same is true of the environment.

6

The Silence of Nature

Artifacts and Humans

The literal social constructionism I am proposing emphasizes, as I have indicated, the concrete and socially organized processes of building that have produced the environment we inhabit. It understands humans fundamentally as organisms who change the world through their activities and who therefore create their own world. No anthropocentric distinction is intended here between humans and other organisms, though—*all* organisms create their worlds, and thus the environment we inhabit is the product of the activities of all the creatures that make it up. And crucially, as I have argued, to say we construct the world through our activities is not to say we control it or are its masters, nor is it to fall prey to the idealism that what might be called the linguistic form of social constructionism seems to threaten. We do not "think" of a world and then magically bring it into existence; the world is perfectly real and material, just as real and material as our activities are. It is not the product of our language or our worldview or our ideology or our discourse or our social imaginaries: it is the product of our work, of what we *do*, and not what we think or hope or desire or imagine.

Thus in the two previous chapters I emphasized the importance of "artifacts," which is to say of items that have been built by human beings. Artifacts are the Rodney Dangerfield of environmental thought. It's easy to be concerned about the protection of animals, plants, ecosystems, Leopoldian biotic communities, and so forth, and even about the protection of rock faces or mountains, but when the moral or ontological status of "mere things" is considered the examples employed rarely include things we have built (which of course are precisely the things by which we are most immediately "environed.") No one seems to care about them; indeed, hardly anyone even seems to take any note of them at all.

The possibility that their character as things both *produced* by us but also (because they are physically real) *independent* of us might cause a problem for environmental ontology is rarely considered. But I think the question of the status of artifacts raises a fundamental difficulty for the distinction between humans and the "natural" on which so much environmental argument relies. Artifacts are *things*, they're *real*, they have properties that their designers never intended or expected them to have, and the properties those designers did intend came to be possessed by the artifacts through the operation of forces the designers could never fully grasp. Once one realizes all this about them it becomes clear that drawing a distinction between the human world and the "natural" one in the way environmentalism has traditionally done, where the latter is supposed to be a more-than-human realm independent of us, makes very little sense, mistaking a difference in genesis for a difference in ontological status. What we create are *things*, just as physical and material as all the other things that surround us, and those things *are* beyond us in the sense that we never fully understand or control them, any more than we fully understand or control the processes by which we create them. And yet in a deeper sense still it is more correct to say that they are not beyond us at all, for to see them as beyond us is still to imagine an "us" that does *not* build things and is not itself a physical organism but rather something mysterious and supernatural, something to which materiality itself is "other" or "beyond." If we are physical creatures whose fundamental character is to act in the world, and if action in the world is itself always physical, then this character of our artifacts—their reality and difference from our ideas and intentions—is not "beyond" us any more than spiderwebs are beyond the spiders that spin and inhabit them. The moment of "independence" in our artifacts, or in the spiders' webs, is simply the moment of realness, and in that sense is analytically implied by the very notion of making something, or for that matter of acting in the (real) world. To build real objects that are independent of us is *what we do*: what else *could* we do? What would it be to build real objects that are not independent of or "beyond" us in this sense?

And so, as I suggested in chapter 4, the point of my constructionism is not simply to point out the "artifactuality of nature," the ways in which what we take as natural can always be shown to possess something of the mark of human action behind it, but rather, and equally important, to talk about the "nature of artifacts," the way in which the items we have built themselves possess the same sort of ontological independence as the unexamined wildernesses, the wild mountain crevasses, the depths of the ocean, the untrammeled other planets that are always mentioned in opposition when constructionists express skepticism about "nature." The distinction between the natural and the artificial is ontologically meaningless: this is the central point I am trying to make. Of course, we can distinguish between things that humans make and things they don't—they make toasters and shopping malls, they don't make rocks or mountains—and we can even distinguish among various "degrees" of human-madeness—there's much more human work involved in the construction of a skyscraper than in the building of a hut in the Black Forest, and there may have been more involved in building the hut than there was in rendering habitable a Neolithic cave. But none of these distinctions has any *ontological* significance: there are doubtless occasions where it might be useful to draw them so as to indicate the relative role played by different organisms in an item's genesis, in the same way, for example, that one might want to distinguish soil that has been well fertilized and aerated by earthworms from soil that has not, but there is nothing ontologically fundamental implied by these distinctions. In particular, *all* (real) items "escape" the human or are "other than" the human or are "more-than-human," if these terms are meant to express the fact that they are subject to forces that humans cannot control, do not fully understand, and are unable fully to predict: this is a characteristic of *reality*, of materiality, and not some ontologically mysterious property that human beings can somehow (even more mysteriously) extinguish by thinking about or working on something. When I take a piece of flint and shape it into an arrowhead, I do extinguish its "not-made-by-a-human"-ness, to be sure, but this is true merely by definition: there's nothing *else*, nothing ontologically deep, that I extinguish in addition—and the same is true when workers hired by the Taubman Company take a piece of land in downtown Columbus and transport steel and concrete and copper and marble and chrome there and shape them into a shopping mall.

It is a mistake, I am suggesting, to treat the world of artifacts—the urban world, the technological world, the built environment—as though it were somehow a world subject to human control and prediction in which human beings were safe and only ever confronted themselves. Artifacts as much as "natural" entities escape that control and prediction precisely because, as much as "natural" entities, they are *real*. And again, this is not to say that differences of degree do not exist: it's true, of course, that I'm probably safer sleeping in my home than I am when camping in the wilderness, and that is partly the result of the fact that many characteristics of my home have been designed to help increase (not "ensure") my safety. And many events are more predictable there, too—the ringing of the alarm clock, the constancy of the ambient temperature, the absence of predatory animals. But these are merely contingent facts about those particular contexts, not the inevitable result of the greater role that humans played in building the one than the other. City streets can be quite dangerous and unpredictable under certain circumstances, as anyone who lived in New York in the 1970s or Baghdad in the 2000s can attest, and the tedious sameness (and so predictability) of certain "wilderness" locations (in Antarctica, say, or in the middle of the Pacific) has often been remarked on. The human is not (necessarily) the "controlled" or the "regularized"; the nonhuman (the "natural") is not the "wild" or the "unpredictable." There's one world, not two: the real one, in which humans, their natural artifacts, and their artifactual nature all exist together.

But to say all this is not to say that human beings are somehow indistinguishable from any other entity in the world. There are characteristics that seem to be unique to humans—although in saying this I do not mean to assert any necessity, conceptual or otherwise, to that claim, which is merely an empirical and fallible one. Among these characteristics are language use, first of all, as well as what might be called the realm of the political. We speak, and we act together to decide what to do, and these characteristics seem linked. The practices we engage in, I have said, are always *social* practices, which as I have suggested means they are always normatively structured, and both this sociality and this normativity are typically mediated through language. The realm of the political is the place where social decisions are made about what practices to engage in and what the norms governing those practices ought to be. The problem mentioned in chapter 4 of relativism, of how a postnaturalist environmental theory could find a normative standard for judging our practices without any appeal to a nature outside those practices, requires a shift toward the consideration of political and ethical questions; but a turn to politics and ethics cannot avoid as well an examination of the question of language. In this chapter I want to consider, first, a number of recent "materialist" discussions of nature and the politics of nature that seem to me to fail adequately to grasp the role of human practices in constructing the environment, and then to turn specifically to the issue of language and its relation to ethics. Questions of practice arise *in* language, I will argue, and can only be answered there as well, and so language users have a unique role to play in deciding such questions. "Nature" is silent; *we*—you and I, the ones who can talk—have to decide what standards should guide our practices, because there's no one else who can.

Materialism, Vitalism, and Language

Another word for the position I have been arguing for might be "materialism." It is the *material* character of our artifacts that I have emphasized in the last few chapters—a material character that in one sense is obvious (what could an artifact be except material?) but that seems to be forgotten when artifacts are treated as though they were merely a reflection of human intention or thought or rationality, somehow outside nature and fully subject to human control and understanding. And to say that they are material—just as material as rocks or lakes or the atmosphere or Mars, and just as material, too, as anything alive—is to say they possess the kind of irreducible independence from human beings and human purposes that I argued in the previous chapter characterized the City Center Mall. What sets artifacts apart from other, supposedly more natural entities is not any lack of materiality or lack of independence but rather the fact that human *action* (not human thought) was required to produce them—human action that is itself *material.* The point then is not (merely) that real objects such as toasters or shopping malls are in fact subject to complex and unpredictable physical forces at every moment but, and more important, that the processes by which they were built required for their very possibility the operation of such forces, and that the builders themselves counted on the operation of such forces at the very same moment that they did not, could not, understand or enumerate or control them. Bruno Latour writes of what he calls "the slight surprise of action," the way in which "whenever we make something *we* are not in command, [but rather] are slightly *overtaken* by the action," and adds (as I have, earlier), "every builder knows that." "I never *act,*" he writes; "I am always slightly surprised by what I do."[1] This is what I called in chapter 4 "the gap": action (real action, in a real world) always requires the operation of forces that intervene, as it were, between the actor and the action's result, forces that again by virtue of their own materiality aren't fully understandable or predictable by the actor but that are required in order for the action to take place.

This emphasis on action, on the material practices through which material artifacts are produced (and therefore also by which the environment itself is produced), distinguishes the view I am developing from the sort of "new materialism" recently proposed by thinkers such as Jane Bennett. Bennett's book, *Vibrant Matter: A Political Ecology of Things*, emphasizes what she describes as the "vitality" of matter, and uses the concept of "thing-power" to describe an approach according to which matter and material objects are seen not merely as a source of difficulty or recalcitrance in frustrating human purposes but also as a productive source of action and change in the world. Her "vital materialism" treats matter as possessing a kind of agency and effectivity that (she says) it has traditionally been denied; she proposes thinking of the world as consisting of "assemblages" of "actants"—"living, throbbing confederations that are able to function despite the persistent presence of energies that confound them from within," with "uneven topographies" and "not governed by any central head."[2] Bennett offers a new metaphysics—she calls it an "onto-story"—strongly influenced by Spinoza, Deleuze, Guattari, Serres, and others, according to which matter is redescribed not as the inert and passive substance of traditional metaphysics but rather as "vibrant, vital, energetic, lively, quivering, vibratory, evanescent, and effluescent."[3] At another point she adds that "an active becoming, a *creative not-quite-human force capable of producing the new*, buzzes within the history of the term nature. This vital materiality congeals into bodies, bodies that seek to persevere or prolong their run."[4] The language here suggests some of what I have spoken of above with respect to artifacts such as the mall—that is, the inevitable complexity and unpredictability of anything real and physical in the world, whether made by humans or not. But the role of humans in the making of those things—and more particularly the role of this same sort of "vital" "creativity" in that very making—receives very little analysis in Bennett's discussion.

Bennett is concerned above all to break down the distinction between human subjectivity and the objective world of material things as a "counter to human exceptionalism," and with such a goal I certainly agree.[5] But if one pays close attention to the structure of the arguments she employs, one sees that she does this not by emphasizing the (active) materiality of humans but rather by projecting human characteristics onto the material world. As a result, she ends up emphasizing the *humanity of materials* rather than the *materiality of humans*. Matter turns out to have human qualities, especially the qualities of intentionality and agency. Thus, for example, Bennett writes that "other [nonhuman] forces in the world approximate some of the characteristics of intentional or purposive behavior on the part of humans."[6] She notes repeatedly that her arguments depend on an "anthropomorphism" that is looking to find "creative agency" outside human actions—that is, to see human characteristics in material things.[7] It might be worth "running the risks associated with anthropomorphism," she writes, mentioning among those risks "superstition, the divinization of nature, romanticism," because "oddly enough, [anthropomorphism] works against anthropocentrism: a chord is struck between person and thing, and I am no longer above or outside a nonhuman 'environment.'"[8] But this isn't true, or rather it makes one's metaphysics depend on a kind of narcissistic fantasy, which *is* the risk in anthropocentrism: the fantasy that all the world is really *like me*, that wherever we look we will find the very same capacities for active and intentional transformation of the world that we find in ourselves, and so there is nothing other than us at all. Here the metaphor of seeing oneself reflected everywhere does indeed seem to apply. *We* are "vital," "creative," "energetic"; our actions are the basis of "an active becoming"—and Bennett's goal seems to be to show that everything else in the world is just like us. Matter is here being reinterpreted as really human, not the other way around.

But in any case her arguments aren't very persuasive: there's no real evidence anywhere in her book that (nonhuman) material objects engage in "intentional or purposive behavior," and that's because they don't unless "intention" or "purpose" is so radically redefined as to lose all ordinary meaning. And Bennett herself acknowledges as much. "The vital materialist," she writes, "must admit that different materialities ... will express different powers. Humans, for example, can experience themselves as forming intentions and as standing apart from their actions to reflect on the latter," whereas other things in the world do not.[9] A bit later she offers what she calls a "theory of distributive agency" that "does not posit a subject as the root cause of an effect," and that "see[s] human intentions as always in composition and confederation with many other strivings, for an intention is like a pebble thrown into a pond, or an electrical current sent through a wire or neural network: it vibrates and merges with other currents, to affect and be affected. This understanding of agency does not deny the existence of that thrust called intentionality, but it does see it as less definitive of outcomes."[10] She is surely right that the material nature of human action in the world means that human intention is never "definitive of outcomes," because in such action there are always material forces at work that exceed the ability of humans to understand and predict them: I have made the same point repeatedly above. But that is not the same as saying those forces are themselves "purposive" ones. Her mistake, repeatedly, is to take the recognition that human purposes are always subject to material forces as meaning that material forces themselves should be understood as purposive.

Bennett is trying to "counter human exceptionalism" by showing that specifically human characteristics (such as intention or purpose or "creative agency") are found in pure matter itself; but this is just false. We simply do not find human characteristics such as intentionality everywhere in the world, any more than we find bird characteristics such as flight or tree characteristics such as trunks, and Bennett's very interesting discussions of "assemblages" involving "actants" such as the electrical grid, food, metals, stem cells, and so forth offer no serious indication otherwise, and don't even try very hard to do so. What they seem much more concerned to show, and are much more persuasive in showing, is not the quasi-*human* but the quasi-*living*, quasi-*animate* character of all matter: the view Bennett really seems to be defending isn't a kind of panpsychism but rather a panvitalism or hylozoism. She talks repeatedly of a "*vital* materialism," of thinking "beyond the *life*-matter binary," of her view as harking back to "a childhood sense of the world as filled with all sorts of *animate* beings," of wanting "to articulate the elusive idea of a materiality that *is itself* heterogeneous, itself a differential of intensities, itself *a life*."[11] It is the extension of the category of *life* across all of matter that is really the guiding idea of her book, not the extension of the specific characteristics of human beings.[12]

I call it a panvitalism because—as her discussions of thinkers such as Driesch and Bergson (not to speak of Deleuze and Guattari) show—she is not only sympathetic to the vitalist rejection of the appropriateness of "mechanistic" or "deterministic" accounts of living things owing to their possessing some sort of vital force irreducible to the mechanical, she also sees the range of that force as extending beyond the biological realm and therefore as characteristic of matter as such. By viewing all matter as quasi-alive (as "vital") in this sense, she wants to emphasize the active, creative, unpredictable, transformative character of material objects, and does this well.[13] But is that all that is meant by her "new materialism"? Materialism is not simply (indeed, it's not at all) an account of what matter *is*: more important, it's a kind of monism, asserting that the supposedly "immaterial" characteristics of human beings are in fact mundanely material ones.

Bennett's argumentative strategy, it seems to me, is backward. A materialist account isn't one that reveals the "humanness" or "vitality" of matter but rather one that emphasizes the materiality of humans. The point wouldn't be to show that *our* characteristics are to be found everywhere in matter but that matter (understood as Bennett does as creative, unpredictable, transformative) is to be found in *us*: that our creativity, unpredictability, and transformative capacities are not indications that we possess some special immaterial souls but rather are simply the effects *of our materiality itself.* Bennett doesn't make this move, betraying her own failure to fully learn the lesson of a "vital materialism." For her the materiality of humans means something like their impotence, their entanglement in assemblages larger than they are, their inevitable frustration by nonhuman forces that demand "recognition" in an "expanded collective." The view of humans as actively shaping the world they inhabit is exactly what she wants to reject, seeming as it does to her to involve a traditional anthropocentric dualism whereby humans are the active ones while "mere matter" is inert and passive. ("The association of matter with passivity still haunts us today," she writes, "weakening our discernment of the force of things."[14]) She tries to replace that view with one in which the positions are reversed: matter is active and purposeful, whereas human claims to agency are repeatedly undercut—a functioning electrical infrastructure requires the "cooperation" of nonhuman actants such as power stations, switches, and electrons; the foods we eat make us fat; I cannot write without the operation of the graphite in my pencil or the electricity in my brain or my laptop; the crook of my elbow is an ecosystem of more than six types of bacteria.

All of these things are true, of course, but by emphasizing them while speaking of nonhumans primarily in terms of their activity and even agency, the lesson of materialism for humans is forgotten. Materialism doesn't mean that *humans are not active* but rather that *human activity is itself material.* Similarly, the point isn't to remove agency from human beings, nor is it to revise the concept of agency so that it applies in an indiscriminate way to everything, but rather to recognize that *agency is always material agency.* The error in traditional dualistic accounts of humans as actively imposing their will on inert matter isn't in the idea of activity, it's in the (nutty) idea of this activity (and of the "will" behind it) as *immaterial.* We *do* transform the world (though to be sure we are not alone in doing so), but we do so *materially,* concretely. As I have been arguing all along, we construct it, and we do so not by thinking about it or imagining it or "constituting" it or "intending" it but by actually building it.

Latour and the Passage to Words

Bennett's view owes a great deal to the work of Bruno Latour, but Latour's version of materialism is more sophisticated and points more closely in the direction of the kind of activist view I am concerned to defend. Latour does not insist so much on a magical vitality in matter but rather on the irreducibly material character of the processes through which we gain knowledge of the world: his enemy isn't—as Bennett's seems to be—a view of material things as passive or static but rather the dualism that views human consciousness or culture as outside the world of matter, part of a spiritual realm distinct from the realm of nature. Latour's point is always about the materiality of science. Thus, for instance, in the tour de force that is the second chapter of *Pandora's Hope*, he emphasizes the physical processes, and the key role of the physical artifacts, that are necessary to make possible the publication of a scientific result. An area of land in the Amazon is divided up and marked off by cotton threads, thereby imposing a Cartesian order on it; plants are removed from the land and tagged, then sent to an office in a university far away where they can be placed in a wooden cabinet with cubbyholes again organized in a gridlike structure; samples of soil are dug out of each segment of land and placed in a "pedocomparator" once more strictly divided into rows and columns; the color of each sample is compared to a reference color by means of a special notebook with holes in the pages under which the sample can be placed, allowing a standard "Munsell code" number to be assigned to it; the texture of each sample is determined by a process of "earth tasting" in which a researcher spits on a bit of soil and then rubs it between his or her fingers and assigns a specific technical description to it (sandy, clayey, sandy-clayey, etc.). Only after all this work and all these mediations by tools (thread, tags, notecards, cabinet, pedocomparator, Munsell notebook) is it possible to produce a diagram that stands, Latour suggests, *in place of* the area of land under investigation (but does not, he says, "resemble" it), and only after the diagram is drawn is it possible to write and publish the article that presents the knowledge about the rain forest that has been obtained.[15]

I call Latour's view closer to an activist materialism because there's much emphasis in his discussion of all that has to *happen* for a scientific "discovery" to be made: the threads must be laid out, the plants must be cut down, the holes must be dug, the holes in the notebook must be superimposed on the samples, the earth must be rubbed between the investigators' fingers. There is thus more of a recognition than in Bennett's account of the role of what I have been calling practices in the processes Latour is describing. But to say that things have to happen is not quite the same as saying that things have to be *done*, which would require doers, agents: there are places where Latour seems to deemphasize the role of *human action* in the processes he recounts. Thus, for instance, when he criticizes (analytic) philosophy for ignoring all the work required to produce a "truth" in discourse, pointing out that "in all [the philosophers'] demonstrations the world simply awaits designation by words whose truth or falsehood is guaranteed solely by its presence" and that for them "the 'real' cat waits quietly on its proverbial mat to confer a truth-value on the sentence 'the cat is on the mat'," he contrasts this with the idea that "to achieve certainty the world needs to stir and transform *itself* much more than *words*."[16] Yet it is not the world that has mysteriously "transformed *itself*" in Latour's story recounting the many steps from rain forest to published article; it is in particular *humans* who have transformed it, by their acts of measuring and laying thread and digging and cutting and comparing and rolling clods of earth between their fingers. And that distinction is an important one because it points to the role of *practices*, and thus of human action, in making possible the expression of knowledge in language, a role that has implications both for the practice of language use itself and for the moral status of those creatures who engage in it.

Still, Latour's materialist point is significant: the relation between knowledge and reality is not a relation of resemblance or correspondence between items belonging to two different realms (one real and the other symbolic or mental) but rather is something produced through material processes. The "whole tired question of the correspondence between words and the world," he writes, "stems from a simple confusion between epistemology and the history of art. We have taken science for realist painting, imagining that it made an exact copy of the world. The sciences do something else entirely.... Through successive stages they link us to an aligned, transformed, constructed world."[17] The published article about the rain forest is the product of what Latour calls a "chain of references" in which land is replaced by a grid of squares marked off by thread, each square in turn is replaced by the soil sample taken from it, the soil sample is replaced by the Munsell number of its color and a verbal description of its texture, the numbers and descriptions are replaced by a diagram, and the diagram is finally replaced or "articulated" by the article itself and the result that it announces. These replacements could be described as processes of abstraction whereby a truth of the physical world is mysteriously turned into an element of knowledge, but Latour's emphasis on the materiality of the process and on the work involved in it, and further on the number and complexity of the intermediate steps between "world" and "knowledge," shows how misleading such a description would be. In fact, as he points out, each stage in the chain of references can be described as having a more "material" and a more "formal" pole, but these terms are merely relative: the soil samples taken from the holes that have been dug, for instance, could be described as "representations" or "abstractions" of the "real" soil in the ground at that point, but then as the pedocomparator is used those samples themselves appear as the "reality" that is then "abstracted" into the Munsell numbers reported in the investigator's notebook. What is called abstraction here is not a move into an ideal or mental realm but rather remains within the realm of the concrete: it is simply the formation of the chain of references that makes it possible for scientists far away from the rain forest to come to know something by reading an article about it. (And note that reading too is a material and concrete activity, involving paper and ink or an e-reader and pixels.) When the investigator on the ground picks up a clump of soil and puts some of it into a square in the pedocomparator, Latour writes, "we should never take our eyes off the material weight of this action. The earthly dimension of Platonism is revealed in this image. We are not jumping from soil to the Idea of soil, but from continuous and multiple clumps of earth to a discrete color in a geometric cube coded in x- and y-coordinates."[18]

Yet the chain of references is not simply something that is *found* in the world, nor is it something that just *happens*: it is something, as Latour's investigations clearly show, that is *constructed* through the activity of humans. And there is a key step in the construction of that chain—a step without which the chain might well remain pointless—that Latour in my view assimilates too quickly and completely to all the others, the step he calls "the passage to words." Language too, Latour wants to argue, functions in the same way as the pedocomparator or the Munsell-coding notebook, providing another link in the chain of references but not an ontologically unique one, not one that allows a leap across a fundamental metaphysical boundary from the real to the idea, from world to knowledge. "This new leap [to language] is no more distant than the preceding one," Latour writes: "There is nothing privileged about the passage to words, and all stages can serve equally to allow us to grasp the nesting of reference."[19] I do not disagree with this formulation, which seems fundamental to any kind of materialism, and yet I think Latour fails in part to grasp what *is* unique about language here, in a way that leads him astray in important respects when drawing political consequences from his view.

His discussion of the passage to words begins with a description of the process of "earth-tasting" by which the pedologists decide whether the sample's texture ought to be described as clayey or sandy or something else. Here, unlike the earlier steps in the chain in which land was marked with threads or a sample was dug from a hole or a Munsell number was assigned to a color, words are used. There is no instrument or standard code such as the Munsell code available for making the judgment in this case, Latour tells us, and so the investigators must examine the soil by hand, rolling it between their fingers and employing their years of experience to assign a character to it. The judgment, he says, is necessarily a qualitative rather than quantitative one, but still it ultimately produces a link in the chain (from sample to word) not fundamentally different from the others (from sample to Munsell number, say, or from hole to sample). And yet there is a moment in the process that differs, at least as Latour describes it, from the other steps mentioned. For there are *two* pedologists at work, and they do something that the Munsell code notebook or the pedocomparator does not: they talk. And the way language is used between them does, in my view, introduce a new element. They speak *with* each other, *about* the sample. Indeed, they *argue*: "sandy-clay or clayey-sand?," one asks, and the other rejects both answers, and then they both discuss it for a while—the first one saying "mold it some more, give it some time," suggesting that more practice, more activity, is needed—until finally they reach agreement (in Portuguese): "*areno-argiloso a argilo-arenoso*."[20] The words they end up attaching to the sample (just as the Munsell number is attached to it) stand in the same relation to the sample, on the one hand, and to the later diagram on the other as all the other stages in the chain, and in this sense Latour is right that there's nothing unique about the passage to words. But something else took place in this interaction, perpendicular to the chain, perhaps, that was not merely a matter of words but of language *use*, of discourse, that was different. Words were not merely attached, as tags or symbols: something was *said*. A claim was made—in fact, several claims were made, and discussed, and questioned, and then the two scientists agreed together that *something was the case*, and that their claim about it could be justified by the physical experience of earth-tasting they had both undergone. This is different from the digging of a hole, which by itself asserts or claims nothing, and is different too from the drawing or the printing of a diagram. None of these is a speech act, none makes a claim that can be true or false and is subject to criticism and justification. It is this element of language use that I think Latour consistently neglects.

In using language, in speaking, a speaker makes a claim, and claims can be true or false. This introduces a moment of normativity into language use that is lacking in the other elements of the chain of reference. Threads on a field or holes dug in the ground make no claims, and have no truth-value. Assertions *about* those things, of course—"that thread is crooked," "this sample doesn't accurately exemplify the plot it comes from"—do make claims, but to say this is to see the difference between language use and the practices that generate the other items in Latour's chains of reference. He treats "*areno-argiloso a argilo-arenoso*" as though it were these words alone—ink on a page, sounds in the air—that served as the linguistic link in the chain. But the moment, external in a way from the chain and yet fundamental to it, when the scientists decide to jointly assert *that* the soil is between sandy-clayey and clayey-sand, is the one that introduces normativity—which is to say truth—into the considerations here and reminds us that part of what the scientific enterprise is attempting to do is to find out *how the world is*, which requires *saying something true about it*. Similarly, the diagram in the published article is merely a drawing; what needs to be *said* is that this diagram is an accurate depiction—or, to use Latour's term, "articulation"—of the situation on the ground back in the rain forest.

To make a claim is to claim that something is *true*, and thus to claim as well that there are good reasons to believe that it is true, reasons that one could point to if challenged. Claims are subject to questioning, to criticism, and to justification—and they are subject as well to being abandoned if they turn out to be mistaken. They are thus essentially bound up not only with normativity but also with *intersubjectivity*, because questioning, criticism, and justification are above all acts that one performs with and for another. To speak, to make a claim, is to imagine an interlocutor to whom one is speaking and whom one is attempting to convince—or rather, whom one *could* convince if one were asked to: an interlocutor who is capable of rejecting or of accepting one's claims, and who at any moment could ask one to justify or redeem them. It is this element of language use that Latour fails to notice or elides, but it is a crucial one, and it considerably complicates his repeated talk about extending the realm of discourse, and therefore of politics, to nonhumans.[21]

The pedocomparator may well, as Latour suggests, "articulate" a "proposition" in the quasi-Heideggerian sense of disclosing or revealing a particular state of affairs, but it *says* nothing, asserts nothing, makes no claim. It cannot be questioned, it does not offer reasons or evidence for what it says; it offers no opportunity for discussion. Others can make claims about it, or about what it shows, and those others can themselves be questioned about those claims and can defend them or, when faced with serious criticisms, withdraw them. There is no "convincing" of a pedocomparator, nor can it be dissuaded or argued with or rendered uncertain. And this is because pedocomparators do not use language.

In this sense the "passage to words," the "new leap" to language, bears more significance than Latour acknowledges, a significance that has both political and ethical implications.

In another section of *Pandora's Hope* Latour discusses Frédéric Joliot's work on nuclear chain reactions, arguing against the kind of dualism that would fundamentally separate Joliot's political interactions with the ministers and industrialists who must be brought on board to build the reactor he is planning from the scientific work involved in designing that reactor and putting it into operation: these two elements, Latour suggests, can no more be distinguished in terms of their epistemological function than the laying of the cotton threads or the digging of the holes in the rain forest can be considered epistemologically separable from the scientific result presented in the published paper. I have no quarrel with this conclusion, let me note, and admire Latour's ingenious ways of arguing for and explaining it, but when he writes that "Joliot's labors could not of course be confined to ministerial offices" and that once he had approval from those offices to build his laboratory, "he now had to go and negotiate *with the neutrons themselves,*"[22] I think his argument goes wrong, and in a way that is telling. For neutrons, of course, do not negotiate. Negotiation is a form of language use and once again involves making claims, asserting that such-and-such is true, or is right, or would be useful; it also involves hearing and responding to counterclaims; and finally, it ends (if successful) in the reaching of an agreement in which all the parties involved decide to accept—and therefore to assert—some common claim the reasons and justification for which they have agreed to share. Neutrons do not do this, but ministers do. That fact does not vitiate Latour's rejection of the dualism between internalism and externalism in discussions of science, I believe, any more than does the fact that neutrons can split nuclei while ministers cannot. But it does indicate a difference that Latour fails to acknowledge between language users and those "objects" about which language users make claims. Elsewhere, interestingly, he does concede it, although it's not clear he recognizes the implications of that concession: in his well-known example of the way in which "sleeping policemen" or speed bumps are used to replace posted speed limits as a way to get drivers to slow down, he writes that the "drivers, used to dealing with negotiable signs, [are] now confronted by nonnegotiable speed bumps."[23] Speed bumps, apparently unlike neutrons, are here explicitly said not to be able to negotiate. Again, Latour's intended point has to do with what he calls the "delegation" by traffic engineers of a program of action oriented toward slowing traffic into the form of asphalt, and with the way in which the speed bump, despite its nonlinguistic form, still remains a "meaningful articulation" of that program. And yet here he is forced to acknowledge that in the move from language use to asphalt something is lost: the moment of negotiability, of questionability, of justification, of a normativity that a driver could in principle reject.

This point is an important one, and puts into question a familiar trope in certain kinds of environmental theory that I want to consider and to question: the trope that brings the idea of the "moral considerability of all things" together with the idea of democracy. In Latour's work the trope is given the name of the "Parliament of Things," but elsewhere it takes the form of a call to extend or expand our notion of democracy to allow us to "hear the voices" of those natural entities that are currently excluded from the polis.[24] In this form the idea of universal moral considerability with democracy is mediated by way of the notion of language: nature speaks, we're told, but the trouble is that we don't listen, that we have forgotten (or never knew) how to hear it. We need to learn to listen to nature, hear what it has to say to us, in order to recognize its value and its equal moral status, or so the claim goes. To listen to nature, to recognize that it speaks—though in a kind of speech quite different from human speech but morally just as significant—would be to see it as part of the moral community, and hence as something with a role to play within the politics of that community: a role not as the mere object of the community's deliberations and policies but rather as itself a full member of it. Latour, to be sure, would not put the issue this way; he is as skeptical as I am about the idea of "nature" and as aware of the (political) dangers that appeals to that idea bring in its wake. And yet his talk of wanting "to redistribute the capacity of speech between humans and non-humans," and of bringing "things" into the political "collective," brings his view perilously close to one that treats nature as a speaking subject to whose voice we must attend and to whom we therefore owe the obligations of respect and noninterference that all such subjects deserve.[25]

Listening to Nature

The more standard move in critiques of anthropocentrism, of course, is to deny the relevance of language use to moral considerability: "The question is not," Jeremy Bentham famously wrote in his discussion of the moral status of animals, "can they talk?" but rather "can they suffer?" But some authors go in the other direction, conceding that the ability to speak is morally relevant and denying that nonhumans lack it. The line of argument is doubtless familiar: the problem with the modern world, it suggests, is that we have convinced ourselves that only human beings speak, and as a result we can no longer hear the other voices that surround us. Nature appears to us as mute, with no inner life and nothing to communicate, and so we think we can do with it whatever we wish. Because we do not hear what nature has to say, or even that it is saying anything at all, we treat natural entities as mere things rather than as other subjects with whom we share a common world. But if we listened carefully, and expanded our conception of what speech and language involve, we would come to see, or rather to hear, that nature and natural entities in fact do speak, and so do deserve moral respect.

I agree (contra Bentham) that there is a close connection between the ability to use language and ethics, but I do not believe that "nature speaks"—or rather (since a lot depends on what is meant here by language and by speech), I do not believe that it speaks in a way that has the ethical implications the argument just outlined suggests.[26] Speakers, that argument seems to imply, can tell us about their needs and goals; in hearing them speak we learn to understand them as experiencing subjects, as sentient beings, as creatures with "a good of their own." Speech thus serves as evidence of their possession of the characteristics we associate with moral considerability. But there is more to the idea that that language use is morally relevant than the idea that language users can report on their experiences, for those reports are also being made *to* someone, and that someone must be a language user as well. For there to be speakers there must also be hearers, and those hearers are capable of being speakers too. If "we" learn something about other entities through their speech, then "we" too—the ones to whom the speech of those entities is said to provide evidence—must be language users, else that speech would not be understandable and so would not be evidence at all. Speech is *conversation*: it is not subjectivity that is uniquely revealed by the ability to use language so much as it is *inter*subjectivity. To speak is not merely to express oneself out loud, it is to *converse*; discovering that an entity uses language means realizing that it is *someone with whom I can talk*. When an entity speaks—not simply *to* me but *with* me—I find myself connected to it, in a relationship that is built and confirmed in the conversation itself. In our talking I learn not just about my interlocutor but also about myself, as well as about the world we inhabit together. It is through talking with others, indeed, that I come to be who I am, that I come to understand the world we share, that I come to see those others as like me or unlike me (but even in the latter case as tied to me in that we are talking together). And it is also, importantly, through talking to others that I come to think about what's right and wrong.

The key thing I learn in real conversation is a lesson of symmetry, and therefore of reciprocity: I learn that just as you appear to me as an other, as an interlocutor, so too do I appear as other to you—that indeed to *you,* you are "I" and I am "you." This startling recognition teaches me that there is no built-in privilege to my perspective over yours (since to you, your perspective is also called "mine"). And this means in turn that whatever happens to me must also be understandable as potentially happening to you, and so whatever reasons I might have to justify what I do (for myself, for instance, or to you) must also be reasons that you could offer to justify doing the same (for yourself, or to me). To speak with an other is thus to recognize that other as an equal, in a way that already points toward an ethical principle of universalization. Those with whom I can speak are those to whom I owe the obligation of respect; to fail to respect them would be to violate the very terms that make our speaking together possible. It is in *dialogue* with others, and in the intersubjectivity that such dialogue both grounds and confirms, I am suggesting, that the connection between language use and ethics is found.[27]

Some years ago Scott Friskics published an essay whose title, "Dialogical Relations with Nature," suggests an understanding of this point. In it, Friskics makes a series of very strong claims about nature's speech. "As I reflect on my own experience," he writes, "it seems the most obvious thing in the world that things speak."[28] He begins with a personal account of a mountain near his home, describing his daily walk to sit by it. He goes, he says, because the mountain "speaks to me, calls me up out of my cabin and beckons me to sit in its silent, hulking presence."[29] Friskics suggests that all things in the world can be seen as calling to us in this way. "That things speak," he writes, "that they present themselves and disclose their presence as speech, is an insight shared among poets, philosophers, and religious thinkers alike."[30] But the trouble today, he adds, is that "we aren't very good at listening," and so we miss the voices of natural objects.[31] Nature's speech has been lost, he suggests, drowned out by the human world.[32] To be able once again to hear the voices and respond to the call of the natural creatures with whom we share the earth, Friskics says, requires what he calls "faith," by which he means a kind of openness to them, a responsiveness to the being of the beings we encounter. Here is the basis of our ethical responsibility to the natural creatures that surround us: it is "response-ability," based fundamentally on "responding, being responsive to the address of the other."[33]

This is an evocative and eloquent account. But there's something odd about its conception both of nature's speech and of the appropriate response to that speech. For despite Friskics's repeated appeal in his essay to the notion of *dialogue*, one looks for it in vain in his discussion of what happens when nature talks. His conception of the ethical obligation generated by the recognition that nature speaks seems merely to be that we should *listen*, never that we too should speak.[34] Thus his relation to the mountain is one in which it calls him and he comes; no dialogue seems to occur at all. "A dialogue, by definition," Friskics writes, "requires the active participation of both speaker and listener," and this is surely true, but he leaves out of the definition the equally important clause that the roles of speaker and listener must be *reciprocally taken up by both parties in turn*.[35] Although Friskics criticizes the contemporary world as being stuck in monologue, in fact his own view seems to be quite monological itself: it's nature that does all the talking. The moment of symmetry crucial to real use of language is simply missing: we are called to respond to the speech of entities in nature, but they are never called to respond to us. Friskics describes "dialogue" as a relation in which "we *give our full attention* to the address of the beings and things we meet, *engage* them as self-speaking presences, and *respond to their claims* wholeheartedly and without reserve,"[36] but do the self-speaking presences we attend and respond to in nature ever themselves give *us* their full attention in this way, engage *us*, respond to *our* claims?

Of course they don't; they can't, as we all know, and it would be a silly category mistake to ask them to do so. But then it follows that the relation between us and such nonhuman entities is not and cannot be a *dialogical* one—which means in turn that the "speech" that nature is supposedly engaging in is not real dialogic speech at all. Nature does not, on Friskics's account, actually use language, because to use language is to converse, and nowhere in his account does conversation take place. As Friskics describes it, nature does not talk with us, it talks at us: we respond to it like silent subjects listening to the commands of a monarch, not like participants in a dialogue who develop mutual understanding and respect through repeatedly and alternately taking up the positions of speaker and listener. The monarch's commands cannot be questioned, and for Friskics neither (apparently) can the call of the mountain, or of anything else in nature. But conversation also means dispute and disagreement, because of the ever-present possibility that the way things seem to me will not be the way they seem to you. Language use makes possible the articulation of competing claims while at the same time positing the possibility of a procedure for resolving them. Once you and I learn that we disagree, we also see that we each need both to explain to the other why things seem to us as they do and to respond to the other's criticisms of those explanations; in doing so we both implicitly express the hope that the other might be brought to see things differently while also admitting the reciprocal possibility that we ourselves might be brought to see things differently as well. Here is another way that ethics and language are connected, for it is in language—by which I mean language *use*, conversation—that claims, including ethical claims, find justification.

Yet on Friskics's account there is no room for competing claims, or for justification. The claims of nature are absolute. They assert that modern humans are selfish and that their failure to listen to nature reveals this selfishness. If the views of humans conflict with those of the mountain, it is perfectly clear who Friskics thinks is right: the mountain. Yet the claims Friskics discusses about the selfishness of humans, or about the rightness of the mountain are themselves ethical ones. How are *they* to be justified, and who can justify them? And who, one might ask, makes these claims? Is it the mountain that makes them—and if so, in what sort of ethical conversation, marked by what sort of obligation to offer reasons? Or is it not in fact someone else making them: Friskics himself? And then the question becomes: in the evocations of nature's speech, who is it who is really speaking?

The Ethics of Language Use

Language, I have been arguing, is essentially dialogue, conversation. If we want to understand the relationship between language and ethics, then, we need to pay attention to the ethics of conversation. For conversation does indeed have an ethic, tacitly accepted by anyone who engages in it. It is an ethics of *reciprocity*, based on the fundamental symmetry of dialogue, as interlocutors constantly alternate between the position of speaker and hearer, and acknowledge that what is permissible (or obligatory) for me as speaker must also be permissible (or obligatory) for you as speaker as well, and that the same is true for each of us as hearers. One expects sincerity from one's interlocutor, for example, and so to be engaged in conversation is to be committed to being sincere oneself. One expects one's interlocutor to be attempting to speak the truth, and so one is committed to attempting to do so as well. And, crucially, one expects that what one's interlocutor says is something he or she has good reason to believe, and expects therefore that if challenged he or she could justify it; and thus again one must be committed oneself to be able to provide justifications for one's own assertions. To speak is to make claims about the way the world is, but to make such claims is at the same time implicitly to promise that if challenged, one could explain why one thinks the claims are true. In conversation one is responsible, therefore, for what one says—for genuinely believing it, first of all, but also for being able to provide reasons to justify that belief. And that responsibility is an intersubjective one: it is a responsibility *to* one's interlocutor, which the interlocutor at any moment has the right to ask one to redeem. *That* is what "being responsive" to the other means: not simply hearing the other's claims, but also, and most important, acknowledging and answering the other's questions and requests for justification.

This ethic of reciprocity and responsibility, of questioning and justification, seems to me to be central to the ethical meaning of language. But it is an ethic that the nonhuman entities whose "speech" Friskics and others want us to learn to hear do not and in fact cannot acknowledge. If those entities were really interlocutors of ours, they would have to be called *irresponsible* ones, because they never respond to our questions by offering explanations or justifications of their claims; indeed, they never even acknowledge that those questions have been asked. But of course they are *not* irresponsible interlocutors, because they are not interlocutors at all. They do not engage in dialogue or conversation with us, and in this sense, as I have already suggested, it is simply a category mistake to assert that they speak. The notion that in speaking one implicitly takes on the responsibility to speak the truth and to justify what one says is one that seems to have no meaning for them, nor does the notion that they might ask us to justify our own claims. Indeed, as I have suggested, it is the very notion of a "claim" that they seem to be lacking.

But then a danger arises if we treat nonhuman entities as if they *were* interlocutors, as if they *were* making claims—the danger that such claims, just because they can't in fact be questioned, will be treated as *unquestionable* in the sense of being unquestionably *true.* David Abram, whose expressive and fascinating book *The Spell of the Sensuous* argues very strongly for the thesis I am rejecting here—that nature speaks, and that we have lost the ability to hear it—offers as an example an account of storytelling in several "pre-alphabetic" cultures that emphasizes the normative and linguistic role that the natural landscape plays for them. Thus the Dreamtime songs and stories of Australian aboriginal peoples, he writes, "provide the codes of behavior for the community; they suggest, through multiple examples, how to act, or how *not* to act, in particular situations.... [They] offer a ready set of guidelines for proper behavior on the part of those who sing or hear those stories today.... And it is the land itself that is the most potent reminder of these teachings, since each feature in the landscape activates the memory of a particular story or cluster of stories."[37] Indeed, as Abram emphasizes, it is the land itself that is understood as the speaker, or singer, of these tales. Yet because the "speech" engaged in by a landscape can never be dialogue in the sense I have described above, lacking in particular any acknowledgment by the "speaker" of the responsibility to speak the truth and to be able to justify its assertions, its claim to normative authority seems unwarranted. What reasons are there to believe that the "codes of behavior for the community" provided by the Dreamtime stories and songs are right? (What do they say about gender relations, or about how to treat strangers, or the disabled? Is it possible to question the codes? What happens to those who do so, or to those who reject them?) My point isn't that the codes here aren't right (I have no idea) but rather that when normative claims are understood as being made by a landscape and not by a human speaker, the possibility even of raising such a question cannot arise.

But those claims *are* being made by human speakers—the ones who *actually* sing the Dreamtime songs. Elsewhere in his book Abram gives the example of a type of Apache narrative called "*'agodzaahi.*"[38] These are brief stories meant to illustrate a moral point, he says, and are always tied specifically to a particular location where they are supposed to have taken place. "The telling of such a tale," Abram writes, today "is always prompted by a misdeed committed by someone in the community"; at some communal event an elder will tell the story in such a way that the person at fault will know himself or herself to be the target, and ever afterward when that person passes by the referenced location he or she will be reminded of the story. The location is said to be "stalking" the person.[39] Abram takes this as illustrating his general point that preliterate societies such as the Apache find speech everywhere, and do not distinguish between humans and nonhumans as speakers. "Places are not just passive settings," he writes. "A particular place in the land is never, for an oral culture, just a passive or inert setting for the human events that occur there. *It is an active participant in those occurrences.*"[40] But to say that something is a participant is not to say that it is a speaker: speaking, as we have seen, requires dialogue and the possibility of justification. And yet of course there *is* a speaker, a human speaker, of the *'agodzaahi* story, but Abram glosses over this fact, as perhaps the Apache do as well: it is the elder, after all, not the land, who actually tells the story. Like a ventriloquist, though, this human speaker makes it seem that something else is doing the speaking, thereby removing from the real speaker the responsibility to be able to justify the normative claims he or she is making. Those claims then appear as facts of nature, built into the landscape, instead of what they really are: the questionable claims of a fallible human being within a particular social order. A truth-claim is being made, a speech act is taking place, but the real speaker is being systematically hidden, and his or her voice is being thrown in a move we're familiar with from *The Wizard of Oz:* the speaker here is depending on an illusion to avoid the obligation to be responsible for defending what he or she says.

In language use something is asserted *about* the world (which means that the assertion has content, and can be *true*), *by* a subject (which means, since subjects are necessarily limited in perspective and therefore fallible, that the assertion can also be *false*, and deserves to be questioned and tested). In the Dreamtime and *'agodzaahi* examples, however, the truth-telling and contentful character of language is employed but its fallible character, the fact that the assertions being made are merely assertions and so might be false, is being hidden, because the real speaker is being hidden. *This* is the deepest danger in the idea that nonhuman entities can speak—and it is a political danger. Because they speak no human language, in order to understand what such entities say we need people to translate for us: and yet what claims to be a translator might turn out to be nothing but a *ventriloquist*, and we have no good way to distinguish one from the other.[41] Abram writes repeatedly about the importance in pre-literate cultures of special figures like shamans or magicians who serve as "intermediaries" between the human and the nonhuman world, and underscores the power such a position entails.[42] But it is hard not to glimpse in his examples a political meaning quite different from the one he emphasizes—a meaning about the power of the shamans *over* those in their community, deriving precisely from their claimed role as "intermediaries" or translators. An intermediary is necessarily very powerful, especially if there is no possibility of direct contact with the thing it claims to be mediating for us.

This is what happens when things are said to speak that many of us find ourselves unable to hear: a special class of hearers arises whose members claim to be able to translate for the rest of us the otherwise incomprehensible words of those things. To be a member of that class is then inevitably to hold a special sort of power, not open to questioning or amenable to justification. The claims those intermediaries make, whether about how we ought to behave or about how the world is, are supposedly not their own; they are merely made through them, by the apparently wordless entities that the intermediaries say they have learned to understand, and so they are not claims for which the intermediaries need take any responsibility. But precisely for this reason they are claims of which we ought to be suspicious, and we ought to be suspicious too that the ones who claim merely to be translating are really the ones speaking—speaking, without acknowledging responsibility for what is said. The power to command without the responsibility to justify: that is the power of the shaman, and it is a power of which we ought to be skeptical.

Latour, strikingly, makes precisely this sort of point in his own critique of "nature" and the use to which this concept is put in contemporary discourse. He emphasizes that the appeal to nature is always in fact an appeal to something that may not be questioned, and hence functions as a way to avoid the messy introduction of discursive politics into "Science."[43] The "Constitution" of modernity, he says, divides the world into two "houses"—a human one filled with speech (but impotent) and a natural one consisting of objects "that have the property of defining what exists but that lack the gift of speech." It is the "scientists," the experts, who (like the shamans Abram writes of) hold the power here, he adds, for they are the ones "*who can move back and forth between the houses.... They can make the mute world speak, tell the truth without being challenged, put an end to the interminable arguments through an incontestable authority that would stem from things themselves.*"[44] Their words are incontestable because they are claimed not to be *their* words but rather those of the things, and so they get to escape the process of questioning, skepticism, and justification that speech normally requires. They claim to be *speaking for* the things, but in fact they may be nothing other than ventriloquists. What's astonishing to me is that Latour understands this crucial point and yet still insists that things *should* speak, and should even be members of a parliament named after them, even though he has just shown what the dangers of such a parliament—which could be nothing other than a parliament of ventriloquists—would inevitably bring. It's not nature that produces these dangers, it's nature's silence.

Translators and Ventriloquists

Let me say more about the distinction I am drawing between translators and ventriloquists. Translators, in my sense, are those who speak *for another speaker*, saying the words that speaker is for whatever reason unable to say herself (possibly, but not necessarily, because her language is different from ours). A ventriloquist, on the other hand, is someone who speaks for something that is *not* a speaker, projecting her own words onto a mute object and then pretending that it is that object that is speaking and not herself. The trouble with ventriloquism follows from the fact that in dialogue, a certain privilege is granted to first-person reports. My obligation to respect my interlocutors, which derives from my obligation to be able to persuade them of the truth of my assertions, requires me to assume the accuracy of their reports about their own beliefs: I may try to convince them that their opinions are *wrong*, but in conversation with them it makes no sense for me to claim that these opinions are not *theirs*, that they do not really hold them.[45] But when my interlocutor is no interlocutor at all but rather a speechless entity (let's call it a dummy) mouthing the words of another, then what seem to be first-person reports are really at best third-person reports, and third-person reports have no such privilege.

This is so even if the ventriloquist is sincerely expressing what she believes the dummy *ought* to be saying, or even what it *would* be saying if dummies could talk. For in the case of third-person reports, the question of the accuracy of the report is absolutely relevant. When I talk to you about the validity of some truth-claim one of us has made, we must assume—if this is a real dialogue—the sincerity of each of our expressions of our views. Those assumptions serve as the background conditions for our talk, and without them the talk could not take place. But when I talk to you about some *other* party, about what that party believes or what is best for that party, then these matters are themselves the topic of our talk; no longer a background condition for our assertions, they are part of the content of those assertions, and their truth is precisely what we are concerned in the discussion to decide. To give one person's claims about those matters a privilege would be to predecide the conversation's outcome and thus to render it superfluous.

Now, sometimes in a conversation one of the parties is unable to speak, for what are essentially contingent reasons. It may be because the party speaks a different language, or it may be because the party is at the moment unable to speak at all, perhaps because of some sort of physical or social disability. In either case some other party may sometimes speak *for* the incapacitated one, saying the words the latter party would be saying if she were not currently unable to speak. We might call such a speaker a translator, expanding the normal meaning of the term only slightly. The speech of such a translator—speech that occurs within quotation marks, one might say—is no doubt a third-person report too, and hence does not enjoy the privilege that a speaker's direct speech possesses. And surely such a report may be mistaken or mendacious; it may be a mistranslation. Yet we know what it would mean for the report to be false: a bad translator is one whose account of someone else's speech fails to present accurately what was said (or, in the case of disability, what *would* have been said if the person were not disabled). And we know—in principle, anyway—how to decide the question of accuracy: we would simply ask the (real) speaker herself whether the translator correctly reported her speech. (In practice, of course, such a procedure requires our or the speaker's learning a new language, or requires the disability to be removed, but both those things are in principle possible.) And if the speaker says yes, the translation was correct, then the speaker has thereby taken upon herself the speech, removed it from the quotation marks, and so turned it from a third-person report to a first-person one. In the case of translation, that is, the question of the adequacy of the translation, which is to say of the truth of the third-person report, always points back toward the possibility of a first-person report. This is the ethical basis of translation: the translator's implicit claim to the accuracy of the translation is always founded on the possibility of replacing it by first-person speech.

But in the case of ventriloquism that possibility is lacking. The dummy does not and cannot engage in first-person speech, not even in principle. The question of mendacity or even of error does not arise: it would be a category mistake to accuse a ventriloquist of *incorrectly* or *misleadingly* expressing the views of the dummy. The danger—which I have suggested earlier is a political danger—arises when *a ventriloquist presents herself as being a translator*, pretending to speak for an entity who is merely contingently unable to speak rather than throwing her own voice onto something speechless. For the ethical basis of translation—its foundation in the possibility in principle of being replaced by first-person speech—means that we are justified in treating the translator's words with the same respect we give the words of other speakers, subject naturally to a fallibilist understanding that the translation may turn out to be inaccurate. But the words of a ventriloquist do not deserve such respect because there is no first-person speaker to whom they ultimately refer. The political danger arises when we are led to grant the ventriloquist's words (which we mistakenly think of as the words of the dummy) the same respect we grant the words of real speakers, because in doing so the ventriloquist gets a power other speakers do not have: the power to make truth-claims without the responsibility to provide first-person justifications for them.[46]

My reference to the "accuracy" of translations might lead to an objection here. There is of course no such thing as an accurate translation if we mean by that term something like a perfect expression of exactly what the speaker meant to say. Not even the speaker herself is capable of such a thing. Accuracy in this sense is impossible not merely because the differences between languages mean they are never entirely intertranslatable but because even within the speaker's own language, the question of what her words mean can only be answered in a hermeneutic context. The translator has no direct access to the speaker's meaning but rather must come to understand it within a circular hermeneutic process. That process is one in which dialogue plays a crucial role, as the translator asks the speaker to explain what she means, raises questions about the use of certain terms, tries through the back-and-forth of conversation to get a clearer sense of what the speaker intends, and so on. The speaker's answers to these questions too will require further understanding, which may require further questions as well. The structure here is a familiar one. But to remark on it is also to recall that it is not unique to translation. The hermeneutic situation of trying to understand another's words, and of having nothing other than other words to use to develop that understanding, is built into *all* dialogical use of language. And this is precisely why the ultimate reference to first-person language use is crucial. For when I try to understand the meaning of words I must take them to be the words *of* someone; the hermeneutic process I engage in is a process of trying to understand what they meant *to* the person who spoke them. In a case in which the actual speaker is merely a translator, the person I am trying to understand, of course, is not that translator but the person whose speech is being translated. But in the case of a ventriloquist pretending to be a translator, there *is* no person whom I am trying to understand, and so the process of understanding is blocked.

A ventriloquist, I am suggesting, is something different from a deceptive translator. A deceptive translator tells us things about someone's intended speech that could at least in principle be discovered to be wrong. A ventriloquist tells us things about the intended meanings of someone who in fact intends no speech at all. The deceptive translator could be unmasked were the real speaker to find a way to enter the conversation—not to tell us what she "really" means but rather simply by beginning the hermeneutic dialogue where we work out together what we mutually believe. The ventriloquist cannot be unmasked in this sense because there's no one to do the unmasking—no "real speaker" to enter the conversation and reclaim her words for herself. What makes something a dummy—an object of ventriloqual action—and not simply someone who is being mistranslated, that is, is that rather than someone incorrectly speaking for it at the moment, it is the sort of thing that could *never speak for itself,* because first-person (dialogical) speech by it is not even possible *in principle.*

But this is the situation of animals, and birds, and mountains, and the other nonhuman entities that Abram and Friskics discuss. And it is also, I think it is clear, the situation of the "things" that Latour intends to bring into a "parliament." Their incapacity to enter into dialogue with us—into, that is, a hermeneutically structured dialogue oriented toward mutually figuring out what the world is like—means that any claim to speak for them is necessarily a ventriloqual claim. When someone claims to speak *for* such an entity, the problem is not that we do not know whether the speaker is doing so accurately but rather that we do not even know what accuracy means here, for there is no possibility even in principle of asking the entity being spoken for whether it would accept the claim as its own. Any attempt to check the putative translation would simply require another translation, by another speaker. The ultimate reference to a first-person report is missing. The difficulty isn't that there's a kind of deep uncertainty as to whether the people who claim to speak for animals or other nonhuman entities are correctly representing them, it's that the notion of representation itself doesn't make sense in this kind of case, since something can be represented only if it is in principle possible for it to speak for itself. And that's exactly what's not possible in the case of these nonhuman entities. It's not that they speak very softly, or speak some other language with a particularly complex syntax that only certain experts can grasp. It's that they do not speak *at all*, and so translation is not the right model for what goes on when humans attempt to tell us what they are supposed to be saying.

Nature's Silence

To say that nonhuman entities in "nature" do not speak, it is important to note, is not to say that they do not possess intrinsic value, or that they do not have rights, or that they do not deserve human care or protection, or that they are mere means for human ends. It does not mean that we have no ethical duties toward them, or that they possess no moral status. There may be lots of very good reasons to believe that such entities are valuable in their own right, and that the traditional assumption within Western ethics that the only significant ethical relationships are those that arise among humans is mistaken. All I have been arguing is that the claim that "nature speaks" does not provide such a good reason because in fact nature does *not* speak, at least not if speech is understood as involving the kind of dialogue that grounds the link between language and ethics.

As far as we know, only humans speak in this sense. But then, since language *is* linked to ethics, there is no avoiding the implication that humans possess a moral status that—again, as far as we know—is unique. As we humans speak with each other, the moral relationship that arises between us is different from any that may arise between us and the nonspeaking entities we encounter. Yet to say that we possess a unique moral status because we speak is not to assert a metaphysically based anthropocentrism. That humans seem to be the only animals who use language is a contingent fact of the world, and one that we could certainly imagine discovering to be false.[47] (But for us to discover it to be false, some nonhuman entities would have to speak *with* us, and speak *for themselves*; and this, I have been claiming, they at the moment seem not to do.) And if there is a logocentrism here it is not a metaphysically based one, either. My point is not that humans are an especially wonderful species, or that being able to use language is an especially wonderful characteristic, and that therefore humans or language users are due an especially grand degree of ethical respect; nor is it that language use puts us in some ontologically unique category. My point is simply that questions of ethics arise *in* language, and can only be resolved there, and that there is no way around this fact. I am using language now, as I write these words, just as Abram does in his books and Friskics in his article, and just as critics of anthropocentrism and logocentrism do when they offer their criticisms: the inevitable role of speech and speakers in ethics (and in critique) cannot be eliminated or plausibly ignored.

The project of determining our obligations to nonhuman entities, of deciding whether and to what extent such entities deserve our respect and care, is itself part of the broader intersubjective project by which language users come to learn about the world. Claims about how we ought to treat such entities, and indeed claims about whether "nature speaks" or not, are themselves claims raised *in* language, and thus are subject to language's (ethical) requirement that such claims be defended and justified through the giving of reasons in a dialogue in which all participants are treated equally and with respect. Such a dialogue, however, is one in which nonhuman entities seem not to be able to take part. Until such entities are capable of making and defending claims, we humans have no choice but to raise and discuss claims about them ourselves, not because we prefer ourselves or think we're at the center of the moral world but because we seem to be the only ones talking here and we don't know how to figure out what's true without talking.

There's no alternative, I am suggesting, to us language users as the arbiters of ethical questions. We have no special access to ethical truths beyond the ones we come to in our conversations. *I don't know* the answer to the question of what sort of moral respect animals or other nonhuman entities deserve, and so I discuss the question with *whomever I can*, not limiting my discussion partners to members of any particular species nor in any other way predeciding it: and it turns out that the only entities (so far) with whom discussion is possible are humans. The mountain and the wind and the wolf make no claims about the question, and certainly don't offer any justifications, nor do they respond to my claims either by questioning them or by pronouncing themselves persuaded, and so they offer no discursive help to me with respect to my question.[48] I discuss it with those with whom I can discuss it; there's nothing else I can do. And if some humans tell me that natural entities do have things to say about the issue, as Abram and Friskics (and, according to Abram, shamans) do, then—since I myself don't hear it—I have to ask *them*, those humans, what it is that the nonhuman entities are saying: which puts us back into the problem of translators and ventriloquists, and in any case leaves us still within a discussion among humans.

The "silence of nature," then, simply means this: that there's no way to avoid or short-circuit the necessity of discourse and the giving of reasons to decide what our ethical duties are, and that the apparent inability of nonhuman entities in the world to take part in that discussion entails that our duties to such entities, rather than arising implicitly *in* that discussion, must themselves be a subject matter *of* that discussion. And to say that is already to say that "nature" cannot help but have a different moral status from those who use language to try to figure out what moral status it has. The duties we owe to nonhuman entities in the world are not the ones we owe to fellow speakers but rather ones we and our fellow speakers mutually determine, in a discursive process that depends on (and grounds) an ethical relationship among us in which "nature" does not share. As we speak, we implicitly acknowledge reciprocal responsibilities to provide justifications, to respect the first-person authority of those who offer such justifications, and to accept nothing as true that could never be found persuasive by all those taking part in the discussion; those responsibilities are prior, I have been arguing, to any that we may decide we have toward those who do not take part in it, because we only come to know the latter through that discussion.

But this also means that environmental questions are, and can only be, *political* questions: nature, being silent, cannot answer them (and neither can Nature). *We* have to answer them, we language users who have to decide, together, how to act. It makes no sense to talk about a Parliament of Things because things cannot speak, cannot "parley," and hence cannot serve in any parliament—again, not because they should be banned from entering its doors but rather because, once inside, they would in fact remain, perhaps uncomfortably, silent. When Latour writes about the Parliament of Things he really seems to mean something different: a political discourse in which scientific questions, or questions about "nature," have an accepted place, rather than being treated as nonpolitical or "extraparliamentary" issues about which scientific experts have to be given the last word. I have no quarrel with *this* idea, the idea that what I would prefer to call the environment (not nature) must be part of our political discourse and can't be viewed as somehow outside it or as dictating to it, but to say that is not to say that the environment is itself a *participant* in the discourse (with all the rights and responsibilities appertaining thereto). To suggest the latter is to misunderstand what discourse, or language use, really is. Or more precisely it is to misunderstand politics. Latour's point is that nature, the physical world, is as appropriate a subject matter for politics as anything else, but this means exactly that *we*, the speakers who engage in politics, are the only ones who can make decisions regarding that world—that those decisions can no longer be left to experts who claim to speak "for" things or for Nature or for God. Only those creatures capable of *speaking for themselves* are the ones whose choices are determinative, because only they are capable of requesting and then accepting or rejecting the justifications that provide legitimacy for those choices a political community makes.

7

Democracy and the Commons

Alienation and the Tragedy of the Commons

Nature doesn't speak; only we speak. And so the questions raised by the problem of the environment are questions that can be answered only by us; sadly, there is no one else to help us answer them. Recognizing this makes clear that the problem of the environment is a political matter: the central claim of postnaturalism is that *environmental questions are political questions*. They can't be answered by Nature, or nature, or for that matter by God or metaphysics, but rather have to be answered in the only appropriate way for political questions to be resolved: through democratic discourse. This is the most important consequence of what I have been arguing throughout. If the environment is "socially constructed," which is to say if it is something we build through our social practices, then the recognition that what we have built is awful, unsustainable, ugly, harmful to its inhabitants, and so on means first that those practices have to change, but second that the question of what those changes should be, and how to organize them, is a question that cannot help but be *up to us*. It is a social question, and requires a social solution. I argued in chapter 3 that our alienation from the environment consists in our failure to recognize both its builtness and its sociality. In chapters 4 and 5 I focused most directly on builtness. In this final chapter I want to examine sociality, asking what it is about the social character of our practices that has produced the terrible environment we find surrounding us today, and what changes in that character, and in those practices, might make it possible to build a better one in the future.

In chapter 4 I criticized the identification of an artifact with the intention of its creator; something can be built through our practices, I pointed out, without our having intended to build it. In fact, in chapter 5 I suggested that all building, and therefore all artifacts, inevitably escape our intentions, as there is always more to the building than was intended by the builder or than the builder can grasp. Global climate change, to choose the most obvious and currently most important example, is something we have built: it is, in the sense I have been using the term, an artifact, constructed by us through our practices. But it is certainly not something anyone *intends*, and indeed it is something many people fear and wish to eliminate. Yet it is also not—at this point—any longer an "unexpected" side effect of our practices: it is well understood, basically predictable, and its consequences are the object of considerable investigation and discussion.[1] For an environmental philosophy after the end of nature, this is the form environmental problems most typically take: they are not caused by the attempt to dominate or replace nature or by a violation of nature's dictates but rather by social practices whose unintended effects on the world around us are harmful and therefore undesirable ones. No one intends the world to become warmer; no one intends for water to be polluted; no one intends cities in developing countries to be choked with smog; no one intends suburban sprawl to deaden the experiences of those who live there. There is no one specifically to blame for these consequences because no one specifically produced them. The practices that created them were engaged in by private individuals attempting to achieve private goals: to drive to work, to expand a business, to live in the country. Yet when aggregated, the consequences went far beyond what those individuals intended, and may even have been contrary to their intentions. Our practices build artifacts different from the ones we intend to build: we cannot help that, as I have argued already, but we certainly can attempt to mitigate it—and yet we rarely seem to do so.

The phenomenon at work here, it should be clear, is the same one discussed in chapter 3, where I associated it with what Marx called alienation, or with what Smith called the invisible hand. Individuals operate as private persons making private choices for private goals, but the overall consequences of their actions turn out to be distinct from those goals and beyond them. Smith thought that in a free market those consequences in general were good ones—the promotion of the public interest; Marx was not so sure. I'm not either, and my suggestion is that it is just this phenomenon that is at bottom responsible for our environmental difficulties. We saw what Marx said about this, in chapter 3: "The social power, i.e., the multiplied productive force that arises through the co-operation of distinct individuals ... appears to those individuals, since their cooperation is not voluntary but has come about naturally [*naturwüchsig*], not as their own united power, but as an alien force existing outside them, of the origin and goal of which they are ignorant, which they thus are no longer able to control."[2] Where individuals operate privately, the aggregated consequence of what they do appears to them not as "cooperation" but rather as something that takes place independently ("naturally") and beyond them, and therefore as something over which they have little control. The result is that the "environment" itself, which as I have suggested is always the product of their practices, appears instead like something independent of those practices. Unable to control the consequences of what they do in the market, they find themselves faced by a built environment that is harmful, dangerous, and ugly in all the ways we experience today.

This paradox of private individuals with private intentions producing, through their aggregated practices, effects quite different from what they desire is a familiar one in discussions of environmental problems and has a well-known name: the tragedy of the commons. Garret Hardin's famous parable of herdsmen whose cattle share a common pasture possesses precisely this structure.[3] The act that is rational for each herdsman to perform—adding additional cattle to his herd—nonetheless when generalized has consequences for all of them which none of them desire but which they are unable to avoid, leading as it does to overgrazing and therefore the destruction of the pasture. Hardin's model is clearly relevant to a series of environmental problems; in particular, its application to the problem of climate change is obvious.[4] An individual factory owner has to decide whether to increase production and therefore emit more pollution into the atmosphere; an individual fisherman has to decide whether to use a new technology that allows significantly more fish to be caught; an individual commuter has to decide whether to drive to work and burn fossil fuels. In each case the benefit of performing the action considered is great, and the cost (in pollution, in loss of fish species, in greenhouse gas emissions) of the individual action is tiny, although it is large in the aggregate. The environmentally conscious industrialist or fisherman or commuter faces the problem of the commons: he or she may genuinely desire to decrease pollution, protect the fish, or prevent global warming but is aware that forgoing the new factory, the new fishing technology, or the drive to work by itself will have no significant impact on achieving these goals on the one hand, while it will deeply and negatively affect his or her own situation on the other. It would be irrational (and often economically suicidal) to refuse to perform the action considered, *and this would be so even if every actor had the same individual commitment to progressive environmental goals*. Left to their own devices, which is to say functioning as private individuals, the actors have no rational choice but to act in ways that they are fully aware have disastrous environmental consequences.

I want to emphasize here that the problem does not arise from the selfishness or short-sightedness of the actors; on the contrary, I am hypothesizing that (as a private matter) each of them is strongly committed to protecting the environment. The problem rather has to do with the private character of the decision with which they are faced. Operating within a market economy, they have to act as private individuals whose acts are independent of the actions of others. If they had a way to decide *together* what they were going to do, they could act in concert to produce the result they all desire, but under a market system all decisions are private ones. Their problem isn't their selfishness, it's their isolation: unable to act together for the goal they all desire, they are forced to act separately and thereby produce a consequence none of them wants. Although Hardin's account is sometimes taken as a call to "privatize the commons," this does not seem correct to me. I think he has accurately described a problem endemic to market economies as such, whose (paradoxical) structure is exactly the structure that Marx described under the name of alienation.

Global warming is a social product; it is the consequence of a series of human decisions and human practices. But it appears to each of the humans who produce it as an unalterable fact independent of their private choices. The tragedy of the commons arises because my own individual actions, when aggregated with those of my fellow citizens, have public consequences, but since each of us acts *as* a private individual those consequences appear to each of us as something beyond us, beyond our control and our ability to affect—as an "alien power." Global warming is in this sense a symptom of alienation: it is a process on which our private choices can have no significant impact and thus about which we can do nothing other than passively respond—thinking about how to live in a warmer world, worrying about the consequences for future generations, and burning fossil fuels on the drive to work each day nonetheless.

The environment, I have argued, is "constructed" in our social practices. But under alienation those social practices look to those who engage in them more like a series of individual practices, and so the environment doesn't appear like "our" social product at all. As a society we shape the world, but not in a way we have, as a society, chosen. Neither the social whole nor the individuals who make it up ever have the opportunity consciously to decide among alternative visions of what the world could be, or to provide justifications for the alternatives that come to pass. Instead the world takes the form it does as the result of an aggregation of individual acts that occur under the sign of alienation—which is to say, an aggregation of acts each of which paradoxically takes the aggregation itself as given and unalterable. This is what Marx means by saying that "our own deed" comes to be an alien power against us.

The tragedy of the commons is one version of a well-known problem in the theory of collective action. Two elements seem crucial to the story. One is that the choice the individual herdsman has (to add or not to add a cow) has essentially no impact on the overall result—because, presumably, the number of herdsmen is so large. The second is that there is no procedure for the herdsmen to enter into a serious binding agreement to limit the size of each herd. (These two elements are related: the more herdsmen there are, and therefore the smaller each one's individual impact, the more difficult it becomes for a binding agreement to be reached or to be effective.) Both elements are present to a very high degree in the case of global warming, or more precisely with respect to the problem of an individual's carbon footprint. I live thirty-five miles from my place of work, in an area with no public transportation. Each morning I make an implicit decision about whether to drive to work or not: driving generates a certain amount of carbon dioxide and therefore helps to increase the future temperature of the planet. Not driving would cause me to lose my job. I might be willing to sacrifice my job if that would end global warming, but simply quitting now because of my carbon footprint would be quixotic at best. The amount of warming would in fact remain the same whether I stopped driving to work or not, but quitting my job would produce a significant loss to me both financially and in terms of happiness. ("Total utility," that is, would decrease, not simply my own happiness.) We could hypothesize that as a matter of private fact, everyone else feels exactly the same way—they are all willing to make significant sacrifices to solve the problem of climate change. Even if this were so, each would be in exactly the same situation that I am: without some sort of public guarantee that others will actually make the sacrifice there is no justification for making it themselves.

But that guarantee, of course, is lacking. This is why Hardin says the only solution to the tragedy of the commons—beyond a privatization of the sort that is fairly unimaginable in the climate change case—is "mutual coercion, mutually agreed upon."[5] The formulation is somewhat tendentious, but the idea is clear: there needs to be some community-level guarantee that all will make the sacrifice before I will be willing to make my own. If that guarantee is in place, the problem is solved; without it, a solution seems impossible. A standard example makes the point: without catalytic converters, automobile exhausts would generate (and did once generate) significant amounts of dangerous and unpleasant pollution into the air. A catalytic converter costs (let's say) $300. We can imagine a situation where every driver is willing to spend $300 to enjoy clean air and perhaps to know that her fellow citizens enjoy it as well. Still, this fact would provide no reason for such a driver to purchase a catalytic converter on her own: simply placing it on one's own car would have essentially no impact on the general level of smog if others did not do the same. The solution is to *require* it, that is, to pass a law (democratically!) obliging all automobiles to have catalytic converters built into them. Note that no one would be required to do anything he or she was not (by hypothesis) willing to do in the first place; all the legal requirement does is to provide the needed guarantee that an individual's act (purchasing the catalytic converter) will in fact be aggregated with the acts of all other drivers, and so will not turn out to be insignificant.

It's the absence of this sort of collective decision that produces cases like the tragedy of the commons. Without a law requiring antipollution devices on every car, or—to go back to my decision to drive to work—in the absence of public transportation or other communal policies that could produce a meaningful general reduction in the emission of greenhouse gases, no *individual* decision can prevent tragic consequences from arising: they will arise even if a private individual purchases the catalytic converter, and even if I give up my job. And of course, in both cases the individual concerned will himself or herself be worse off—which, in the absence of any other change, means the community will be worse off (although only slightly) as well. That's what I mean by saying that the problem does not arise from greed or selfishness on the part of individuals: it's not a matter here of an act that will improve the world but that the selfish car-owner is declining to perform owing to his or her unwillingness to sacrifice for the common good. The acts under consideration here—the employee refusing to drive to work, the car owner purchasing the catalytic converter without being legally required to do so—will not enhance the common good, and in fact will detract from it: nothing will happen to global warming, no change will occur in air pollution, but the driver's life will definitely be harmed, by losing her job in the first case and by losing $300 in the second. There's no sense in calling an act a sacrifice if it *worsens* the world or *increases* disutility, and if in fact the world would be clearly better off if it were not performed. But to say this is not to deny that the same act, if performed in concert with all one's fellow citizens, *would* improve the world, *would* help bring about the common good—and that failing to perform it under *those* circumstances would be selfish. This paradox, that the very act that would be helpful if engaged in by the community as a whole would be harmful if engaged in by a single member (and harmful not just to herself but to overall utility), is precisely the tragedy of the commons.

This point is frequently missed, it seems to me, in discussions that criticize citizens of developed nations for their environmental failures. In a 2012 collection of essays, *Ethical Adaptation to Climate Change*, for example, one finds Jason Kawall bemoaning what he calls the "modest greed" of those who are "wealthy by global standards" (that is, those of us who live in the First World) and whose patterns of consumption are responsible, he argues, for significant environmental and social damage.[6] He defines greed as involving an "excessive" pursuit of a set of goods and a "vicious" overestimation of the value of those goods or underestimation of the value of other goods, and then points out that one can be greedy by this definition even if the goods involved aren't particularly "luxurious" or the desires for those goods particularly "intense." (Those are the cases in which he calls the greed "modest.")[7] And then he suggests that under this definition you and I are (modestly) greedy:

> Consider a middle-class American who regularly drives to the mall, and buys a shirt here, a DVD there, foods imported from around the world, and so on. Each individual desire and pursuit seems mild enough, but when we look at the *cumulative* effect, it is what we would expect of a greedy person. This agent is still having comparatively large impacts on the environment. She is still encouraging ongoing shipping of goods across the world (with the associated carbon emissions and other impacts), devoting more land to growing cash crops (with the associated loss of habitat or local subsistence crops), and so on.[8]

Yet what is written here is, if taken literally, simply false. Such an individual does *not* have "comparatively large impacts on the environment," as one can see if one imagines this person suddenly dying or suddenly deciding on a life of ascetic locavorianism, neither of which would produce any change whatsoever in the global environmental situation. She does not "encourage" the shipping of goods across the world or the extension of cash crops to more and more land; to her, rather, the possibility of that shipping and the extension of those agricultural practices are unalterable facts of the world—ones that make it possible for her (and indeed could be said to encourage *her*) to purchase certain items that she (mildly) desires, if she wishes, but not ones that would somehow disappear were her desires to change and become less greedy. She is in precisely the same situation as Hardin's herdsman: she gets a benefit by purchasing the goods she wants, although the consequences of many people getting that benefit, for her and for them, are ultimately harmful ones—yet those consequences will occur whether she takes the benefit or not, and so she is better off (and no one is worse off) if she takes it.[9]

The problem isn't greed, and it isn't egoism, either—it's not that the actors are putting their own needs ahead of those of the society they're part of. Derek Parfit's canonical discussion of these sorts of collective action problems in his *Reasons and Persons* is misleading on this score. He succinctly presents one version of the dilemma involved using the language of egoism and altruism, describing it as a case in which "each has two alternatives: *E* (more egoistic), *A* (more altruistic). If all do E that will be worse for each than if all do A. But, whatever others do, it will be better for each if he does E. The problem is, for this reason, each is more disposed to do E," and so the optimal result that all do A can't be attainied.[10] But there's no reason to insist here that those who do E do it for egoistic reasons—as long as E produces benefit for *anyone* (including others, or for that matter the community as a whole) no matter what others do, E would seem to be the rational thing for an individual (including a strictly altruistic one) to do in the absence of any communication with the others involved.[11] The difficulty doesn't come from the fact that an agent in this situation is putting her own needs ahead of the needs of her community but rather that whether she is altruistically community-minded or not, she has no way to coordinate her actions with those of others, and hence has to treat those others' actions as "natural facts" about which there is nothing she can do. The problem isn't that the individuals in the tragedy of the commons are *egoists*, it's (simply) that they're *individuals*, unable to act collectively and hence forced to treat the actions of their fellow citizens as things they cannot affect or modify. Whatever their goals are, altruistic or egoistic, they have no way to achieve them except through individual action, and that's the source of their dilemma.

And finally, the problem does not arise from ignorance any more than it does from greed or egoism. Part of what makes Hardin's story of the commons a tragedy is precisely that the herdsmen may be perfectly aware of what the consequences of their actions will be, but *even so* it remains reasonable for each of them to add additional cows to their herd. Similarly, we can assume that the commuter driving to work understands full well what causes global warming, what its consequences will be, and the responsibility of the culture of the automobile for producing those consequences—but nothing about that knowledge changes the structure of the situation he faces. The environmentally concerned factory owner, faced with the decision about whether to install new scrubbing devices on smokestacks, may completely understand the toxic consequences of the pollution such factories emit, but at the same time she knows the cost of the devices and the effects on her business of incurring such costs when her competitors do not: if she's bankrupted by the additional costs, nothing is gained in terms of pollution reduction. Knowledge in these cases in no way lessens the problem but rather in certain ways renders it more acute and even poignant.

The problem of the commons, I am suggesting, is very appropriately called a tragedy, in the classical sense. The agents are faced with an implacable and unavoidable destiny of which they are themselves the authors: it is their own acts, engaged in for the best of reasons and in the fullest understanding of their consequences, that bring about the effects that destroy them—and that appear to them, in the form of an aggregate that they produce but that they have no way to collectively determine, as Fate. The other name for Fate here, however, is the market. The tragedy is the central structural fact, it seems to me, of laissez-faire capitalism. The acts of private individuals transacting with each other in the market produce effects ("externalities") when aggregated that none of the individuals intended. Sometimes those effects are called "prices" or "wages" or "profits"; sometimes they're called GDP or the unemployment rate; and sometimes they take the form of pollution or global warming or the other unintended consequences of economic development.

The problem here, I'm arguing, doesn't derive from people's character flaws or their ignorance but rather ultimately from their alienation, in Marx's sense. No matter what the individuals desire or know as individuals, without any way to act together as a cooperative whole the consequences of their actions appear to them like facts of nature to which they must merely adjust themselves—driving to work, adding more cows to their herds, releasing smog into the air, in full and tragic knowledge of the harms such actions (when aggregated) cannot help but bring about. An economy based on private individuals engaging in private transactions with each other in a free market, I am suggesting, produces a social world whose contours and institutions were chosen by no one but were produced by all. This is the dark side of the invisible hand, and it seems to me to be the fundamental source of what are called environmental problems in general. Whether it is global warming, air or water pollution, toxic wastes, species extinction, or any of the other problems we talk of when we worry about the environment, in each case the problem arises not fundamentally because of ignorance or selfishness but because the actions of individuals produce consequences, when aggregated, that none of the individuals necessarily intend but which, in the absence of any public forum in which those actions could be effectively coordinated, they have no way of preventing.

Dale Jamieson, in an early essay on the ethical and political difficulties of responding to climate change, suggested that often they arise from the complexity of assigning moral responsibility for the harms it will produce. Our paradigm case of responsibility, he writes, involves an individual agent whose action causes a specific harm to another (local) individual. But "this paradigm collapses," he asserts, "when we try to apply it to global environmental problems, such as those associated with human-induced global climate change."[12] This is why, he claims, we have trouble thinking about the moral issues involved: "conventional morality would have trouble finding anyone to blame," he writes, for harms caused by climate change, "for no one intended the bad outcome or brought it about."[13] And this is certainly true, among other things for the reasons I have been discussing. But Jamieson's approach suggests a novelty and uniqueness to this kind of problem that misses, it seems to me, the frequency with which it arises and indeed the central role played by the structure it exemplifies in our social system as a whole. For the sort of distributed and therefore anonymous responsibility for an outcome Jamieson highlights is actually something with which all of us are quite familiar: it is nothing other than the phenomenon of the market's invisible hand, that is, of what Marx called alienation. The difficulty in assigning responsibility for climate change has the same structure as the difficulty explaining the movements of the S&P 500, or of interest rates, or of prices in general: we *all* are responsible, although for each one of us these things seem like external facts we cannot change but to which we must adjust ourselves. But there's another step here. For everyone knows the name of the realm we cannot change and to which we must adjust ourselves: its name is nature. That's the form "sociality" takes, under capitalism: *it seems like nature*, like something unmodifiable and external to us, but in reality it is nothing but our own act, having escaped our control. Taking it back under human control, to whatever extent that is possible, is what acknowledging the sociality and builtness of the world that surrounds us would require.

Inconsequentialism

Of the two elements required for a tragedy of the commons—that the marginal contribution of a single individual's decision to the overall effect is infinitesimal, on the one hand, and that there is no procedure in place for all of those involved to make (and enforce) decisions in common on the other—it is the first that has received more discussion. Sometimes called the problem of inconsequentialism, the issue has been examined both with respect to climate change in particular but also as a more general question about how to attribute moral responsibility to individuals for their contribution to a group effect when the group is large and each individual's contribution seems negligibly small. Walter Sinnott-Armstrong wrote an influential essay focusing on the case of climate change in 2005 whose title, "It's Not *My* Fault," was apparently not meant ironically. Using considerations similar to those I've suggested above (but without referring to Hardin), he examines a number of standard arguments designed to show why an individual has a moral obligation not to wastefully burn greenhouse gases (by, in Sinnott-Armstrong's example, taking a gas-guzzler out for a Sunday drive just for the fun of it) and shows them all to be wanting. Thus, for instance, he writes that in such a case,

> my act of driving does not even make climate change worse. Climate change would be just as bad if I did not drive. The reason is that climate change becomes worse only if more people (and animals) are hurt or if they are hurt worse. There is nothing bad about global warming or climate change in itself if no people (or animals) are harmed. But there is no individual person or animal who will be worse off if I drive than if I do not drive my gas guzzler just for fun. Global warming and climate change occur on such a massive scale that any individual driving makes no difference to the welfare of anyone.[14]

There simply is no moral obligation not to unnecessarily emit greenhouse gases at the level of the individual, Sinnott-Armstrong concludes.

But of course, this seems a paradoxical conclusion: surely the profusion of drivers who enjoy such gas-guzzling Sunday drives is at least part of what produces global warming, and so it seems there must be some sort of moral obligation on *someone's* part to try to reduce or eliminate such drives. Sinnott-Armstrong agrees, but the obligation, he says, is on the part of "the government": "Even if individuals have no moral obligations not to waste gas," he writes, "*governments* still have moral obligations to fight global warming, because they can make a difference. My fundamental point has been that global warming is such a large problem that it is not individuals who cause it or who need to fix it. Instead, governments need to fix it, and quickly."[15] A government can have a responsibility, Sinnott-Armstrong argues, that is not borne by its citizens; if a public bridge, for instance, becomes unsafe because of overuse by traffic, the government has an obligation to fix it, but this does not mean that I as a citizen have an obligation to go out and attempt the fix myself.[16] It's not clear, though, what the reference to "the government" is supposed to mean here. Sinnott-Armstrong's formulation seems to suggest merely that there are other sorts of moral agents in the world—"governments" rather than people—that are capable of larger impacts and are therefore subject to different sorts of moral obligations. What's partly obscured by this notion is the idea that "the government" (at least in a certain kind of democracy) might be the name not just for another agent but specifically for a *collective* agent, of whom the individual who takes the joyride, or imagines fixing the bridge, ought to see herself as a member (citizen). I return to this idea below.

For some, though, Sinnott-Armstrong's conclusions—both the idea that individuals are not morally obligated to reduce their emissions and the related suggestion that perhaps the obligation is limited (and so perhaps can be left) to "the government"—are counterintuitive and even infuriating. The conclusions seem to let the individual off the hook, joyriding in her SUV and crying crocodile tears about how her own miniscule emissions make no difference so what can she do? The intuition many have is that to engage in activities that clearly contribute to climate change, even if on an individual basis (that is, on the margin) the contribution is infinitesimal and therefore negligible, is nonetheless to act immorally. The trouble is in explaining why this is so.

One way to defend the intuition here is to point to the role of individual acts as *models for others*: thus one's environmentally proper behavior, even if in itself it makes no significant difference toward producing an actually sustainable world, nonetheless serves as an exemplar of behavior to those who become aware of it, and hence assists in building something like a "green culture" that ultimately might be able to change behavior on a wider, and therefore more consequential, scale. Sinnott-Armstrong responds to this kind of objection by pointing out that it's hard to imagine that one's own individual acts would have so much influence on others as to make any more of a difference than one's own self-limitation on emissions would.[17] I have some trouble with this answer because I think it relies on an analogy between the inconsequential character of one's impact on the climate and the supposedly inconsequential character of one's impact on other social agents that fails to distinguish between the *causal* impact of one's actions and their *persuasive* impact; the latter, I would note, have a cognitive and linguistic dimension that is significant and that the former lacks. But nonetheless I agree with Sinnott-Armstrong that the sort of modeling behavior involved here would be unlikely to have the consequences claimed for it, at least not under the sort of social structure marked by alienation that we currently inhabit. No matter how impressed my neighbor might be by my willingness to give up my car (and with it my job) in order to minimize my carbon footprint, she remains faced with the same problem she faced beforehand—a system that requires the use of automobiles and that cannot be modified by individual action, and not by the action of two individuals either. She may respect me, but nonetheless I still look (and in some sense I still am) crazy to do what I am doing.

Instead of putting the issue in terms of modeling, another possibility is to argue more directly that no matter what the specific consequences of one's own individual acts are, the real moral question has to do with character. Ronald Sandler and Dale Jamieson, among others, have argued that the problem of inconsequentialism reveals the limits of standard act-utilitarian views, and have suggested that this sort of difficulty shows the superiority of virtue-ethical approaches.[18] The idea here is that while someone who burns a lot of fossil fuels isn't directly causing an increase in global warming, there is nonetheless something wrong with being *that sort of person*. Yet, as is frequently the case with virtue-ethical positions, the basis for the claim that character traits involved here are virtuous or vicious seems thin, and based more on intuition than anything else. Sandler in his essay on inconsequentialism writes that "a character trait is a virtue to the extent that its possession is generally conducive to promoting the good," while a vice is a trait that is "detrimental to promoting the good," but he offers no account as to why a gas-guzzling joyride is detrimental (nor does he explain how "the good" is to be defined).[19] The argument seems circular, or empty: given that the original question was why one should abstain from engaging in these sorts of behaviors in the first place, it doesn't help much to say that the answer is that doing so is vicious because such behaviors are "detrimental to the good."

Jamieson has even less to say on this question. He writes that virtues are "non-calculative generators of behavior" and sees this as the central advantage of a virtue-oriented approach over a straight utilitarian one.[20] The idea seems to be that if an individual calculates what would lead to the best outcome in a tragedy of the commons situation, she is inevitably led to the action that produces disaster for all, whereas if she acts on the quasi-habitual or dispositional basis of a "green virtue" she will choose not to add the extra cow or take the joyride, and will thereby help avoid that disaster. But she only avoids the disaster in this latter case if the others do too, which is to say the virtue is only conducive to a good outcome if it's generally shared across the society, and so the problem of inconsequentialism reappears: these green dispositions are virtues only if others possess them as well, and so it isn't clear why they are virtuous for *me*.

Sandler does a better job of justifying his account of the virtues in his excellent book *Character and Environment*, in which he provides what he calls a "pluralistic teleological account" that defines virtues as character traits that make humans "well fitted" for a series of ends such as survival, species-continuation, autonomy, a well-functioning social group, a meaningful life, and so forth.[21] But the same problem that Jamieson faced arises: Sandler doesn't explain why a disposition to private actions that by hypothesis will have only inconsequential effects (refraining from driving, say) should be taken as an indication that the agent who performs them is any better fitted for these ends than someone lacking that disposition. What happens here, as in many of these discussions, is that a moment of something like universalization (that is, aggregation) is implicitly assumed, in the sense that if many agents had this disposition they would be more likely to achieve such ends, but no account is given of how *my* having the disposition alone helps me achieve them. But universalization can't be presupposed in a virtue theory, since its point is precisely to show why *each* agent individually is "better" if she acts virtuously.

What's striking, in fact, about the arguments Sandler and Jamieson offer is that they each emphasize as one of the intellectual advantages of virtue theory what they call its "noncontingency," by which they mean (as Sandler puts it) that "evaluation of an agent's actions is not overly contingent on the actions of others,"[22] so that (for instance) reducing one's own carbon footprint is morally admirable independent of what others do. Yet while making morality depend on something explicitly disconnected from the actions of others (as well as from the actual consequences of one's own actions), the theory here nonetheless still attempts—as it were behind the backs of the actors—to produce a set of consequences that are indeed the best *for all* (and indeed defines virtue in terms of those consequences) while still pretending that only individual character matters. The theory thus doubles down, one might say, on the very individualism that in my view generates the problem in the first place, and tries to produce virtuous agents whose actions will be effective because they match up with those of others by paradoxically leading them to believe that the actions of those others are irrelevant to their own virtue. But I would argue that whether an individual's acts are moral or not (and for that matter, whether an individual is virtuous or not) in fact *does* depend on the actions of others—indeed, one might suggest that a failure to consider other people's behaviors in deciding how to act is itself a kind of vice, or, more to the point, that a society in which the actions of others had no moral relevance to one's own actions would itself be a vicious society. The impulse is somehow to blame a person's character for engaging in acts whose significance, as long as they remain private and not part of a general practice, is really entirely symbolic; it's an example, I would say, of something like blaming the victim of alienation. The solution to the problem of inconsequentialism doesn't derive from placing the moral burden on a private individual to quixotically and self-sacrificingly do what she can even though all involved know that doing this makes no difference unless others do so as well, but rather requires finding a way to *restore the discursive connection to others* that a system based on alienation (and on the replacement, via market mechanisms, of "relations between people" by "relations between things") has rendered impossible.

Restoring that connection, it seems to me, might require first of all recognizing that although *I* as an individual have no way of overcoming the tragedy of the commons, *we*—the community as a whole—might together be able to do so. And this in turn requires understanding that in a certain sense the community is, or can be, something like a *collective agent*, capable of a kind of moral responsibility, and that such responsibility is not merely a matter of summing the responsibilities of the individual members of the community. In a good essay on the problem of inconsequentialism with respect to global climate change, Joachim Sandberg makes this latter point clearly. After considering the question of whether a person who chooses to fly from Stockholm to Paris can be morally blamed for doing so because of the consequences for climate change, he writes:

> My suggestion is that we have a *collective* obligation to change *our* ways, and this collective obligation may be partly separate from the obligations of individuals. While my own flying makes no difference, it should be noted, climate change could be averted if we all changed our ways. But then it seems plausible to say that we act wrongly as a *collective*, even though no individual driver or flyer may be doing anything wrong. This view could be further explained by saying that moral questions can be asked on at least two different levels, with implicit reference to different sorts of agents. It is one thing to ask "What should *I* do?" but quite a different thing to ask "What should *we* do?" and the answers may not always converge.[23]

But again—as I suggested with respect to Sinnott-Armstrong's idea that "the government" is responsible for solving climate change—this formulation threatens to make it sound like the individual is simply off the moral hook and all moral responsibility lies elsewhere, on some different moral "level." For the "we," of course, is made up of "I's," and in order for the collective to do anything the individual I's who make it up must do some things as well. Still, these need not be the same things as the ones under discussion up till now—driving less, taking fewer airplane trips, minimizing emissions, and so forth. Instead we (that is, each of the I's) might be under an obligation to *build the sort of community* capable of averting further climate change. This is the conclusion Sandberg comes to: "Since my driving and flying are seldom harmful, it is seldom morally wrong for me to drive or fly," he writes. "But I should not use this fact as an excuse for giving up on environmentalism altogether. Instead I should direct my efforts towards other lines of action that are more likely to make a difference."[24] Baylor Johnson, in what I think is the most persuasive essay on the inconsequentialism question with respect to global warming, puts the point this way: "One has an obligation in an impending T[ragedy] of [the] C[ommons], and it is to 'do the right thing' without waiting for others. The 'right thing' is not, however, a fruitless, unilateral reduction in one's use of the commons, but an attempt to promote an effective collective agreement that will coordinate reductions in commons use and therefore avert the aggregate harms."[25] The tragedy arises precisely from the lack of such an agreement; preventing the tragedy requires, then, working toward such an agreement. *This* is my obligation, under the alienated conditions that characterize the tragedy: an obligation to move, we might say, *from the realm of the market to the realm of politics*. It is in that move, I want to suggest, that the alienation whose tragic effects we have been tracing can ultimately be overcome.

In this sense, to call the problem underlying the tragedy of the commons a problem of inconsequentialism is a misnomer. The problem doesn't arise from the inconsequential character of one's individual actions when aggregated but rather from the character of the social structure through which that aggregation takes place. Those who find the conclusion that individuals have no moral obligation to limit their emissions as individuals absurd, thinking that it lets everyone off the hook for the actions they take that do, in the aggregate, cause the harms of global warming, misunderstand the relevance of inconsequentialism to this kind of case. They fail to see the difference between the inconsequential character of my decision to cut my emissions *in the absence of a general agreement by all others to do so* and the inconsequential character of a decrease in my emissions *as part of such an agreement*. In the first case nothing happens to improve climate, and so I have made no "contribution" to such an improvement, while in the second case presumably global warming is eased and my acts have indeed contributed to that easing. The problem isn't that the effect of one's individual's actions on a social aggregate is inconsequential: that's true more or less by definition. The problem is that one's individually "inconsequential" actions to cut emissions can only have a consequential effect, and hence count as morally valuable "contributions," if they are coordinated with the (again individually inconsequential) actions of many others. The problem here is not simply a version of the paradox of the heap, where the difficulty has to do with how inconsequential changes turn into significant ones, but rather a problem having to do with a social structure where coordination with others is difficult or impossible to arrange. My obligation isn't to engage in what are essentially symbolic, "modeling," or virtue-evincing but globally ineffective behaviors, as Johnson says; it's to *change that social structure* to make the kind of real coordination possible that will lead to actual protection of the climate.

Out of the Market, Into the Forum

Jonathan Glover, in a 1975 essay on issues associated with inconsequentialism, introduced a (rather distasteful) thought experiment that has turned out to be influential in the literature and is worth reconsidering in the context of what I have been calling alienation.[26] One hundred inhabitants of a village on the verge of starvation are about to eat a meal which for each of them consists of one hundred cooked beans. Suddenly one hundred invaders appear in the village, and each of them steals the beans of one of the villagers; the consequence is the death by starvation of everyone in the village. Clearly, each invader has done something terribly wrong. But now we are to imagine that—perhaps because of a newfound moral compunction on the part of the invaders, and their being persuaded of the inconsequentialist principle that if one's own act causes only an imperceptible harm, it cannot be wrong—as they plan their next attack on the next village (which again consists of one hundred starving villagers with one hundred beans each) they decide to change their modus operandi. Each attacker now takes *one* bean from the bowl of *each* villager, thus again ending up with one hundred beans but now having personally done no significant harm to any individual. (We assume here that the loss of a single bean from a bowl of one hundred causes no noticeable harm.) Those who defend the claim that inconsequential acts cannot be blameworthy seem forced to conclude that in this second case, unlike the first one, no attacker deserves any blame. But of course, the overall effect is exactly the same: each attacker gets one hundred beans, and all the villagers are left to starve.[27]

The moral seems clear: just because the consequences of one's individual action are miniscule, still if when they are combined with the actions of others they cause harm one is individually at fault. The change in procedure between the first and the second case is morally irrelevant: if they do wrong in the first case they do wrong in the second one as well. But then this would seem to apply to the case of the commuter or the herdsman too. It is true that their actions play an individually inconsequential role in global warming or commons depletion, but nonetheless they appropriately bear moral blame for it. It makes no more sense for them to conclude from the small impact of their acts that they can avoid such blame than it would for the bean stealers to think their shift in tactics could get them off the moral hook. And yet there are certain differences between the bean-stealing story and that of the commuter that are worth noting, involving the degree of premeditation and coordination involved in the collective act, and those differences, I would suggest, indicate that an important role is played here not just by the sorites-like problem of how individual acts contribute to a social aggregate but by the *political* problem of how that aggregate (and the society in which it arises) is actually organized.

For we can imagine a variant on Glover's story of the invaders, an unlikely one to be sure but one that shows the role of coordination and organization in eliciting our moral intuition here. If a single visitor, perhaps starving himself, were to enter the town alone and surreptitiously remove a single bean from each of the bowls without being noticed—again, assuming that the loss of a single bean produces no significant harm to anyone—we might well be inclined to say that nothing terribly wrong has been done and that the starving visitor deserves no, or not much, moral condemnation. And then if we imagine one hundred such visitors, each one unaware of each other's existence (and somehow each able to steal a bean from a bowl without noticing that others are simultaneously doing so as well), we end up imagining a situation where we would surely bemoan the loss by all the villagers of all their beans but still would not be so ready to blame the visitors, ignorant as they are that the effect of all their actions together is starvation in the village.[28] The point here is that the moral blame that accrues to the culprits in Glover's story derives in significant measure from the coordinated and premeditated way they go about their business—from the fact that they *collectively plan* and *intend* the effects they produce, and that they *consciously cooperate* in producing them (and therefore also know that their acts will be aggregated). In the absence of that degree of social organization, I'd argue, we do not see the individual actors here as morally responsible for their aggregated act in the same way.

One might be inclined then to conclude that the more organized the actors are, or perhaps simply the more one is aware of the intended actions of one's fellow actors, the more culpable one will be for the aggregated results of the acts one engages in along with them. Yet the situation is more complicated even than that, I think. To find an analogy to the sorts of everyday experiences of life under a market economy I have been discussing—the experiences of the commuter who regrets his carbon footprint or the fisherman who knowingly contributes to overfishing—one has to imagine yet a third variant of Glover's story, one perhaps harder still to imagine but more relevant to the situation of alienation. For let us at this point imagine the hundred hungry visitors each intending to take one bean from each villager, but now on the one hand no longer ignorant of the existence of the others, instead fully aware of what the other ninety-nine intend, but on the other hand (for some reason) *unable to talk with them or prevent them from carrying out their intention*. Hungry and isolated, let's suppose, I need the hundred beans to keep from dying and know both that I can remove one bean from each bowl without causing any harm to the villager whose bowl it is, but also that there are ninety-nine others like me in the same situation and with the same intention, and that nothing I can do can change their behavior. Here, of course, the situation closely resembles the tragedy of the commons. My own act, which is needed to preserve my very life, is by hypothesis in itself inconsequential, but in the context of the other acts I know are going to occur (and am powerless to prevent) the consequence is going to be the starvation of the villagers. But that consequence will arise whether I act or not—and so I'm sorely tempted to do my deed and, perhaps with dirty hands, make my escape.

If I do, am I morally blameworthy? Perhaps I am. But if I am, it won't be because I lack virtue, or because I'm greedy or ignorant or wanton or "the scum of the earth"—it will be precisely because of the tragic situation I'm in, whereby the act I need to perform—essentially blameless in itself—will, when aggregated with the acts of others I cannot modify or prevent, cause harm as a consequence. It will be, that is, because I am faced with something like the tragedy of the commons. The problem arises from the way our acts are organized, or rather are not organized. More precisely, it is an effect of alienation, and is characteristic of a system whereby social practices are determined by the mechanisms of the market. When individuals are left to make individual decisions about their own practices, and when they find themselves unable to take part in public decision-making processes with each other about the *communal* consequences of those practices, the result is a series of consequences that no one desires but no one can prevent.

The central issue here has to do with the relation between individual and collective responsibility under different forms of collective organization. We saw Sandberg and Sinnott-Armstrong arguing that there could be collective responsibility for a phenomenon without that responsibility accruing in the same sense to individual members of the collective. The three versions of Glover's tale of the bean robbers show how complicated the conceptual situation is here, though. The first version shows that one cannot escape responsibility by appealing to the "inconsequential" nature of one's actions, but the second one suggests that that's only clearly true when the collective is a well-organized one whose actions can be seen as (collectively) intentional. And yet in the third version—whose structure is that of the tragedy of the commons—the collective is *not* well organized and intentional, at least not in the standard sense, but now it is exactly that lack of organization itself that leads to the harmful consequences.

But even that way of putting it might be misleading, for the "lack of organization" in the third version, the way no individual can affect the acts of the others but rather must simply take those acts as given, evinces a form of "organization" that is arguably indeed quite familiar to us—the form of organization associated with a laissez-faire market, which is to say the form of organization imposed by the invisible hand. The "collective" behaviors of this community are simply the product (or more exactly the sum) of the behaviors of all the individual members of the community; the community *itself* does nothing but what all the individuals do. But rather than this allowing the individuals full freedom, as libertarian individualism would suggest, such a form of organization (as Marx points out) leads to a set of social consequences that no individual freely chose or would freely choose, and indeed appears as a nature-like *constraint* on individual freedom.

Virginia Held wrote a very interesting essay in 1970 asking the question "Can a Random Collection of Individuals Be Morally Responsible?" and raising the issue of how the degree of organization of a collective might affect ascriptions of moral responsibility to it.[29] Although intuitively it seems plausible to make moral judgments about certain organized collectives, Held points out, praising or criticizing the collective as such for its actions—a club that acts in a racist manner, an army that systematically commits atrocities, a corporation that engages in price-fixing—it's harder to imagine it being reasonable to make such judgments made unorganized or "random" collectives. In the latter case (Held mentions, for example, the set of passengers in a train carriage) one would be much more inclined to defend the reductionist claim that moral responsibility for actions could only accrue to the various individuals involved, not to "the passengers" as such. And yet, she points out, there are cases even of the latter sort where one's intuition suggests something like collective responsibility. She imagines, for example, passengers in a subway car who see an assault taking place, where it's obvious that together they would be able to subdue the assaulter without suffering any serious injury themselves, although perhaps no individual person in the car could be confident of being able to do so. It does seem fairly clear that the "random" group here does have a moral responsibility to cooperate so as to stop the assault—a responsibility that is distinct from the one any individual would have alone.[30]

In this relatively simple sort of case, it's pretty evident what the individuals need to do, and all that's required is that sufficiently many of them do it. More complex cases, though, might require more planning and therefore more coordination. Held describes, for example, a situation in which a small group of pedestrians witness a building collapse that leaves an injured person pinned and in danger of bleeding to death. Various beams must be moved to free the victim, but no individual is strong enough to do this alone, and furthermore the question of which beams to move and in which order has several plausible answers. In such a case, Held argues, not only does the "random" collective have an obligation to act together to save the victim, it has an obligation to *decide* how to do so, and to coordinate the actions of its members to achieve its goal. Earlier, though, Held had defined the difference between "organized" and "random" collectives precisely as having to do with the possession by the former and not the latter of a "decision method," that is, some procedure (whether it be voting or a choice made by officials of the group, etc.) for deciding how the group should act: "The possession of such a decision method, by a collection of individuals, is, we might say, that which transforms a random collection of persons into an organized group or collectivity," Held writes.[31] Thus in the case of the collapsed building, she concludes, the random collection of witnesses has the moral responsibility precisely to organize itself into a nonrandom one—to turn itself from a set of unconnected individuals into a collectivity capable of deciding and acting *as* a collectivity.

The relevance of this argument to the problem of the commons as I have been interpreting it should be clear. The problem arises from the fact that those who face it are "unorganized" in Held's sense: they face the problem as individuals and have no procedure for deciding *together* what they are going to do. I have suggested repeatedly that as individuals they do not really bear moral responsibility for the harmful consequences of their aggregated actions, at least not in the sense that they can be accused of greed or selfishness or even thoughtlessness or ignorance. But the *collective* of which they are a part can be criticized precisely for its *failure to be an organized one*, its failure, that is, to employ a "decision method" that would allow its members to mutually agree on behaviors that, engaged in now intentionally and collectively, would make it possible for them to avoid the consequences that none of them wishes to see but that none of them, as individuals, can prevent. They have to, that is, *become* a collective—or, if we allow some collectives to be unorganized or "random" ones, they have to become a *self-consciously organized* collective, and it is in their failure to do so that their moral blameworthiness consists. And Held is right, I think, that what makes a collective self-conscious and organized has something to do with its ability to make decisions *as* a collective, and not just as an agglomeration of individual decision makers.

The unpleasant cartoonish example of witnesses to a building collapse arguing with each other while the victim bleeds to death is more appropriately replaced by the tragic example of people who genuinely want to do the right thing and know what it is but have no way to form an agreement with each other to make sure it happens. *What's lacking in the commons case is a forum in which the various actors can come together and organize themselves into a self-conscious community.*[32] But the key characteristic of a forum is that in it, people *speak*: a forum is a locus in which decisions are made by interlocutors who talk with each other to decide what they should together do. And with that we are back to the significance of language that was the focus of chapter 6. Left to their own individual devices—left to the market—individuals facing the tragedy of the commons can, as it were, only signal to each other regarding their activities, by engaging in various individual transactions. They cannot *speak with* each other about what they should *jointly* do.

The tragedy of the commons arises when a collective "organized" only as a set of private individuals is unable to turn itself into a true collective that decides together, using language, how to act. The key role of language is illustrated even more clearly in the other and even more famous version of the kind of collective action problem under consideration here, the prisoners' dilemma.[33] Two innocent prisoners, each informed of the private advantage to be gained by falsely confessing but aware as well of the even greater, and mutual, advantage of each refusing to confess, are forced by the logic of their situation into an outcome they each realize is worse for both. This is a two-person version of the commons problem. It lacks the element of inconsequentialism, as each prisoner's choice will certainly affect the outcome significantly. But it maintains the element that because the actors' decisions are made independently of each other, a result is achieved that neither one prefers and that if they could only act in concert they could both avoid. The metaphor of the prison, though, illuminates the source of the tragedy, which lies precisely in their isolation and (especially) their silence. Cut off from communication with each other, unable to discuss together their situation and how to resolve it, they are effectively rendered mute, and this muteness is what leaves them doomed to produce the result they do not want while fully aware that that's what they are doing.

For if they could speak, they could form an agreement that neither one will confess to something she didn't do. Speaking, as chapter 6 argued, is essentially *dialogue*; the real moral of their situation is that the isolated prisoners have no access to dialogue and so are left to make their decisions monologically, and that this is the source of their dilemma. Dialogue, the story shows, is preferable to monologue, not for the standard Millian reasons about being open to other opinions and therefore being more likely to hit on the truth, but rather (or in addition) because dialogue actually transforms the social and political situation and thereby makes certain solutions possible whose value individuals are capable of monologically recognizing but which they cannot by themselves put into practice. Once they speak, the relationship between the prisoners itself furthermore takes on a different moral status, for the reasons adduced in chapter 6, because to speak—to assert, to question, to persuade, to agree, and finally to promise—is to undertake a responsibility toward one's interlocutor, especially the responsibility to speak the truth and to keep one's word. As solitary prisoners (and maybe strangers) they arguably have no responsibilities beyond the bare one of personal survival. The two of them do not form a collective or community in any serious sense—each is a private individual, alone in a cell, unable to enter into conversation with anyone about what is right to do and therefore left with no alternative but to act for her own benefit alone; and the result, as in the commons case, is—tragically because foreseeably—disaster. In the commons case, too, it is precisely the failure of the herdsmen to form an agreement together that leads to the tragedy. If instead of acting independently to add cows they were to *talk together* about how they should collectively use the commons, the problem would disappear—they could determine together how many cows the commons could support and then decide on a fair division of that number among the herdsmen in the group. But to talk together, to decide together, is *to form a self-conscious community*, an "organized collective" in Held's language, where before there was only a "random" one. Hence the solution to the various collective action problems here consists exactly in the act whereby the collective *makes itself into a real collective* instead of remaining an unorganized group of individuals without what Held calls a decision method.

I take it this is the real significance of the conclusion that Johnson and Sandberg each come to in various ways—that our moral obligation as members of a community whose aggregated actions are producing significant harms to global climate is *not* to act as individuals to minimize our own individual emissions but rather to engage in the sort of political action that would help generate a *collective decision* on the part of the community itself to change the sorts of social practices (and the form of social organization) that leads to those harms. (And as we've seen, something like this is Sinnott-Armstrong's conclusion too, except that he fails to note that in a democracy, what he calls "the government's" responsibility is really a responsibility of its citizens as a collective.) In doing so we *form ourselves into a real community*, one with a discursive "decision method"—we decide together what it is we will do (in the forum), instead of each deciding separately (in the market) and then allowing whatever aggregated social effect might result to turn out however it does.

The key move, as I have already suggested, is a move from the market to politics. Instead of individual decisions being made by independent participants in the market whose relation to all the other participants is essentially the same as that between the prisoners in the prisoners' dilemma, in the political realm decisions are made by members of the collective *together*. To make them together, furthermore, is to make them discursively; the implicit norms that operate within the political sphere are the discourse-ethical ones described in the previous chapter, not the instrumental-rational and individualist norms of the marketplace. I am tempted here to start using Hegelian language: a collectivity organized only via market mechanisms is what might be called a community in itself but not yet for itself. The collectivity does things, to be sure—the actions of its members produce a certain level of prices, of unemployment, of interest rates, and so forth, just as they also produce a certain level of carbon emissions and therefore of climate change—but it does not do them consciously, and thus its acts take place behind the backs of the actors involved. But in the (democratic) political realm, the community acts *self-consciously as* a community: in that realm it directly chooses what it does, as the result of a common decision reached by the members talking together about what would be best for the community as a whole, not for each individual by him- or herself. In Hegel's terms, the community is now a community *for itself*.

As mentioned, Hardin says that without privatization, the tragedy of the commons can only be avoided by what he calls "mutual coercion, mutually agreed upon," but the use of the word "coercion" here is misleading. The driver who is happy to spend $300 for a catalytic converter as long as she can be guaranteed that others will do so too is in a certain simplistic sense "coerced" by a law requiring all cars to have catalytic converters, but in a deeper sense what happens here is that the passage of the law provides the condition that makes it possible for her to achieve the goal she wishes to achieve. (Hegel would say in this sense the law offers her freedom, rather than anything like limitation or coercion.) And the "coercion" involved might take other, noncoercive, forms as well: it's perfectly possible, as Elinor Ostrom and others have pointed out, for groups to agree on communal solutions to the problem here that employ more informal techniques of enforcement than the passage of laws or other forms of hard coercion.[34] If we imagine a community that democratically decides together that it wishes to engage in a certain form of action—an action that all the individual members agree is the right one—then when they each engage in the practices that together cause that action to take place, it seems odd to call the decision a case of coercion. They've all done what they agreed to do, and (assuming a discursive model of democratic decision making) what they thought was the right thing to do. In what sense have any of them been coerced?

This is the answer to the frequent objection that communal agreement does not resolve the kind of collective action problem exemplified by the tragedy of the commons because it simply replaces it with a new one, the problem of preventing free riding. Even after the herdsmen agree on a new cooperative regime for sharing the commons, and even after the prisoners are allowed to meet to discuss their plans, they still face an incentive, the objection runs, to secretly increase their herd or to confess despite the agreement. The fact that "defection" is advantageous to them remains true no matter what they say they will do. "Covenants, without the sword, are but words," as Hobbes writes in the canonical expression of this idea, "and of no strength to secure a man at all."[35] (Virtue theorists such as Sandler emphasize this issue, using it to downplay the point Johnson and others make about the priority of political action over the development of individual character.[36]) Yet this objection fails to note that the normative situation here is entirely different from the one that obtains prior to the formation of an agreement. The isolated prisoners stand in no moral relation to each other: to each one the other is an independent figure whose actions have to be strategically taken into account in the same way as the laws of nature. Once an agreement has been formed, however, they have entered the moral realm whose foundation lies in language use. They have now made promises to each other, undertaken to perform certain actions, agreed on a common set of cooperative tasks. They don't *predict each other's actions* the way one predicts the behavior of physical objects; rather, they *rely on each other's word.* The relation is no longer strategic but moral. They have formed a community—an "organized collective"—and they are now normatively bound to each other. Hobbes is right, of course, that such normative bonds do not bind us in the way fear of the sword does; when we obey them we do so because we ought to, not because we want to avoid paying the price of punishment. It surely follows that some actors may choose to break the agreement and attempt to free ride. But such an actor has now done something wrong, by violating the normative order that she herself created by her words and her promise. A free rider in *this* situation deserves all the calumny that virtue theorists and others direct at those who insist that "my emissions make no difference": to break an agreement into which one has voluntarily entered and on which others are depending, because one hopes to gain the benefits the agreement produces but is unwilling to perform what one has promised, *is* indeed to act selfishly. The moral problem here doesn't have to do with the consequences of one's free riding (which are doubtless still "inconsequential" in the sense we have been discussing) but rather with the attempt simultaneously to be a member of a discursively constituted community while taking advantage of one's fellow members by treating them strategically.

Free riding by breaking an agreement one has already discursively formed is therefore a *political* wrong; it occurs at the level of politics and violates the necessary normative presuppositions of that level, and is thus morally quite different from the action of a private individual in the realm of the market. In the market one *must* treat one's fellows strategically, predicting their behavior and attempting to maximize one's utility. There's no other choice, and there is no violation of market norms in acting this way. But as we have seen in a situation where only market transactions and market relationships are to be found, the aggregated total of everyone's actions produces a state of affairs that no one wants and that appears to all like a nature over and against them—the phenomenon of alienation. Politics is where that alienation ends, where the community recognizes itself *as* a community and therefore organizes itself as one as well, and thus by forming a communal agreement about what to do is able to take a kind of control over the aggregation of individual acts that market relations do not permit. Of course, it is possible to treat the political realm like the market realm, acting strategically and employing the techniques of rational choice theory to decide on one's course of action, but to do so is to make a kind of moral category mistake, albeit one that our current social system too often encourages us to make.

A similar mistake is made, I would argue, by those (like Sandler) who assert that since political action is as "inconsequential" as market action, the same collective action problem arises in the one sphere as in the other. For as my reconstruction of Glover's example of the bean thieves was meant to show, the difference between self-consciously organized collectives and those whose "organization" is only the nature-like and alienated one that results from an aggregate of solitary monologists trying to predict each other's behavior is morally relevant, and acting strategically out of narrow self-interest has an entirely different significance in the one case than in the other. Not only is the market realm distinct from the political realm, but the path to overcoming the alienation characteristic of the former realm consists precisely in replacing it (or large parts of it) by the latter one. The problem of the commons cannot be solved by market mechanisms—which is to say, by private individuals acting independently of each other. In fact, it is *caused* by such mechanisms. It can only be solved by shifting the level of action to the level of politics—the level at which individuals who know themselves to be members of a community decide together, in language, what behaviors they wish to engage in as a community, and then carry that decision out as a group, thereby showing themselves to be a self-conscious and unalienated community and not simply an agglomeration of isolated individuals.

Thus it is solved by *democracy*, by which I mean a discursive process in which the members of the community discuss the problems they face and examine various possible solutions, and then decide together which of those solutions will be best. Best for whom? The model of democracy I'm proposing isn't one in which each individual attempts to produce the result that will maximize his or her utility: that's simply another way of describing the market relations that lead to the tragedy of the commons.

Instead it's a model in which each individual expresses and attempts to justify his or her view about what course of communal action would be best overall. This procedure will involve individuals expressing their own sense of what the most important values are, which will surely include their own personal good but will likely include as well the good of their families, of fellow members of the community, but also of other humans outside the community, members of future generations, other sentient creatures, living things, and certainly the "environment" that surrounds them all. And whatever views are expressed, of course, have to be justifiable ones—that is, good reasons have to be given for them, where the goodness of reasons is itself a matter to be judged by the discourse. The goal of the discourse, furthermore, is agreement—not a modus vivendi or compromise but the actual moment in which all involved in the discussion come to a consensus on the practices they wish to engage in and the goals they wish to achieve.

I can no longer ignore two related objections that have without a doubt occurred to every reader at this point—first, that market structures do not leave us so entirely isolated from each other as my comparison of them to the prison in the dilemma suggests, and therefore that blaming environmental problems on those market structures is overly simplistic, and second, that my suggestion that the solution to those problems can be found in discursive democracy is overly utopian. Both these objections, frankly, are correct. The previous discussion has been a highly abstract one and is not really meant to be a literal description of the situation of citizens of the technologically advanced nations in the twenty-first century. What I have attempted to offer instead is something like ideal types of two realms of social action, to which I have given the names of the market and of politics, respectively, and which I have attempted to describe in abstract and highly purified terms. In reality, of course, we do not live in either of these realms alone but rather in a complex world in which they are mixed in varying and heterogeneous ways. Although I concede this point, I still think that the basis of my critique is valid.

Thus the claim that under capitalism we are all essentially like the isolated prisoners of the dilemma, forced into the tragedy of the commons because of our inability to communicate with each other so as to make cooperative plans, is surely literally false. Such communication *is* possible, and as a result there *are* ways to avoid the tragedy in certain cases. Certainly under modern conditions in the liberal democracies there is a sometimes significant degree of governmental (that is, political) regulation of markets, associated among other things with the environmental consequences of various technologies, whereby corporations and individuals are required to act in ways that enforce cooperation rather than defection in the face of environmental dangers. Thus automobiles are required to contain catalytic converters, limits are placed on the toxic effluents and air pollutants produced by factories, measures are taken to increase the fuel efficiency of automobiles, to encourage the use of public transportation by commuters, to develop new transportation technologies that will not involve fossil fuels, and so on. But thinking about all these sorts of examples should make clear their limitations, both in terms of what they have achieved up until now and also what difficulties they inevitably face in a system more committed to the "freedom" of private transactions than to providing citizens a sense of membership in a self-conscious community that decides together what it wants to do. My claim is that a social system based on laissez-faire market relations will unavoidably face environmental problems, and that *our* system, in the advanced capitalist nations, faces those problems to the extent that it is such a system. But to the extent that ours is a mixed system, in which government regulation does take place—and to the extent that the government does operate in accordance with discursive democratic procedures—those problems may find partial solutions, although I doubt that they will ever be sufficient for a full resolution. My goal above thus has been to diagnose the source of the problems, not to make specific claims about the political situation in (for example) the United States.

Similarly, it is of course impossible—particularly in a large developed country—to imagine a political system that functions in accordance with the discursive democratic ideals summarized above. But again, it was not my intention to suggest that such a system is a practical possibility for the United States or other developed nations. My goal was rather to define the political as a distinct realm from the market, and to point to the differences between those realms. Discursive democracy is the regulative ideal that should underlie the really existing politics in which we engage as actual citizens, despite our knowledge that such an ideal will never fully be achieved. Still, the point of the argument I have been offering is that environmental questions require *communal* solutions, and that formulating and deciding on such solutions requires citizens giving and defending reasons to each other rather than viewing themselves as isolated individuals privately predicting the expected behaviors of their fellow prisoners of capitalism. In trying to decide which environmental policies we ought to support and work to establish, furthermore, we can be guided by discursive democracy as an ideal. We can, that is, first of all try to imagine what policy would be able to win the assent of everyone involved in a discussion wherein all participants are given an equal chance to speak on the one hand and required to be able to give reasons to justify their views on the other, and in which (in Habermas's eloquent phrase) "no force except that of the better argument is exercised."[37] And second, we can try to work for a political system in which that ideal serves as the guiding one—a system where a premium is placed on discourse (and not simply on the satisfaction of interests) and where ways are found for individuals whose voices have typically not been heard to enter the conversation on an equal basis with those more used to being listened to—and whose outcomes to whatever extent possible will match the ones that a true discursive democracy would reach.

I have avoided so far the problem of what has come to be known as "climate skepticism" or "climate denial." My reconstruction of the forces that both lead to climate change and make it difficult to overcome have located them in the fact that individuals whose mutual interactions are mediated only by the market—and not by the political realm in which they can actually acknowledge themselves and act as a community—find themselves "imprisoned" in a tragedy of the commons that works itself out even if as individuals they feel personally committed to preventing the harms climate change threatens to produce. But it is of course true that for many citizens of the United States today (and to a lesser extent those of other nations as well) this commitment is absent, because they do not agree that climate change is real, or is really caused by human action, or is a real threat. There are many reasons for this, and examining them in detail would take us too far afield. The point of the argument I have been providing is that even if all involved did agree on the answers to questions regarding the reality, origin, and seriousness of climate change, there would still be no effective mechanism within a market system for dealing with it, and therefore that at the deepest level the problem has its source in a set of social arrangements, and not in the greed or stupidity or other character flaws of contemporary humans.

Yet there is no doubt, sadly, that there is a fair amount of greed and stupidity to go around nowadays, and worse, that the short-term interests of certain people with more wealth and social power than most others lead them to act in ways that perhaps intentionally confuse and obfuscate the evidence about climate change and therefore complicate any debate that might actually occur in the fairly debilitated and anemic political sphere that currently exists in the United States. Habermas distinguishes between "communicative action" (the sort of discourse oriented toward truth and justification that I have been describing as central to the ethics of language) and what he calls "strategic action," the sort of pseudo-discourse that both violates language's own ethical presuppositions but also takes advantage of them to attempt to manipulate interlocutors into believing and acting in ways that could not survive actual discursive justification.[38] And it's clear enough that there has been plenty of the latter at play in the "debate" about climate change as it has been taking place over the last decade or so in the United States. To the extent that this has been the case, my call for a move from the market to the political realm, and for discursive democracy as the ideal model we should uphold for finding a way to deal with problems such as climate change, is at the same time a call for such manipulative action to cease so as to make it possible for citizens to decide for themselves what they *really* think is true and what they *really* want to do about it.

But once one imagines that move to the political sphere being made, it becomes clear that at another level, climate skepticism remains a possibility—and here a series of issues emerges that I am not in a position to develop at any length. For the same problems that arose in the previous chapter about the silence of nature—the fact that calls to "listen to nature" require relying on self-described translators who might turn out instead to be dangerous ventriloquists—arise in this situation too with respect to the problem of the role of scientific experts in a democratic polity. There is a danger, in contemporary discourse about climate change, for the experts to be given too much authority, as though their "conclusions" would need to be treated as unquestionable inputs to whatever democratic processes might deal with questions of climate or other environmental issues. Science, it is important to remember, is discursive too, and there is nothing about it that grants its "conclusions" (which always turn out to be tentative and temporary, and hence not always so conclusive as one might think) any fundamental epistemological privilege. Those who genuinely question the scientific "consensus" about climate change, I am suggesting, deserve a seat at the discursive table as well, which is to say "science" itself is part of the democratic discourse.[39] But I will leave this issue to the side, because it would take us in directions I'm not prepared at this point to go.

Toward a Democratic Environmentalism

The pieces are now in place for responding to the central problem of relativism that seemed to render questionable the idea of an environmental philosophy after the end of nature—the fact that without "nature" as a normative standard for determining how we should treat the environment, the danger would arise that anything goes. If there is no nature, if the world we inhabit is always the product of our social practices, then how are we to choose among social practices, and therefore among worlds? Isn't the view I have been describing here simply once again a kind of arrogant anthropocentrism in which humans, viewing themselves as masters of the universe, can feel free to dominate it and transform it in any way they happen to like?

I don't think it is. The first point to make about this caricature of the position is that I have been explicitly denying the power of humans to "dominate" or "master" the environing world. As chapter 5 made clear, the processes of building always escape the ability of builders to plan or anticipate, or even fully to comprehend, what they are doing. And so what Latour calls the "slight surprise of action" is built into every building; we do not have control over what we build. But the second point, which I have been developing in this chapter, is that everything depends on the character, and in particular on the degree of self-consciousness, of the community whose social practices help to produce the environment it inhabits. The terrible environmental consequences that result from our social practices today—and the ever more terrible consequences that can be foreseen if those practices do not fundamentally change—are *not* the result, I have been arguing, of social choices that arrogantly refuse to recognize that the world is not ours to do with as we wish. Indeed, they are not the result of social *choices* at all, at least if choices are understood as the outcome of conscious social decision-making. They are the result of an alienated form of social organization in which all transactions are taken to be private ones, and the question of the social consequences of those transactions as aggregated is treated as irrelevant (as "externalities"). Under that sort of social organization the society cannot be said to choose anything, to refuse anything, or even to act arrogantly, for it does not *act,* in the self-conscious sense, at all.

But it is precisely this failure to act, this failure of the community to act *as* a community, that leads to the appalling and dangerous environment that its social practices produce. Those practices are unchosen, and as a result they turn out almost inevitably to be undesired and undesirable. The ugliness and ecological harm produced by our practices today are not anything that anybody asks for or intends; they are what happens when people act in uncoordinated ways and thereby face the tragedy of the commons. If the community were instead to *choose* its social practices in the realm of a democratically organized politics rather than leaving them to the realm of the market, then the environment produced by such those would be one of which we could approve.

To say, as I have, that the environment around us is always the product of our social practices, and that the idea of a "natural" environment independent of those practices cannot function even theoretically as a standard for measuring the one we inhabit, is not to say that all environments are equally good. For there are practices and there are practices: certain sorts of social practices are self-conscious in a way that others are not. Practices that *know themselves as such*—that involve both a social recognition that they *are* social practices, and a social willingness to take responsibility for them—are superior to those that are engaged in thoughtlessly, unconsciously, without self-recognition. The latter sorts of practices are the ones that I have been describing as alienated: they are practices that do not own up to what they are, do not see themselves as social, and so do not recognize themselves as subject to democratic decision-making processes. Or they are practices that do not acknowledge themselves as practices at all: these are the kinds of practices I discussed toward the end of chapter 3, the practices of a society that does not want to take responsibility for the world it inhabits (or doesn't know how to do so) and so prefers to believe in something called "nature" that is larger and stronger than it and can dictate to it how it ought to live.

The normative standard, that is, for deciding which practices we ought to engage in and which ones we ought to eschew does not lie in "nature" but rather *in those practices themselves,* and specifically in the degree of self-consciousness they evince. All our practices transform the world, which is to say they help to build the environment we inhabit, but those practices that know this about themselves, and that take responsibility for the environment they help produce, are preferable to those that do not.[40] Thus an environmentalism after the end of nature would call not for practices that protect nature (which doesn't exist), or Nature (which doesn't need protection), or even for ones that protect the "environment" (because that would mean protecting shopping malls and coal-burning power plants and all the other horrors that environ us), but rather for practices in which the actors *acknowledge and take communal responsibility for* their transformative effects on the world, doing so via the procedures of a discursive democracy. These would be the practices of a form of social organization that *chose itself*, rather than one that developed through the alienated and nature-like processes of aggregation produced by market relations. Such a form of organization would *know* what I have called the builtness and the sociality of the environment. It would not treat the environment as something other than and beyond human practices, but rather would understand that it is, always already, the product of those practices, and therefore that it ought to be seen as something for which we must take responsibility.

To say this is not to forget the lesson of chapter 5, the one to be learned from the sad story of the City Center Mall. Part of that lesson was that the products of our practices are always beyond our power to understand and to control; it was a lesson in humility. And so the social procedures in which decisions are made about our practices must always remember that predictions are fraught with danger and that the best-laid plans always go at least partly awry. But another part was that allowing those decisions to be made in the market leaves us at the mercy of a thing-like world that looks like "nature" and that functions as an independent power over and against us. To recognize the world instead as something that we ourselves make in our practices would be, according to the sort of philosophy of practice I have been proposing, to start to *make it differently*. Humility does not mean abstention from action. We cannot help but create the environment we inhabit through our practices, but it would be better if we did so knowing that that's what we're doing. To say this is not to say we can make it any way we want, or that our practices will always have the effects we expect. But it does mean that we have to do the best we can, in a spirit of humility and fallibilism but also of hope and self-understanding, using the intelligence we have to try to determine what it would be best for us to do. This is what building means. To recognize that what we build never turns out to be identical to what we expected doesn't mean we ought not to build at all—which is in any case an impossibility, because our every movement in the world, every step, every breath, "builds" the world in a certain way. It means rather that we have to build carefully, humbly, self-consciously. That we cannot determine with certainty the outcome of our practices does not remove from us the obligation to take responsibility for those practices, and to choose together which practices we have good reason to hope will make the world a better place. That obligation is the central "moral standard" applied by an environmental philosophy after the end of nature.

In what sense is this an "environmentalism" as traditionally understood, though? Does the preference for self-consciously chosen practices that know themselves as such over the alienated ones that arise through market processes map in any straightforward way onto the standard preferences for clean air and water, for the preservation of green spaces and "wilderness," for the prevention of species extinction and of global climate change, that we normally associate with an environmentally progressive worldview? I think it does, but the argument for this of necessity will be an abstract one, and has to be marked by the same fallibilism and humble uncertainty I have claimed we must always show toward the likelihood of things turning out the way we hope they do. Two levels have to be distinguished here. At the level of the broad political argument I have been making, all that can be said is that an environmentally good society will be one in which decisions about environmentally significant social practices are made consciously and discourse-democratically by the community as a whole, or—more concretely—that the environmentally correct decision for *us* is the one that such a society would make. Such a formulation rejects the idea that environmental correctness can be defined by some sort of external standard—for example, by what would be required by nature (or Nature), or by God, or by some set of principles not themselves questionable within a discursively democratic process.

This means that in a fundamental sense, the right environment for a community is simply the environment that community would choose in a democratic discourse, a choice that is not subject to being judged by some external standard. This formulation isn't quite correct, though, because as I have repeatedly pointed out, the environment that results from our practices is never entirely up to us. Better would be to say that the right social practices for a community to engage in are the ones that the members of that community would choose in such a discourse, and that the environment produced by those practices would in that sense be "right" for it. The basic idea here is a pragmatist one. "Choice" has to be understood, in accordance with the practice-oriented account I have been offering, as a matter of practice, not simply a theoretical decision: the community's choice *is* its practices, not something prior to those practices that the practices are attempts to bring about. But of course it may happen that the community discovers that the environment that its practices create is one it doesn't like, and therefore decides that those practices must change. The overall point, though, is that there is no way to define what makes a set of practices or an environment the right ones except through the self-conscious decision of the members of the community whose practices it is and whose environment those practices produce.

Yet what guarantee is there that the community will make the right decision? Here is where I can imagine the howls of "hubris" and "anthropocentrism" growing. I seem to be saying that the only judge of the goodness of an environment is whether the members of the human community who inhabits it like it. I can't deny that *something* like this is my view. But the issue, first of all, isn't what they "like": it isn't a matter of their aesthetic judgment or their personal pleasure or desire. To say the community's decision has to be a self-conscious one, I have insisted, is to say it has to be the result of a democratic discourse, in which the key element is the *giving of reasons*—members offering justifications for the proposals they make and answering objections raised in response to those proposals. Thus, whatever decision comes out of the discourse will have to be *justifiable,* to anyone concerned who might take part in the discourse. There's no question here of a bare preference dependent on nothing but some individual's (or group's) whim or personal desire. Yet this doesn't entirely resolve the problem, for a critic might worry about a perverse community all of whose members share the same environmentally objectionable whim and find it justifiable—enjoying the idea of exterminating a species, let's say, or of causing a massive warming of the atmosphere. It's true that on my view, the wrongness of such proposals is nothing that can be determined a priori by appeal to any external standard: there is no standard, I insist, besides the decision of those who take part in the discourse. But it should be noted that this very objection—with its claim that such decisions would be perverse ones, and that their possibility reveals that a democratic discourse could come to an environmentally immoral decision—*is itself a contribution to such a discourse*, and so the objection has something of a performative contradiction about it. For if the objector indeed believes (as I do too) that the choice to exterminate a species or to allow global warming would be wrong, then *she* at least must have what she believes to be good reasons to believe this, reasons that might indeed be offered up in a discourse about whether to engage in social practices with those effects. And to say that she believes her reasons are good ones is to say that she believes they would be taken to be such in such a discourse (because if they wouldn't, then how can she be sure those reasons are good?)—which means the discourse would *not* end up defending those sorts of choices.

This is what I meant by saying that two levels have to be distinguished. At the formal level, the lack of any external standard for decisions by the community about its practices means that nothing can be ruled out a priori about what such a community might legitimately decide. But nonetheless, those of us who consider ourselves environmentalists must believe that the views we hold—about the value of the living green world, about the moral significance of animal consciousness and of species continuity, about the importance of preserving a livable atmosphere for human and nonhuman creatures now and into the future, and so on—are valid ones for which good reasons can surely be given, reasons that could persuade any interlocutor equally committed to rational discourse; and as a result we cannot seriously worry that a legitimate discourse would lead to conclusions other than these—unless we are uncertain, of course, that these are right after all. Thus within the discourse itself—and so at the substantive level—a whole series of familiar arguments will presumably be offered to defend environmentalism, and surely environmentalists must believe that they would be successful. One has to distinguish, that is, the *formal* point that environmental questions can only be resolved by democratic discourse (and not by an appeal to anything beyond that discourse) from the *substantive* contributions that we environmentalists ourselves might make to that discourse as citizens whose opinions deserve the same consideration as those of all others.

Still it must be acknowledged that the discourse-political approach I am taking here at the formal level places a number of constraints on the *sorts* of arguments that are appropriate at the substantive level. In particular, as will be obvious from what has come before, arguments that appeal to "nature" as a source of normative authority superior to the discourse itself can have no role to play here. Such arguments serve to shut down discussion, short-circuiting it by asserting that it doesn't matter what other participants in the discourse believe to be true since nature "requires" some particular set of actions. This is the dogmatism of the ventriloquist, who is in truth simply another participant in the discourse but tries to claim a unique authority for her own views over those of other participants by insisting that the views she expresses derive from some special source of extradiscursive truth. Such arguments are ruled out for the same reason that assertions of special authority for members of particular genders or racial or ethnic groups would be ruled out: because they contradict the necessary formal presuppositions of the discourse itself, and so cannot even be expressed without producing a performative contradiction.[41]

Yet this does not itself mean that neither nature nor Nature would have any role to play in such a discourse. Appeals to nature as moral authority are ruled out because they function as attempts to trump the role of the discourse as morally decisive, but to say nature can't possess moral authority is not to say it cannot possess *value*. There is no performative contradiction involved in claiming within the discourse that nature, or Nature, possesses a special value that deserves our recognition and protection, and it may well be the case that participants in the discourse would make precisely this assertion. I myself think such an assertion requires (and would meet with) rejection as well, but in saying this I am speaking not at the formal but the substantive level. My reasons for doubting that the value of Nature or nature could have much of a role to play in environmental discourse are the ones I have been presenting throughout this book, of course. On the one hand, any talk of the value of Nature (where Nature stands for everything in the world subject to ordinary physical forces) faces the problem that it would end up finding value in everything that exists, including shopping malls and toxic wastes and the burning of fossil fuels. On the other hand, if it is nature whose value is being asserted (where nature means that part of the world that humans have not touched), the problem will be that nature doesn't seem to exist any longer, and I have given some reasons to think that perhaps it never did—or rather, that even if it did once exist, the idea of drawing a distinction between the human and the nonhuman parts of the world, and using that distinction to support the claim that those parts differ in value, itself depends on a hidden anthropocentric metaphysics that views humans as outside Nature.

I don't deny that there might well be a preference expressed by participants in a discourse today for preserving parts of the world where the human trace is not so conspicuous—where nonhuman living things make up most of the landscape, say, and do so in ways that humans have very little role in intentionally organizing or directing. The reasons given for this preference will be varied, but most of them seem quite plausible: the beauty of such landscapes, first of all, but also (on the one hand) the historical significance they possess in terms of the history of the human habitation of the Earth and (on the other) a strong feeling most of us have that nonhuman living things themselves deserve to be able to live and flourish in some relative independence from human will. We are astonished, as inhabitants of a world that we have radically altered so much, to see those parts of it where our alterations have been minimal—in part because we also can see there more clearly the *other* alterations that other (nonhuman) organisms and objects have caused. We appreciate landscapes that are typically called "natural" for reasons that are partly aesthetic, partly historical, partly built into our culture, and these seem reasons enough to justify the claim that we ought to protect them (and even, *pace* Katz, to produce more of them). None of this stands in contradiction to what I have said above. All I want to avoid is the appeal to "nature" as a metaphysically significant category with intrinsic moral implications. Simply to say that so-called "natural" areas are attractive and significant to us for a whole series of reasons, and therefore deserve our concern and care, is fine; the problem is with going further and granting the category a normative priority over what can be discursively justified.

To understand the value of "nature" in this somewhat deflationary way avoids what are the finally pointless sorts of debates that thinkers such as Katz or Elliot lead us into—about what is *really* natural, about *how much* human involvement turns a place into something artificial, and so forth. We need to acknowledge that the preference for what gets called "nature" is *our* preference, not something with deep metaphysical roots, and so acknowledge that here too the human and the so-called natural are not distinct. But another advantage of this deflationary account is that it allows an environmentalism of the urban, of the built environment, to be developed that is fully continuous with the traditional nature-based one. For with respect to cities, suburbs, factories, artifacts, and all the objects in all the landscapes that are indeed the product of intentional human action, the question to be asked is the same one I'm suggesting should be asked about the so-called natural environment: is this the sort of world we want to be environed by? Is a built world consisting of these things a world that humans would genuinely wish to inhabit—by which I mean that they would agree to inhabit if the choice of environments were left up to them and not to the nature-like workings of a market that unavoidably leads to tragedies of the commons? Answering such a question would require insights from fields such as city planning, urban aesthetics, architecture, and the psychology and sociology of place and space—but also, surely, from ecology, biology, and restoration ecology as well. The fundamental environmental question would be a political one: *What sort of environment ought we to live in?* What kind of world would be the best for us—and not just us, but also the many creatures, animate and not, with whom we share it—so that all of our lives can be flourishing ones, and the world we inhabit can be as beautiful as possible? And what practices ought we to engage in, as a community, to help bring that sort of world into being?

To imagine an environmental philosophy after the end of nature is to acknowledge that humans are not separate from the world, and not separate from their own actions in the world either, so that there's nothing fundamentally different between that part of the world that they have walked upon and changed and built and that part where they haven't. The idea that there is such a difference is finally a religious idea, and an environmental philosophy after the end of nature is one that rejects religion, rejects the idea that some spaces are sacred and others are profane or have been profaned by human action. We are not profane, or rather there is nothing to the distinction between the profane and the sacred, which is to say *there is nothing sacred.* The greatest advantage of such a philosophy is that it gives up the idea that there is something beyond us or above us to whose dictates we must submit unquestioningly, whether that something be God, or Nature (or nature), or the market. Whenever such a superior being is referred to, ventriloquism is taking place (and it's the ventriloquism of Oz, the worst kind of all). Our obligation in such cases is always to reveal the real speaker behind the curtains and insist that he or she too join the discourse in the same fallible spirit of humility (but also of commitment to rational justification and consensus) as the rest of us. In the case of God or Nature there's nothing really there except those who claim to speak for them, I think; in the case of the market, as I've tried to show, the situation is a little worse. For the humans behind the curtains in the case of the market are us (as Pogo said): our own actions when they are separated from each other turn into this practical power we feel impotent to overcome. But if we only act together and refuse to be separated from each other by the false idea of an individual action or choice with no externalities whatsoever, we can take that power back and work together to build a world that would be a good one, an environment in which we can feel at home and recognize both our connection to it and our connections to each other. An environmental philosophy after the end of nature would know that the world is nothing beyond us but also is nothing above or superior to us: it is something we are in as well as of, and that we make in all our actions. Our duty is simply to make it together, and to make it well.

Notes

Chapter 1: Against Nature

1. Richard Routley (Sylvan), "Is There a Need for a New, an Environmental Ethic?," in *Environmental Ethics,* ed. Andrew Light and Holmes Rolston III (Malden, MA: Blackwell, 2003), 47. [This essay was originally published in 1973.]

2. Holmes Rolston III, *Environmental Ethics: Duties to and Values in the Natural World* (Philadelphia: Temple University Press, 1988), xi.

3. J. Baird Callicott, *In Defense of the Land Ethic: Essays in Environmental Philosophy* (Albany: SUNY Press, 1989), 63.

4. Paul Taylor, *Respect for Nature* (Princeton, NJ: Princeton University Press, 1986), 3.

5. Christopher Stone, "Should Trees Have Standing?," *Southern California Law Review* 45 (1972): 456.

6. Andrew Light, "Ecological Restoration and the Culture of Nature: A Pragmatic Perspective," in *Restoring Nature: Perspectives from the Social Sciences and Humanities,* ed. Paul H. Gobster and R. Bruce Hull (Washington, DC: Island Press, 2000), 50.

7. Ibid., 64.

8. Bill McKibben, *The End of Nature* (New York: Anchor Books, 1989), 59.

9. Ibid., 58.

10. See Eric Katz, "The Big Lie: Human Restoration of Nature," in his *Nature as Subject: Human Obligation and Natural Community* (Lanham, MD: Rowman & Littlefield, 1997). I return to Katz in chapter 4.

11. But the book is more than twenty years old, and there has been no letup in the human transformation of the world. What was merely a prophecy then might simply be true now.

12. See, e.g., Peter M. Vitousek, and Harold A. Mooney, "Human Domination of Earth's Ecosystems," *Science* 277 (5325) (1997): 494–499.

13. See William Cronon, "The Trouble with Wilderness, or Getting Back to the Wrong Nature," J. Baird Callicott, "The Wilderness Idea Revisited: The Sustain-

able Development Alternative," and Ramachandra Guha, "Radical Environmentalism and Wilderness Preservation: A Third World Critique," all in *The Great New Wilderness Debate,* ed. J. Baird Callicott and Michael Nelson (Athens: University of Georgia Press, 1998). Cronon's critique of McKibben in many ways parallels my own: see pp. 486–487 of his essay.

14. See Roderick Nash, *Wilderness and the American Mind*, 3rd ed. (New Haven, CT: Yale University Press, 1982).

15. See Callicott, "The Wilderness Idea Revisited," 352–353; Cronon, "The Trouble with Wilderness," 482; and William Denevan "The Pristine Myth: The Landscape of the Americas in 1492," all in *The Great New Wilderness Debate*, ed. J. Baird Callicott and Michael Nelson. See also William Cronon, *Changes in the Land: Indians, Colonists, and the Ecology of New England* (New York: Hill & Wang, 1983).

16. Denevan, "The Pristine Myth," 418–429. See also Gary Paul Nabhan, "Cultural Parallax in Viewing North American Habitats," in Callicott and Nelson, *The Great New Wilderness Debate*, 628–641, and Charles Mann, *1491: New Revelations of the Americas before Columbus* (New York: Vintage Books, 2006).

17. Denevan, "The Pristine Myth," 425.

18. Ibid., 417.

19. Callicott, "The Wilderness Idea Revisited," 351–353.

20. Guha, "Radical Environmentalism," 236–238.

21. Callicott, "The Wilderness Idea Revisited," 354–355.

22. Guha, "Radical Environmentalism," 235.

23. Ibid., 240–242.

24. Cronon, "The Trouble with Wilderness," 484.

25. Ibid. Emphasis in original.

26. See Callicott, "The Wilderness Idea Revisited," 354; Guha, "Radical Environmentalism," 239; Cronon, "The Trouble with Wilderness," 484–485.

27. Cronon, "The Trouble with Wilderness," 490.

28. McKibben, *The End of Nature,* 32, 88. ("So what if it isn't nature primeval?" McKibben asks when he finds signs of human habitation such as old lawn chairs and rusted pipe while on a hike by a stream near his house, but he doesn't explain what the answer is to this question. If such indications of human action are only "reminders of the way that nature has endured and outlived and with dignity reclaimed so many schemes and disruptions of man," as he says, it isn't clear why the consequences of changing the temperature by a few degrees might not be a similar reminder.)

29. See Denevan, "The Pristine Myth," 418; see also Cronon, *Changes in the Land,* 49–52.

30. And when *did* the first human appear? And what does "human" mean here —*Homo sapiens*? What about earlier members of the genus? Or primates? Which ones? The "always already" is operative here too.

31. The best discussion of all these issues is Kate Soper's *What Is Nature?* (Oxford: Blackwell, 1995).

32. See Jacques Derrida, "Différance," in *Margins of Philosophy,* trans. Alan Bass (Chicago: University of Chicago Press, 1982), 9.

33. Actually, McKibben is not always that clear. He writes that the "end of nature" does not mean the "end of the world" but rather the end of "a certain set of human ideas about the world and our place in it" (*The End of Nature,* 8); elsewhere he says ideas can "go extinct," and that "the idea in this case is 'nature'" (48). But surely when he says that nature has ended he cannot mean that the *idea* of nature has ended—it obviously has not, otherwise even the title of his book would be unintelligible. The problem with trying to defend nature (or Santa Claus, or the Union of Soviet Socialist Republics) isn't that the *ideas* of these things don't exist, it's that there is nothing (anymore) in the real world that corresponds to the ideas—that they don't *refer* to anything.

34. Ibid., 64. Emphasis in original.

35. See Katz, *Nature as Subject,* 94. The original reference is from Lecture II of William James's *Pragmatism.*

36. McKibben, *The End of Nature*, 68–69.

37. Ibid., 64.

38. One interesting example is in David Kidner's essay, "Fabricating Nature: A Critique of the Social Construction of Nature," *Environmental Ethics* 22 (2000): 339–357. Kidner criticizes "social constructionism" about nature on one page for its anthropocentric image of a "discursively-defined *world ... from which nature is effectively excluded,*" while on the next he criticizes it because it offers "an entirely anthropocentric vision" in which "*all awareness of nature as existing independently of these [discursive] activities [is] denied*" (348–349; emphases added). Is the trouble that nature is *excluded* from the discursively defined world or that its independence (i.e., exclusion) from that world is *denied?*

39. John Stuart Mill, "Nature," in *Collected Works,* vol. 10 (Toronto: University of Toronto Press, 1963), 375. Hume had made a similar point in the *Treatise of Human Nature,* (Oxford: Clarendon Press, 1975), 473–475.

40. Of course, it might be possible for us to "imitate" nature in the second sense. But this would be an odd kind of imitation, where one tries to mimic the behavior of precisely that from which one by definition is entirely excluded.

41. Mill, "Nature," 373.

42. McKibben, *The End of Nature*, 83.

43. Are they concerned not that (lowercase) nature is itself being harmed but rather simply that its range is being limited—that in some sense the *ratio* of "natural" to "human" is decreasing? Frequently it does indeed sound this way, and McKibben's language suggests it too. But then note that the objection has to do with a change in Nature (understood now somehow as the sum of the "natural" plus the human), not with (lowercase) nature itself.

44. C. S. Lewis writes that "if ants had a language they would, no doubt, call their anthill an artifact and describe the brick wall in its neighbourhood as a *natural* object. *Nature* in fact would be for them all that was not 'ant-made.'" *Studies in Words* (Cambridge: Cambridge University Press, 1960), 45–46.

45. Mill, "Nature," 374.

46. And most usually the "actions" involved are those of ordinary sexual intercourse; I'm not thinking here of conceptions involving IVF or other technological mediation.

47. John Nolt, in an article attempting to calculate the harm caused by "the average American's greenhouse gas emissions," notes that exhalation is a source of such emissions, but then says that "for obvious moral reasons," he will not count them in his calculation. It would have been interesting to try to specify what those "obvious moral reasons" are. Do they depend on the idea that exhalation is natural while driving automobiles is not? "How Harmful Are the Average American's Greenhouse Gas Emissions?," *Ethics, Policy and Environment* 14 (2011): 3–10.

48. Katz, *Nature as Subject*, 104.

49. Andrew Brennan, *Thinking about Nature: An Investigation of Nature, Value and Ecology* (Athens: University of Georgia Press, 1988), 89.

50. Katz, *Nature as Subject,* 104.

51. This is the element that Brennan emphasizes, although he also denies that he is defending a distinction based on intention (*Thinking about Nature,* 91).

52. Thus Mill defines nature (in one sense) as "what takes place without the agency, or without the voluntary and intentional agency, of man" ("Nature," 375).

53. See, e.g., Katz, *Nature as Subject,* 122. Brennan thinks that childbirth provides the mother with an experience of "naturalness" because in it one "feel[s] one's body taken over in a way which leaves the agent with little intentional or voluntary control" (*Thinking about Nature*, 91). But anyone who has ever been in a high-speed automobile accident must know the same feeling, without this meaning that automobiles are natural objects or that driving (or crashing) is a natural activity. And after the accident the survivor may not be able any longer to avoid noticing that the absence of control is a necessary element in *all* driving; the laws of physics and chemistry that allow internal combustion engines to move us along highways at high speeds operate whether we intend them to or not. I return to this point in chapter 4.

54. It may in any case not even be true that this is a unique character of humans: the effects of phytoplankton, and (in the early days of life on Earth) of the first photosynthesizing bacteria on climate, for example, are or were immense.

55. Brennan defines natural human activity at one point just simply as "behaviour that is common to humans and other mammals" (*Thinking about Nature*, 88)—suggesting that whatever we do that other mammals also do (make babies, defecate, exhale) is natural while whatever we alone do (build factories, restore prairies, write poetry) is not. Here the anthropocentric claim that we are unique in our unnaturalness becomes tautological.

56. See Callicott, "The Wilderness Idea Revisited," 348.

57. Robert Elliott—to whom I return in chapter 4—compares humans to exotically introduced species that disrupt biological stability. Robert Elliot, *Faking Nature: The Ethics of Environmental Restoration* (London: Routledge, 1997), 122–123.

58. Aldo Leopold, *A Sand County Almanac* (New York: Oxford University Press, 1966), 240.

59. See Katz, *Nature as Subject,* 104; Elliot, *Faking Nature*, 123–124. Katz repeats this point in his recent return to this topic, "Further Adventures in the Case against Restoration," *Environmental Ethics* 34, no. 1 (2012): 76 (and elsewhere), admitting, however, that the reference to various items as lying on a "spectrum" between naturalness and humanness doesn't change the underlying dualism. (He also never makes clear how such a reference coheres with his insistence that "there is a fundamental ontological difference between artifacts and natural entities; they are different kinds of things" [71]. He seems to be willing to soften or relativize the distinction only when pushed.)

60. "A toxic waste dump is different from a compost heap of organic material," Katz writes (*Nature as Subject*, 104). "To claim that both are equally non-natural would obscure important distinctions." And yet he never clarifies what those distinctions are, or in what their importance consists.

61. Mill, "Nature," 377. (Mill denies that this is a third distinct meaning.)

62. Ibid., 385.

63. For a careful examination of this idea, see Holmes Rolston III, "Can and Ought We to Follow Nature?," in his *Philosophy Gone Wild* (Buffalo, NY: Prometheus Books, 1986), 30–52.

64. Derrida uses this phrase, in a context that has much in common with this one ("Différance," 27).

Chapter 2: The Social Construction of Nature

1. Georg Lukács, *History and Class Consciousness: Studies in Marxist Dialectics* (Cambridge, MA: MIT Press, 1971), 130.

2. William Cronon, "The Trouble with Wilderness, or Getting Back to the Wrong Nature," in *The Great New Wilderness Debate,* ed. J. Baird Callicott and Michael P. Nelson (Athens: University of Georgia Press, 1998), 482–483. The point being made here might also be taken—although I doubt Cronon has this in mind—as the sort of critique the young Marx made of Feuerbach.

3. See, e.g., Holmes Rolston III, "Nature for Real: Is Nature a Social Construct?" in *The Philosophy of the Environment,* ed. T. D. J. Chappell (Edinburgh: University of Edinburgh Press, 1997), 38–64; or David Kidner, "Fabricating Nature: A Critique of the Social Construction of Nature," *Environmental Ethics* 22 (2000): 343; or Anna Peterson, "Environmental Ethics and the Social Construction of Nature," *Environmental Ethics* 21 (1999): 339–357.

4. Kate Soper puts this clearly (*What Is Nature?* [Oxford: Blackwell, 1995], 151): "It is true that we can make no distinction between the 'reality' of nature and its cultural representation that is not itself conceptual, but this does not justify the conclusion that there is no ontological distinction between the ideas we have of nature and that which the ideas are about.... It is not language that has a hole in its ozone layer."

5. See, e.g., Eileen Crist, "Against the Social Construction of Nature and Wilderness," *Environmental Ethics* 26 (2004): 5–24.

6. Ian Hacking, *The Social Construction of What?* (Cambridge, MA: Harvard University Press, 1999).

7. Ibid., 6–7, 12–14. On unmasking, see 20, 53–54.

8. See Kidner, "Fabricating Nature," 345.

9. This, by the way, is why it seems quite misleading of McKibben to say that by "the end of nature" he means the end of an *idea*. It's clearly much more than that for him. See chapter 1, note 33.

10. As Tim Ingold, in his marvelous *The Perception of the Environment: Essays in Livelihood, Dwelling and Skill* (London: Routledge, 2000), writes, "First, environment is a relative term.... Just as there can be no organism without an environment, so also there can be no environment without an organism.... Secondly, the environment is never complete [but is] continually under construction.... [And] third ... the notion of environment ... should on no account be confused with the concept of nature. For the world can exist as nature only for a being that does not belong there, and that can look upon it, in the manner of a detached scientist, from such a safe distance that it is easy to connive in the illusion that it is unaffected by his presence. Thus the distinction between the environment and nature corresponds to the difference in perspective between seeing ourselves as beings *within* a world and as beings *without* it" (20).

11. Is it wrong to say "build" here? One could imagine the following objection: of course human beings *affect* their surroundings and have always done so, but that's not the same as saying that they *build* them. Yet building—as I shall argue below—is itself never ex nihilo: to build something *is* to "affect" some material and thereby to transform it into something new—wood into a bookcase, clay into a pot, silicon into a memory chip. Can we be said to build something even though we did not intend the effect our actions had? Sure we can: the failing brakes in a poorly made automobile, the leaky roof of a badly constructed home, the melted-down core of a failed nuclear power plant were all built, although none of them was intended by the builder. The building/affecting distinction, I would argue, is simply another version of the human/nature one, and just as subject to criticism. See chapter 5 for much more discussion of these issues.

12. See Ingold, *The Perception of the Environment,* 20, 188, 199.

13. For insightful criticisms of this kind of view, see Martin Heidegger, "The Age of the World Picture," in *The Question Concerning Technology and Other Essays*, trans. William Lovitt (New York: Harper & Row, 1977), as well as Ingold, *The Perception of the Environment,* chap. 12.

14. See Cronon, "The Trouble with Wilderness," 484: "the place where we are is the place where nature is not."

15. John Locke, *An Essay Concerning Human Understanding*, vol. 1 (New York: Dover, 1959), 390–392.

16. Mostly one finds this view attributed to "social constructionism" in various attacks on straw men. Several particularly egregious examples can be found in Michael E. Soulé and Gary Lease, eds., *Reinventing Nature? Responses to Postmodern Deconstruction* (Washington, DC: Island Press, 1995), such as Paul Shepherd's article in that collection titled "Virtually Hunting Reality in the Forests of Simulacra."

17. David Hume, *A Treatise of Human Nature*. (Oxford: Clarendon Press, 1975), 251–253. I'm oversimplifying a whole series of arguments, of course.

18. Karl Marx, *Theses on Feuerbach* 8. See also *Thesis* 1: "The chief defect of all hitherto existing materialism ... is that the thing, reality, sensuousness, is conceived only in the form of the object or of contemplation, but not as sensuous human activity, practice, not subjectively. Hence, in contradistinction to materialism, the active side was developed abstractly by idealism—which, of course, does not know real, sensuous activity as such." Karl Marx and Frederick Engels, *Collected Works,* vol. 5 (New York: International Publishers, 1976), 3–5.

19. See Georg Lukács's remarkable essay, "Reification and the Consciousness of the Proletariat," in *History and Class Consciousness*. Much of my argument in this chapter (and in this book) can be seen as an application of (some of) Lukács's ideas to environmental philosophy.

20. Is it possible yet to make approving reference to a set of philosophical ideas developed by Marx without readers assuming that one is a "Marxist" in the political sense? Marx's ideas about labor, alienation, and materialism/idealism are all analytically separable, it seems to me, from his economic ideas about the workings, and the future, of capitalism, not to speak of his political ideas about the proletarian struggle to form a communist society. There are doubtless relations among these ideas, but they are not the same. The (catastrophic) failure of "Marxism" as a political force in the twentieth century is absolutely not something that those who appeal to Marx's ideas can ignore, any more than Heidegger's full-throated support of Nazism can be ignored by those who find something valuable and inspiring in his work; but in neither case can the work be simply identified with the politics. Marx, in my view, was (among other things) a philosopher; I'm interested in the value his philosophy might have for the questions being examined here. That his philosophy bears connections to the catastrophes of the twentieth century must never be forgotten, but that fact alone does not allow us to reject it tout court.

21. And there's no doubt that Marx is inconsistent about rejecting this conception. Thus his well-known remark that "what distinguishes the worst of architects from the best of bees is this, that the architect raises his structure in imagination before he erects it in reality" falls back into the kind of dualism I am suggesting needs to be rejected. The architect doesn't raise the structure "in imagination"

(where's that?): he draws it, on paper. *Capital*, vol. 1 (New York: International Publishers, 1967), 178.

22. Martin Heidegger, *Being and Time,* trans. Edward Robinson and John Macquarrie (New York: Harper & Row, 1962), chap. 2.

23. Ibid., 88.

24. Ibid., sec. 16.

25. Heidegger calls this *Mitsein*. See ibid., sec. 26.

26. This is the real point of Marx's 11th thesis on Feuerbach—that philosophy has failed to see that understanding the world *is* changing it, and in that sense itself has failed adequately to understand the world (and therefore of course has failed to change it!).

27. See G. W. F. Hegel, *Science of Logic* (New York: Humanities Press, 1976), 121.

28. Gilles Deleuze and Félix Guattari, *A Thousand Plateaus,* trans. Brian Massumi (Minneapolis: University of Minnesota Press, 1987), 3–25.

Chapter 3: Alienation, Nature, and the Environment

1. Richard Louv, *Last Child in the Woods: Saving Our Children from Nature-Deficit Disorder* (Chapel Hill, NC: Algonquin Books, 2008).

2. A few random examples: J. Baird Callicott, *In Defense of the Land Ethic: Essays in Environmental Philosophy* (Albany: SUNY Press, 1989), 33; Val Plumwood, *Feminism and the Mastery of Nature* (London: Routledge, 1993), 1; Erazim Kohák, *The Embers and the Stars: A Philosophical Inquiry into the Moral Sense of Nature* (Chicago: University of Chicago Press, 1984), chap. 1. There are many more.

3. See G. W. F. Hegel, *Phenomenology of Spirit,* trans. A. V. Miller (New York: Oxford University Press, 1977), 65, 107–110.

4. Ibid., 118.

5. Ibid., 118.

6. Karl Marx and Friedrich Engels, *Collected Works,* vol. 3 (New York: International Publishers, 1975), 272 (hereafter *CW3*). Translation altered: see Karl Marx and Friedrich Engels, *Gesamtausgabe,* vol. 2 (Berlin: Dietz Verlag, 1982), 236.

7. *CW3*, 271–272.

8. Ibid., 276–277. Translation altered: see *Gesamtausgabe,* vol. 2, 240–241.

9. Karl Marx and Friedrich Engels, *Collected Works,* vol. 5 (New York: International Publishers, 1976), 38–39 (hereafter *CW5*). Translation altered: see Karl Marx and Friedrich Engels, *Die Deutsche Ideologie* (Berlin: Dietz Verlag, 1953), 40–41.

10. See chapter 2, pp. 59–63, above.

11. *CW5*, 40; Marx and Engels, *Die Deutsche Ideologie,* 42.

12. *CW5*, 40.

13. *CW3*, 303–304.

14. *CW5*, 47.

15. Ibid., 46–49.

16. Marx refers directly to Smith, ibid., 48.

17. Marx and Engels, *Die Deutsche Ideologie*, 30. It is translated in *CW5* as "fixation" (48).

18. Marx and Engels, *Die Deutsche Ideologie*, 31.

19. The concept of *Naturwüchsigkeit* is an important one in the present context; unfortunately, it is also difficult to translate. Jeremy J. Shapiro in his essay "The Slime of History" translates it as "embeddedness in nature," which doesn't seem quite right. See John O'Neill, ed., *On Critical Theory* (New York: Seabury Press, 1976), 145–163. The word refers to a kind of growth or development—the kind that arises in the absence of conscious human planning or control.

20. It is in the discussions in the *Grundrisse* that the word "alienation" is repeatedly used and that the lines of argument are explicitly (and strikingly) Hegelian ones. See, e.g., Karl Marx, *Grundrisse: Introduction to the Critique of Political Economy,* trans. Martin Nicolaus (New York: Vintage Books, 1973), 450–456, but also passim.

21. Karl Marx, *Capital,* vol. 1 (New York: International Publishers, 1967), 72.

22. Ibid., vol. 1, 71.

23. Ibid., vol. 1, 72. Translation altered: see Karl Marx, *Das Kapital,* Bd. 1 (Frankfurt: Verlag Marxistische Blätter, 1976), 86.

24. Ibid., vol. 1, 74.

25. Marx, *Grundrisse,* 157.

26. Ibid.

27. Marx, *Capital,* vol. 1, 75.

28. See, e.g., John Clark, "Marx's Inorganic Body," *Environmental Ethics* 11 (1989): 243–258, or Val Routley (Plumwood), "On Karl Marx as an Environmental Hero," *Environmental Ethics* 3 (1981): 237–244, or Robyn Eckersley, *Environmentalism and Political Theory* (Albany: SUNY Press, 1992), chap. 4.

29. See chapter 2, pp. 40–41, above.

30. Although again, they are the ancestors of very few of us. The issues here are very deep ones, and discussing them further would take us too far afield.

31. John Locke, *Two Treatises of Government* (Cambridge: Cambridge University Press, 1988), 298; Adam Smith, *The Wealth of Nations* (Baltimore, MD: Penguin Books, 1970), 116–117. See also chapter 2, p. 61, above.

32. The Heideggerian term for such items is the *Zuhanden.* Relating the issue under discussion here to Heidegger's important examination of the everyday environment in the first division of *Being and Time* would take us too far afield. It's worth noting, though, that even at those moments of failure when the *Zuhanden-*

heit of the tool collapses and we are left staring at the useless object in its bare *Vorhandenheit*, it is rare for the *builtness* of the object to come to the fore. "This damn envelope is too flimsy. I should have gone to Staples, not CVS," is a more likely response than an examination and critique of the social processes by which the envelope was made. Yet the fact that such an examination *is* possible, at least with respect to many objects in the environment, suggests an inner connection between *Zeug* and *Mitsein* that Heidegger never carefully investigates, and that might considerably complicate his account.

33. Should a distinction be drawn here between a *product* and an *effect*? We have *affected* the weather by burning fossil fuels; is it a mistake to say that we have *produced* it? I don't think so. The fact pointed out in the previous chapter that building always has some matter on which it works means that *things can only be produced by affecting other things*. The woodworker affects the wood; the product is a finished cabinet, but it could also be called wood that shows the effects of her work. Or does the distinction between product and (mere) effect have to do with what the producer intends? But surely one can produce something without intending to do so, as a factory can produce pollution while intending to generate electricity, or as a worker in the factory can help generate electricity while intending to earn a paycheck. Unintended products are still products—although often they are products of alienation. (See also note 11 of chapter 3, above.)

34. Georg Lukács, *History and Class Consciousness: Studies in Marxist Dialectics* (Cambridge, MA: MIT Press, 1979), 204.

Chapter 4: The Nature of Artifacts

1. Anna Peterson expresses this well: "If there is no 'real' nature, if all nature is constituted by human interpretation or intervention, then we have no grounds on which to evaluate one environment as better or worse or to resist some forms of intervention and support others" ("Environmental Ethics and the Social Construction of Nature," *Environmental Ethics* 21 [1999]: 346).

2. Martin H. Krieger, "What's Wrong With Plastic Trees?," *Science*, n.s., 179 (4072) (1973): 453.

3. Ibid., 451.

4. Ibid., 448.

5. Ibid., 453.

6. Mark Sagoff, "On Preserving the Natural Environment," *Yale Law Journal* 84 (1974): 205; Eric Katz, *Nature as Subject: Human Obligation and Natural Community* (Lanham, MD: Rowman & Littlefield, 1997), 112–113.

7. On terraforming Mars (and inventing ecosystems), see Frederick Turner, "The Invented Landscape," in *Beyond Preservation: Restoring and Inventing Landscapes,* ed. A. Dwight Baldwin, Jr., Judith De Luce, and Carl Pletsch (Minneapolis: University of Minnesota Press, 1994), as well as Keekok Lee, "Awe and Humility: Intrinsic Value in Nature. Beyond an Earthbound Environmental Ethics," *Royal Institute of Philosophy Supplement* 36 (1994): 89–101, and idem, *The Natural and the Artefactual* (Lanham, MD: Lexington Books, 1999), 172–180.

8. See chapter 1, p. 10, above.

9. Robert Elliot, "Faking Nature," *Inquiry* 25 (1982): 91–93.

10. See chapter 1, p. 3. Katz's article later appeared as chapter 8 of his book *Nature as Subject*, which develops his views in much more detail.

11. Katz, *Nature as Subject*, xix (on Kant) and 96 (on Elliot).

12. For details, see William K. Stevens, *Miracle under the Oaks: The Renewal of Nature in America* (New York: Pocket Books, 1995), and Stephanie Mills, *In Service of the Wild: Restoring and Reinhabiting Damaged Land* (Boston: Beacon Press, 1996), chap. 7.

13. Katz, *Nature as Subject*, 101.

14. Ibid., 102–103.

15. "It is impossible to imagine an artifact that is not designed to meet a human purpose, for without a foreseen use the object would not have been created" (ibid., 114). See also 122: "Artifacts ... stand in a necessary *ontological* relationship with human purpose."

16. See, e.g., ibid., 122.

17. See ibid., 95.

18. See ibid., 103: "the natural is defined as being independent of the actions of humanity." For additional discussion of Katz's dualism, see his recent rejoinder to critics (including me), "Further Adventures in the Case against Restoration," *Environmental Ethics* 34, no. 1 (2012): 76.

19. Katz, *Nature as Subject*, 129–130.

20. See ibid., 98; also 114–115.

21. Ibid., 127–129.

22. Ibid., 122, 98.

23. Ibid., 128.

24. See on this point Yeuk-Sze Lo, "Natural and Artifactual: Restored Nature as Subject," *Environmental Ethics* 21 (1999): 259.

25. Katz, *Nature as Subject*, 128–129; see also "Further Adventures in the Case against Ecological Restoration," 78–79.

26. See chapter 1, p. 19, above.

27. This is the line he takes in "Further Adventures in the Case against Ecological Restoration," claiming that the "side effects" of human activity are not artifacts (88). He refers in this context to Helene Siipi's article "Dimensions of Naturalness" (*Ethics and the Environment* 13, no. 1 [2008]: 78), which makes a similar claim. But that artifacts *have* side effects, including unintended ones, significantly complicates the assertion that they have "no nature *of their own*." Are an artifact's unintended side effects not part of its "nature"? Limiting its "nature" only to what its creator intended in it begs the question, making the claim that it has no nature of its own true simply by definition.

28. See Lo, "Natural and Artifactual," 253.

29. Katz's account of restoration sometimes seems misleading. He returns repeatedly to a book by Chris Maser on sustainable forestry to show the unnatural character of restoration, making much of Maser's apparently approving remark that "we are redesigning our forests from Nature's blueprint to humanity's blueprint"—a remark that certainly seems to indicate a desire to turn nature into something built by humans for human purposes and along human lines. Yet it's hard to believe that many of those who engage in restoration projects would accept this account of what they're up to. In fact, this seems a more accurate description of the kind of anthropocentric land management that has led to the environmental problems restorationists are attempting to redress. Instead, restorationists seem more likely to describe their own intentions as re-creating forests precisely *according* to "Nature's blueprint," or rather—since as Katz correctly points out Nature has no blueprint—simply in accordance with what they would have been like had humans never intervened in them. Quoted in Katz, *Nature as Subject*, 99, 125. The original reference is from Chris Maser, *The Redesigned Forest* (San Pedro, CA: R&E Miles, 1988), xvii.

30. Katz, *Nature as Subject*, 126.

31. Ibid., 122.

32. Quoted in Stevens, *Miracle under the Oaks,* 290.

33. In "Further Adventures," Katz describes the comparison between ecological restoration and child-rearing as "at the very least, disingenuous, and more likely, flat out incorrect." Restorers such as Packard, he says, have a "very precise idea of what type of ecosystem" they want to produce, which "is very unlike what parents do when they 'plan' to have a child." Packard, says Katz, was "trying to recreate the oak-savannah of the American mid-west before the arrival of European settlers," and he compares this to parents who aggressively attempt to produce a particular sort of child—a musical prodigy, say, or a doctor—and in doing so dysfunctionally overmanage their children's lives in a way that Katz says does indeed threaten to turn them into "artifacts" (82–83). But the supposed disanalogy here is unconvincing, and in fact is belied by Packard's own experiences: he and his volunteers did *not* intend to produce an oak savanna but rather were working to restore what they thought would be a (treeless) prairie. Like a parent who hopes to raise an athlete but discovers her uncoordinated child instead to be a gifted artist, they found themselves *surprised* by what they had (intentionally) brought into existence, and then, as good—not "dysfunctional"—parents do, they allowed and appreciated this, and did not try to force it to be something that was not in its "nature." See Stevens, *Miracle under the Oaks,* 81, and William R. Jordan, *The Sunflower Forest: Ecological Resoration and the New Communion with Nature* (Berkeley: University of California Press, 2003), 135–136.

34. Robert Elliot, *Faking Nature: The Ethics of Environmental Restoration* (London: Routledge, 1997), 108–110.

35. Ibid., 108.

36. Ibid., 109.

37. Katz, *Nature as Subject*, 109–110 and 116.

38. Katz actually says that "in my lucid rational moments, I realize that [the deer] are not 'wild'" (ibid., 116), but I'm not quite sure how to take this; it seems to suggest (1) that the rest of his essay is not lucid or rational, which is clearly false, and (2) that he has somehow been taken in by a forgery or lie of the very sort he's arguing against. (My view, of course, is that the deer *are* wild, even if they're not "natural." They may indeed be artifacts!)

39. Elliot, *Faking Nature*, 108.

40. Elliot points specifically to this issue in showing how his views remain opposed to those associated with restoration ecology; see ibid., 145.

41. See chapter 2. "Building," of course, in later Heidegger becomes an important and technical term—especially in the essay "Building Dwelling Thinking" (in *Poetry, Language, Thought* [New York: Harper Colophon, 1971, 141–161). My account of building is certainly influenced by Heideggerian ideas, but his key claim in that essay—that "building" is a form of "dwelling"—seems to me exactly wrong: dwelling (the way humans are in the world) must rather be understood as a form of building (of practice). Showing where Heidegger goes wrong in that essay, however, would take me too far afield.

42. And the gap is there too, it is worth noting, in the work of the social planner developing a policy, the entrepreneur starting a company, the developer building a mall, the democratic citizenry deciding on a course of action. I return to this point in the next chapter.

43. Compare on this point Tim Ingold's discussion of weaving and building in *The Perception of the Environment: Essays in Livelihood, Dwelling and Skill* (London: Routledge, 2000), chap. 18.

44. Heidegger, again: "When Dasein directs itself towards something and grasps it, it does not somehow first get out of an inner sphere in which it has been proximally encapsulated, but its primary kind of Being is such that it is always 'outside' alongside entities which it encounters and which belong to a world already discovered" (*Being and Time*, trans. Edward Robinson and John McQuarrie [New York: Harper and Row, 1962], 89). To be-in-the-world is to not find the world "other." I return to the idea of nature as otherness below.

45. See chapter 2 , p. 44, above.

46. See Turner "The Invented Landscape," and Jordan, *The Sunflower Forest*.

47. Andrew Light has argued similarly for the importance of the hands-on character of restoration projects as a way to "restore ... the human connection to nature by restoring that part of culture that has historically contained a connection to nature." See his "Ecological Restoration and the Culture of Nature: A Pragmatic Perspective," in *Restoring Nature: Perspectives from the Social Sciences and Humanities*, ed. Paul H. Gobster and R. Bruce Hull (Washginton, DC: Island Press, 2000), 49–70.

48. Elliot, *Faking Nature*, 145.

49. I have been very influenced in my thinking about this issue by Andrew Light, and in particular by the article cited above.

50. Elliot, *Faking Nature*, 86–90.

51. Elliot at one point briefly asks whether someone might find a value in an artificial wilderness if she knew the artifice, but dismisses the question quickly, writing that he "find[s] it difficult to see ... how art that mimics nature in quite this way would have any value at all" (*Faking Nature,* 89.) But "mimicry" scarcely seems the right word here, given the complexity of what would need to be achieved; only a misanthrope, it seems to me, could fail to find it impressive.

52. See Theodor Adorno, *Aesthetic Theory*, trans. C. Lenhardt (London: Routledge & Kegan Paul, 1984), 108–110.

53. We have considered something like this thesis above. Here it takes on a somewhat different, and more "postmodern," form.

54. See Jürgen Habermas, *The Philosophical Discourse of Modernity*, trans. Frederick Lawrence (Cambridge, MA: MIT Press, 1987), lectures 4 and 6; see also Thomas McCarthy, "The Politics of the Ineffable: Derrida's Deconstructionism," in *Ideals and Illusions: On Reconstruction and Deconstruction in Contemporary Critical Theory* (Cambridge, MA: MIT Press, 1991).

55. Derrida, "Différance," in *Margins of Philosophy*, trans. Alan Bass (Chicago: University of Chicago Press, 1982), 26.

Chapter 5: Thinking like a Mall

1. Aldo Leopold, *A Sand County Almanac* (New York: Oxford University Press, 1966), 137–41.

2. "Mega-Statistics Mark Mall," *Columbus Dispatch,* August 18, 1989, 4H.

3. "Shoppers' Delight—Tens of Thousands Visit Downtown Mall on Opening Day," *Columbus Dispatch,* August 19, 1989, 8D.

4. "Borrowing Success—New Indianapolis Downtown Mall Hopes to Mirror City Center's Triumph," *Columbus Dispatch,* November 10, 1995, 1H.

5. *Business First,* July 7, 1997.

6. "Teen Shot to Death in City Center—2 Held," *Columbus Dispatch,* May 28, 1994, 1A.

7. "There is a mixture between the two shopping centers that gives the consumer the greatest advantage," the general manager of Tuttle Crossing was quoted as saying before it opened. "It is truly a win-win for consumers. Based on where they are and what their needs are, they now have two dynamic shopping centers to satisfy their needs" ("Ralph Lauren Meets Bob Vila," *Columbus Monthly*, August 1997, 99).

8. "Downtown Site Was Death for Mall by '90s," *Columbus Dispatch*, February 4, 2009, 6A.

9. "Timeline," *Columbus Dispatch*, February 4, 2009, 6A.

10. "City Center Turns Vacant Space into Business-Services Center," *Columbus Dispatch*, March 22, 2002, 1F.

11. "Mall Hopes Soaps Will Boost Business," *Columbus Dispatch*, July 12, 2003, 1C.

12. "Accidental Tenants," *Other Paper*, May 2, 2006, 8–9.

13. "Anchor Abandons Ship," *Columbus Dispatch,* September 20, 2007, A1.

14. "GOP Candidate Challenges Coleman on Mall," *Columbus Dispatch,* May 15, 2007, 3B.

15. "Timeline," *Columbus Dispatch*, February 4, 2009, 6A.

16. "Goodbye City Center," *Columbus Dispatch*, February 4, 2009, 1A.

17. "Downtown Playground," *Columbus Dispatch,* May 27, 2011, 1A.

18. "Farewell to Penn Station," *New York Times,* October 30, 1963.

19. I have spent a fair amount of time looking for clear photographs of the mall's exterior, and they're strikingly difficult to find. When I discussed this with the helpful librarians at the Columbus Metropolitan Library they were clear about the answer: "It was so ugly nobody wanted to photograph it," they said.

20. See, e.g., the section "October" in *A Sand County Almanac.* See J. Baird Callicott, *In Defense of the Land Ethic: Essays in Environmental Philosophy* (Albany: SUNY Press, 1989), 17–18.

21. Leopold, *A Sand County Almanac*, 140.

22. When talking about the idea of a "land ethic," Leopold does gloss the idea of "land" in terms of a "biotic community," which suggests the relevance for him of the fact that the mountain is populated by living organisms. But malls are populated by them as well. See notes 23 and 28 below.

23. The article in *Columbus Monthly* welcoming the new mall spoke proudly of the 198,870 bricks, the 80,928 cinder blocks, and the 11,400 light fixtures that made it up—and pointed out as well the 83 planters containing 2,000 plants, the 14 trees, the 600 flowering plants inside the mall. Nature was there, too! ("Here Comes City Center. Ready. Set. Charge!," *Columbus Monthly*, September 1989, 43).

24. A useful set of essays on the topic of nature's autonomy is Thomas Heyd, ed., *Recognizing the Autonomy of Nature* (New York: Columbia University Press, 2005). See also Keekok Lee, *The Natural and the Artefactual* (Lanham, MD: Lexington Books, 1999).

25. "Mall Garage Said Safe Despite Cracks," *Columbus Dispatch,* August 26, 1992, 5B.

26. "A Special Store of Knowledge," *Columbus Dispatch*, September 28, 2004, 1A.

27. Sometimes one's intention in using an artifact might in fact be to frustrate one's own intentions: piggy banks, locks on refrigerators, alarm clocks, wedding rings (sometimes), and so forth. The locus classicus of this sort of thing is Odysseus's ingenious solution to the problem of how to listen to the Sirens. See Max Horkheimer and Theodor Adorno, *Dialectic of Enlightenment,* trans. Edmund Jephcott (Stanford, CA: Stanford University Press, 2002), 45–47.

28. And it's worth noting that some of these processes and properties were biological: the plants inside the mall photosynthesized, the humans inside exhaled, and the atmosphere inside the mall changed.

29. W. Murray Hunt, "Are *Mere Things* Morally Considerable?," *Environmental Ethics* 2 (1980): 59–65, and Kenneth Goodpaster, "On Being Morally Considerable," *Journal of Philosophy* 75, no. 6 (1978): 308–325.

30. See chapter 4, note 7.

31. Katz is clear, too, that life isn't even a sufficient condition for naturalness—as noted in the previous chapter, he calls domesticated animals and bioengineered species "living artifacts," and explicitly states that they "have no place in an environmental ethic since they are not natural entities" (*Nature as Subject: Human Obligation and Natural Community* [Lanham, MD: Rowman & Littlefield, 1997], 129; and see Katz, "Further Adventures in the Case against Ecological Restoration," *Environmental Ethics* 34, no.1 [2012], 79). Keekok Lee similarly writes that "domesticated plants are biotic artifacts." "Is Nature Autonomous?," in Heyd, *Recognizing the Autonomy of Nature*, 72n9. I return to this issue below.

32. Eric Katz, "The Liberation of Humanity and Nature," in Heyd, *Recognizing the Autonomy of Nature*, 82–84. I am grateful to George Mackaronis for first pointing out to me the relevance of debates in the rock-climbing community to these issues, and to Gina Weinberger for discussion of these and other matters.

33. Katz, "The Liberation of Humanity and Nature," 8. The reference is from Herbert Marcuse, *Counterrevolution and Revolt* (Boston: Beacon Press, 1972), 74.

34. Robert Elliot, "Environmental Ethics," in *A Companion to Ethics,* ed. Peter Singer (Oxford: Blackwell, 1993), 288, 291. (At 292 he mentions a "variant of the everything ethic which includes in its scope all natural items," but never mentions any artifacts at any point.)

35. Lee, *The Natural and the Artefactual,* 85.

36. This sort of view—as I argued in chapter 1—always faces the problem that it simply repeats, in an inverted fashion, a quasi-Cartesian dualism that treats humans as at least partly supernatural. Lee tries to solve this problem by calling her view "dyadism" and trying to distinguish it from the anthropocentric "dualism" she criticizes for treating humans as superior to nature; she refers to Val Plumwood's related notion of "hyperseparation" to ground the distinction, connecting it (as Plumwood does) to an Enlightenment modernism that denigrates the natural in favor of the human. But Plumwood (in *Feminism and the Mastery of Nature* [London: Routledge, 1993]) describes "hyperseparation" as "radical exclusion," characterized as involving "not merely a difference of degree within a sphere of overall similarity, but a major difference in kind, even a bifurcation or division in reality between utterly different orders of things" (49–50), which sure sounds to me like what Lee is doing when she describes the difference between the natural and the artifactual as "ontological" in character, and distinguishes it as a "primary" characteristic separate from any "secondary" or empirical characteristics that might be taken to distinguish the two realms. (This last is her way of dealing with the problem raised by Krieger that awakened Katz from his dogmatic slumbers.) Lee keeps repeating that "dualism" treats nature as inferior and insignificant, while "dyadism" treats it with respect; she doesn't see the way in which the latter treats *artifacts* as inferior and insignificant (incapable, for example, of having a

good or a telos of their own), and so could be seen simply as a dualism with the signs reversed. See Lee, *The Natural and the Artefactual,* 180–184.

37. Katz, "The Liberation of Humanity and Nature," 82.

38. Ibid., 84.

39. Goodpaster, "On Being Morally Considerable," 320. See also G. J. Warnock, *The Object of Morality* (New York: Methuen, 1971), 150–152, and Joel Feinberg, "The Rights of Animals and Unborn Generations," in *Philosophy and Environmental Crisis,* ed. William T. Blackstone (Athens: University of Georgia Press, 1974), 51.

40. Feinberg, "The Rights of Animals," 51; Goodpaster, "On Being Morally Considerable," 318–320. It should be noted, though, that Feinberg follows up his remark by adding that "this is a case, however, where 'what we say' should not be taken seriously." See note 42 below.

41. Christopher Stone, "Should Trees Have Standing?," *Southern California Law Review* 45 (1972): 471.

42. Feinberg, in fact, makes the same point, similarly taking it as a reductio ("The Rights of Animals," 51–52). Like Hunt, he offers no argument as to where the absurdity comes from, beyond suggesting that we simply don't talk this way. But we don't usually talk as though plants or animals have rights either, and yet some have suggested that they do. Ordinary language isn't always alright.

43. Paul Taylor, *Respect for Nature: A Theory of Environmental Ethics* (Princeton, NJ: Princeton University Press, 1986), 15–16. By "moral subjects" Taylor means what others would describe as "moral patients" or even (confusingly) "moral objects": that is, entities that deserve moral consideration but may not themselves be moral *agents.*

44. Ibid., 62–63.

45. Ibid., 67.

46. And further, perhaps Mr. Taubman chose to build the mall in Columbus (rather than, say, Indianapolis) because there was a pastry shop in Columbus whose almond croissants he particularly enjoyed, and he knew that building a mall there meant frequent visits and hence frequent opportunities to breakfast at it. That would be *his* purpose, but surely not the *mall's* purpose. Less hypothetically, the revitalization of a depressed downtown was surely one of the purposes behind the mall's construction—but again, it was not a purpose of the mall itself.

47. Taylor, *Respect for Nature*, 61; emphasis in original.

48. R. G. Frey makes a similar point in his article "Rights, Interests, Desires and Beliefs," *American Philosophical Quarterly* 16, no. 3 (1979): 234.

49. Taylor, *Respect for Nature*, 123–124.

50. Ibid., 53; emphasis added.

51. Ibid., 55; second emphasis added.

52. Ronald Sandler and John Basl suggest in a recent article that there is no way to block the move from the claim that nonsentient living things have a "good of

their own" to the same claim about, first, "synthetic" biotic organisms but also, second, even nonliving artifacts, a conclusion to which I'm quite sympathetic. My argument for the conclusion is different, though, and depends on the fact that artifacts escape our control (are wild), not on what Sandler and Basl call the "selection etiology" through which they came to have the characteristics they do ("The Good of Non-sentient Entities: Organisms, Artifacts, and Synthetic Biology," *Studies in History and Philosophy of Biological and Biomedical Sciences,* 2013, http://dx.doi.org/10.1016/j.shpsc.2013.05.017).

53. Taylor, *Respect for Nature*, 66.

54. Ibid., 66–67.

55. See Jennifer Price, "Looking for Nature at the Mall: A Field Guide to the Nature Company," in *Uncommon Ground: Rethinking the Human Place in Nature,* ed. William Cronon (New York: Norton, 1996).

56. Taylor, I must concede, might offer a different objection here: he is quite insistent that his view finds moral considerability only in *individual* organisms, not in larger wholes such as ecosystems of which individual organisms are simply viewed as members (*Respect for Nature*, 118–119). The quasi-teleological character I am claiming for the mall might depend on the sort of holism that he rejects. But frankly, he doesn't offer much of an argument against that holism, beyond rhetorically asking how we could have an obligation to consider the good of a whole unless we already had an obligation to consider the good of the organisms that constitute it. This scarcely seems convincing, first because individual organisms are also in a certain sense wholes (and respecting the good of a tree doesn't require respecting the good of its branches), and second because in any case, nothing said here—or for that matter by a Leopoldian holist—denies that individual organisms too might be morally considerable. To say we should consider City Center morally doesn't imply that we shouldn't also consider, say, Abercrombie and Fitch.

57. I don't actually know if this *was* the cause of its demise. But it might have been.

58. Leopold, *A Sand County Almanac*, 254.

59. Robin Attfield, "The Good of Trees," *Journal of Value Inquiry* 15, no. 1 (1981): 39.

60. Ibid., 41–42.

61. Man is born from man, Aristotle famously says, but bed is not born from bed (*Physics,* II.1 193b9). This is supposed to be the difference between natural entities and artifacts. And yet malls do seem to bequeath other malls, and there even turns out to be a family resemblance between parent and child. (Just as Starbucks apparently bequeath other Starbucks, like dandelions on an untended field.) Furthermore, some men, or more to the point women, cannot bear children at all, and require technological assistance to do so. (And the same is true of mules, and corn, and fruit trees.) In any case, why should ability to reproduce be the key factor in determining whether something has a "nature of its own" or not, without begging the question?

62. Attfield, "The Good of Trees," 42.

63. See Richard (Sylvan) Routley, "Is There a Need for a New, an Environmental Ethic?," in *Environmental Ethics,* ed. Andrew Light and Holmes Rolston III (Malden, MA: Blackwell, 2003), 49–50.

64. Mary Midgley, "Duties Concerning Islands," in *Environmental Ethics,* ed. Robert Elliot (Oxford: Oxford University Press, 1995), 89.

65. Relevant here is the marvelous book by Alan Weisman, *The World without Us* (New York: Thomas Dunne Books, 2007).

66. Like Keekok Lee. See "Awe and Humility: Intrinsic Value in Nature. Beyond an Earthbound Environmental Ethics," *Royal Institute of Philosophy Supplement* 36 (1994): 96, where she explicitly asserts that "even the most beautiful, exquisite or complicated human artifact, like the Pieta, the Alhambra or a nuclear power station," could be destroyed in a last person situation without any loss of value from the world.

Chapter 6: The Silence of Nature

1. Bruno Latour, *Pandora's Hope: Essays on the Reality of Science Studies* (Cambridge, MA: Harvard University Press, 1999), 281.

2. Jane Bennett, *Vibrant Matter: A Political Ecology of Things* (Durham, NC: Duke University Press, 2010), 23–24.

3. Ibid., 112.

4. Ibid., 118; emphasis in original.

5. Ibid., 34.

6. Ibid., 29.

7. Ibid., 98–100, 119–120.

8. Ibid., 120.

9. Ibid., 31. Bennett goes on to say that nonetheless, "it may be relevant to note the extent to which intentional reflectivity is also a product of the interplay of human and nonhuman forces," quoting Bernard Stiegler on the role played by tool use in the constitution of human psychological "interiority." Stiegler's point is a good one, but to refer to it here is a non sequitur: the issue isn't whether intentional reflectivity requires nonhuman material objects in order to come into existence—surely it does—but whether it exists *in* those nonhuman material objects themselves. It's silly to suggest that it does the latter.

10. Ibid., 31–32.

11. Ibid., 20, 57. Most emphases added.

12. See ibid., 4, e.g., where Bennett writes that the upcoming pages "will highlight the extent to which human being and thinghood overlap, the extent to which the us and the it slip-slide into each other. One moral of the story is that we are also nonhuman and that things, too, are vital players in the world." The latter sentence presents itself as a symmetrical inversion, but actually it isn't: humans are said to

also be thinglike, but things are only said to *vital,* which is not the same as saying they're human.

13. Bennett repeatedly speaks (e.g., 63–64, 76, 77) of "calculability" or "quantification" as the problem with nonvitalist views, which strikes me as a mistake; I have spoken above of the difficulty of predicting what matter will do, or of the necessary operation of forces that one does not understand or conceptually grasp, but I don't see that this is a matter of improperly using quantitative methods or otherwise "calculating." Quantification and calculation face the same difficulties, as the Pythagoreans were perhaps the first to notice.

14. Ibid., 65.

15. For the threads, see Latour, *Pandora's Hope,* 43–44; pedocomparator, 47–54; notebook with the Munsell code, 58–61; "earth-tasting," 61–63. For a discussion of the diagrams, see 56–57 and 64–67.

16. Ibid., 48–49.

17. Ibid., 78–79.

18. Ibid., 49. And see 60, where Latour similarly writes of "the practical Platonism that turns dust into an Idea via the two callused hands firmly holding a notebook/instrument/calibrator."

19. Ibid., 64.

20. Ibid., 63. The literal conversation as quoted by Latour is a little confusing. I've tried to make sense out of it but might have gotten it wrong. The structure of disagreement followed by consensus is clear, though.

21. See, e.g., Bruno Latour, *We Have Never Been Modern,* trans. Catherine Porter (Cambridge, MA: Harvard University Press, 1993), 142–145, and *Politics of Nature: How to Bring the Sciences into Democracy,* trans. Catherine Porter (Cambridge, MA: Harvard University Press, 2004), esp. chap. 2.

22. Latour, *Pandora's Hope*, 89.

23. Ibid., 187.

24. *Non*-natural entities, such as artifacts, are rarely included here, as I have pointed out.

25. Latour, *Pandora's Hope*, 140–141. The argument that we have to learn to "listen to nature" is a familiar one; for examples, see Val Plumwood, *Environmental Culture: The Ecological Crisis of Reason* (London: Routledge, 2002), 189–195, and John Dryzek, "Green Reason: Communicative Ethics for the Biosphere," *Environmental Ethics* 12, no. 3 (1990): 195–210.

26. And by "nature" here I mean, of course, nonhuman entities in the world.

27. The key figure in contemporary philosophy who has emphasized this point is Jürgen Habermas. See, e.g., "Discourse Ethics," in *Moral Consciousness and Communicative Action*, trans. Christian Lenhardt and Shierry Weber Nicholson (Cambridge, MA: MIT Press, 1990), or "What Is Universal Pragmatics," in *On the Pragmatics of Communication*, ed. Maeve Cook (Cambridge, MA: MIT Press, 1998).

28. Scott Friskics, "Dialogical Relations with Nature," *Environmental Ethics* 23, no. 4 (2001): 391–410.

29. Ibid., 392.

30. Ibid., 394.

31. Ibid., 399.

32. Friskics claims that artifacts speak too. "We live in an incredibly noisy world," he writes, in which "the quiet whispers and silent speech of [natural] things can't be heard over the clamor of our engines, computers, TVs, radios, and all the rest." But when artifacts speak, "they lack the eloquence and depth of creatures.... They don't speak of themselves. Instead, they speak primarily of the function and purpose for which they have been made" (ibid., 399).

33. Ibid., 396.

34. He quotes Henry Bugbee as describing our relation to other beings as one of "*appel et réponse,*" and then says that "our being-together [with such beings] might best be described in terms of a dialogue" (ibid., 395). Yet call-and-response is not dialogue but something quite different: the relation of an authoritative speaker and an awe-filled respondent.

35. Ibid., 397.

36. Ibid., 395–396; emphases added.

37. David Abram, *The Spell of the Sensuous: Perception and Language in a More-Than-Human World* (New York: Pantheon, 1996), 175–176.

38. Ibid., 156–162.

39. Ibid., 158–159.

40. Ibid., 162; emphasis in original.

41. I am grateful to my former colleague David Goldblatt, whose work first helped me see the philosophical significance of ventriloquism. See his *Art and Ventriloquism* (New York: Routledge, 2005).

42. See, e.g., Abram, *The Spell of the Sensuous*, 7, 88, 256.

43. See Latour, *Politics of Nature,* 9–10.

44. Ibid., 14; emphasis in original.

45. This is not to say that I cannot come to the conclusion that the opinions my interlocutors express are *not* genuinely theirs: perhaps they are joking, or under hypnosis, or repeating what they have been trained to say by the corporation they work for. But such a conclusion would mean that what we are doing can no longer be understood as engaging in dialogue, and so my appropriate response would be something else—to laugh, to undo the hypnosis, to speak to someone able to take (justificatory) responsibility for corporate policy, and so on.

46. Donna Haraway offers a different although related objection to ventriloquism in "The Promises of Monsters: Reproductive Politics for Inappropriate/d Others," in *Cultural Studies,* ed. Larry Grossberg, Cary Nelson, and Paula Treichler (New York: Routledge, 1992), 311–312. In my view, though, she fails to draw the key

distinction between translation and ventriloquism, and (like Latour) fails to give sufficient attention to the significance of language-use and its absence.

47. Thus I am not asserting that it is conceptually impossible to imagine any nonhuman capable of speech; surely that's not the case. The point is simply that as an empirical matter, nonhuman entities do not appear to be capable of the sort of dialogical speech I have been discussing, and that this incapacity seems not to be the result of any "disability" on their part or of our failure to understand their language. If it turned out that animals, or shopping malls, *could* engage in dialogue, then the situation would be quite different—and we would be obliged, I would say, to treat them in the same way we do all other potential interlocutors.

48. Again, they may provide me with *evidence* for or against my claims. But whether the evidence is *good* evidence I can only decide by talking to *you*, not to them.

Chapter 7: Democracy and the Commons

1. Of course, there are those who deny its existence or reject standard accounts of its causes. Their skepticism, it seems to me, is based on a bad epistemology, or on unexamined prejudices, or sometimes on bad faith. The philosophical problems raised by climate change denial are actually complicated ones, but I cannot deal with them fully here. Throughout most of this chapter I ignore the issue of "deniers," and assume—as is the case for the vast majority of those who examine the question—that the reality and the seriousness of the phenomenon of global warming are well understood by all. Later, though, I will return briefly to this issue.

2. See chapter 3, note 18.

3. Garrett Hardin, "The Tragedy of the Commons," *Science* 162 (3859) (1968): 1244.

4. See Stephen M. Gardiner, *A Perfect Moral Storm: The Ethical Tragedy of Climate Change* (Oxford: Oxford University Press, 2011), for a detailed analysis of climate change and other environmental problems in terms of collective action problems. Gardiner offers reasons to believe that the intergenerational aspect of climate change problems (and the time-asymmetry that it introduces) makes those problems even more intractable than standard commons problems or prisoner's dilemmas. A full investigation of that issue is beyond the scope of this book.

5. Hardin, "Tragedy," 1247.

6. Jason Kawall, "Rethinking Greed," in *Ethical Adaptation to Climate Change: Human Virtues of the Future,* ed. Allen Thompson and Jeremy Bendik-Keymer (Cambridge, MA: MIT Press, 2012), 223.

7. Ibid., 224–229.

8. Ibid., 228. Emphasis in original. Although Kawall *almost* notes that the fault lies in the *cumulative* effects of one's acts, not in the individual acts themselves, he's clearly imagining here an aggregation of the effects over one lifetime, not over many different agents.

9. Similarly in the same volume Jeremy Bendik-Keymer calls contemporary Americans "wanton" for the "thoughtlessness" with which their behaviors are leading to the mass extinctions of species, while Stephen Gardiner writes an essay whose title poses the incendiary question "Are We the Scum of the Earth?" and makes clear throughout that the obvious answer is yes. See Jeremy Bendik-Keymer, "The Sixth Mass Extinction Is Caused by Us," in Thompson and Bendik-Keymer, *Ethical Adaptation to Climate Change*, 266–269, and Stephen Gardiner, "Are We the Scum of the Earth?," in Thompson and Bendik-Keymer, *Ethical Adaptation to Climate Change*, 241–259. Philip Cafaro gives a kind of summary of this sort of reasoning in his essay "Gluttony, Arrogance, Greed, and Apathy: An Exploration of Environmental Vice," in *Environmental Virtue Ethics*, ed. Ronald Sandler and Philip Cafaro (Lanham, MD: Rowman & Littlefield, 2005), 153: "Why do we harm nature? Because we are selfish. Because we are gluttonous, arrogant, greedy, and apathetic. Because we do not understand our obligations to others or our own self-interest." I think almost every word of this is wrong.

10. Derek Parfit, *Reasons and Persons* (Oxford: Clarendon Press, 1984), 62.

11. Suppose, for example, the agents are all strict altruists and E is some sort of self-sacrificial act. (Six altruists are left on a sinking ship, say, with a lifeboat that holds only five. They each go to their rooms to prepare, where each has a gun, and must each decide whether to commit suicide or not.)

12. Dale Jamieson, "Ethics, Public Policy, Global Warming," in *Morality's Progress: Essays on Humans, Other Animals and the Rest of Nature* (Oxford: Clarendon Press, 2002), 83.

13. Ibid., 84.

14. Walter Sinnott-Armstrong, "It's Not *My* Fault: Global Warming and Individual Moral Obligations," in *Perspectives on Climate Change: Science, Economics, Politics, Ethics,* ed. Walter Sinnott-Armstrong and Richard B. Howarth (Burlington, VT: Emerald Group Publishing, 2005), 293. The limitation of the idea of "harm" to individual humans or animals isn't crucial to the argument here. McKibben, for instance, sees the harm caused by global warming as consisting in part in the destruction of "nature" in the sense of a world unaffected by human action, but doing so doesn't prevent the same problem from arising: my own individual Sunday joyride does essentially nothing to *further* destroy nature more than it would be destroyed if I stayed home.

15. Ibid., 304. Emphasis added.

16. Ibid., 287.

17. Ibid., 292.

18. Ronald Sandler, "Ethical Theory and the Problem of Inconsequentialism: Why Environmental Ethicists Should Be Virtue Oriented Ethicists," *Journal of Agricultural and Environmental Ethics* 23 (2010): 167–183, and Dale Jamieson, "When Utilitarians Should be Virtue Theorists," *Utilitas* 19, no. (2007): 160–183.

19. Sandler, "Ethical Theory and the Problem of Inconsequentialism," 176.

20. Jamieson, "When Utilitarians Should Be Virtue Theorists," 167.

21. Ronald Sandler, *Character and Environment: A Virtue-Oriented Approach to Environmental Ethics* (New York: Columbia University Press, 2007), 28.

22. Sandler, "Ethical Theory and the Problem of Inconsequentialism," 176; see Jamieson, "When Utilitarians Should be Virtue Theorists," 167.

23. Joakim Sandberg, "'*My* Emissions Make No Difference': Climate Change and the Argument from Inconsequentialism," *Environmental Ethics* 33 (2011): 241. For a similar argument (without the reference to climate change), see Frank Jackson, "Group Morality," in *Metaphysics and Morality,* ed. Philip Pettit, Richard Sylvan, and Jean Norman (Oxford: Basil Blackwell, 1987).

24. Sandberg, "'*My* Emissions Make No Difference,'" 247.

25. Baylor L. Johnson, "Ethical Obligations in a Tragedy of the Commons," *Environmental Values* 12 (2003): 284.

26. Jonathan Glover, "It Makes No Difference Whether I Do It: Part I," *Proceedings of the Aristotelian Society*, Supplementary Volumes, 49 (1975): 174–175. Parfit (*Reasons and Persons,* 511) explicitly refers to it as the foundation of his discussion, and Jackson too refers to it ("Group Morality," 96–98). (Jackson raises the number of villagers and beans and robbers to one thousand).

27. Glover, "It Makes No Difference Whether I Do It," 174–175.

28. And to make the point even more decisively, we could imagine not one hundred but ten thousand hungry visitors, each of whom merely steals a single bean from a single bowl.

29. Virginia Held, "Can a Random Collection of Individuals Be Morally Responsible?," *Journal of Philosophy* 67, no. 14 (1970): 471–481.

30. Ibid., 476–477.

31. Ibid., 479. See also 471.

32. I'd rather talk here of the absence of a forum than the absence of a "decision method." Decision methods themselves have to be chosen (have to be, one might say, decided upon); prior to the employment of a decision method, that is, there needs already to be some process in which the members of the group agree as to what that method will be. It's that process that I'm calling a forum. See Jon Elster, "The Market and the Forum: Three Varieties of Political Theory," in *Deliberative Democracy,* ed. James Bohman and William Rehg (Cambridge, MA: MIT Press, 1997), 3–33.

33. I'm changing the traditional account here to highlight the point I want to make. One change is small, but significant: it's the prisoners' dilemma, not the prisoner's dilemma. It's *one* dilemma, faced by a collective of two. It's not two dilemmas faced by two individuals. The problem arises for them *together*—although to be sure it only arises as a dilemma because they are kept separate from each other, and so they cannot solve it together but have to do so monologically. The other change doesn't affect the structure of the problem, but is meant to show its moral poignancy: I'm assuming that they're innocent.

34. See Elinor Ostrom, *Governing the Commons: The Evolution of Institutions for Collective Action* (Cambridge: Cambridge University Press, 1990).

35. Thomas Hobbes, *Leviathan* (New York: Collier Books, 1962), 129.

36. See Sandler, "Ethical Theory and the Problem of Inconsequentialism," 172n5, also 169.

37. Jürgen Habermas, *Legitimation Crisis,* trans. Thomas McCarthy (Boston: Beacon Press, 1975), 108. And, of course, the "participants" here—the "everyone involved"—include all those capable of taking part in the discussion. See chapter 6.

38. See Jürgen Habermas, *Moral Consciousness and Communicative Action*, trans. Christian Lenhardt and Shierry Weber Nicholson (Cambridge, MA: MIT Press, 1990), 58.

39. This has been a central point of Latour's for many years, and I am absolutely in agreement with him about it. See especially *Politics of Nature: How to Bring the Sciences into Democracy,* trans Catherine Porter (Cambridge, MA: Harvard University Press, 2004), chap. 1, as well as his *Love Your Monsters* (Breakthrough Institute, 2011), Kindle.

40. Why? Because self-consciousness is better than unconsciousness. I have nothing deeper to say on this point than that.

41. To say they are "ruled out," of course, is not to say that they are *prohibited*, since freedom to express *any* view is itself one of those necessary procedural presuppositions. It is simply to say that they do in fact possess this self-contradictory character, which would presumably become clear to all those involved in the discourse once it is noticed.

Bibliography

Abram, David. *The Spell of the Sensuous: Perception and Language in a More-Than-Human World*. New York: Pantheon, 1996.

Abram, David. Between the Body and the Breathing Earth: A Reply to Ted Toadvine. *Environmental Ethics* 27 (2) (2005): 179–180.

Adorno, Theodor. *Aesthetic Theory*. Trans. C. Lenhardt. London: Routledge & Kegan Paul, 1984.

Adorno, Theodor. *Äesthetische Theorie*. Frankfurt: Suhrkamp Taschenbuch, 1990.

Aristotle. *Basic Works*. New York: Random House, 1941.

Attfield, Robin. The Good of Trees. *Journal of Value Inquiry* 15 (1) (1981): 35–54.

Baber, Walter F., and Robert V. Bartlett. *Deliberative Environmental Politics: Democracy and Ecological Rationality*. Cambridge, MA: MIT Press, 2005.

Baden, John A., and Douglas S. Noonan, eds. *Managing the Commons*. 2nd ed. Bloomington: Indiana University Press, 1998.

Baldwin, A. Dwight, Jr., Judith De Luce, and Carl Pletsch, eds. *Beyond Preservation: Restoring and Inventing Landscapes*. Minneapolis: University of Minnesota Press, 1994.

Basl, John, and Ronald Sandler. The Good of Non-sentient Entities: Organisms, Artifacts, and Synthetic Biology. *Studies in History and Philosophy of Biological and Biomedical Sciences*, 2013. http://dx.doi.org/10.1016/j.shpsc.2013.05.017.

Bendik-Keymer, Jeremy. The Sixth Mass Extinction Is Caused by Us. In *Ethical Adaptation to Climate Change: Human Virtues of the Future,* ed. Thompson and Bendik- Keymer, 263–280.

Bennett, Jane. *Vibrant Matter: A Political Ecology of Things*. Durham, NC: Duke University Press, 2010.

Bennett, Jane, and William Chaloupka, eds. *In the Nature of Things*. Minneapolis: University of Minnesota Press, 1993.

Biro, Andrew. *Denaturalizing Ecological Politics: Alienation from Nature from Rousseau to the Frankfurt School and Beyond*. Toronto: University of Toronto Press, 2005.

Biro, Andrew, ed. *Critical Ecologies: The Frankfurt School and Contemporary Environmental Crises.* Toronto: University of Toronto Press, 2011.

Brennan, Andrew. *Thinking about Nature: An Investigation of Nature, Value and Ecology.* Athens: University of Georgia Press, 1988.

Brown, Charles S., and Ted Toadvine, eds. *Eco-Phenomenology: Back to the Earth Itself.* Albany: SUNY Press, 2003.

Cafaro, Philip. Gluttony, Arrogance, Greed, and Apathy: An Exploration of Environmental Vice. In *Environmental Virtue Ethics,* ed. Sandler and Cafaro, 135–158.

Callicott, J. Baird, ed. *Companion to A Sand County Almanac.* Madison: University of Wisconsin Press, 1987.

Callicott, J. Baird. *In Defense of the Land Ethic: Essays in Environmental Philosophy.* Albany: SUNY Press, 1989.

Callicott, J. Baird. The Wilderness Idea Revisited: The Sustainable Development Alternative. In *The Great New Wilderness Debate*, ed. Callicott and Nelson, 337–366.

Callicott, J. Baird, and Michael P. Nelson, eds. *The Great New Wilderness Debate.* Athens: University of Georgia Press, 1998.

Cameron, W. S. K. Tapping Habermas's Discourse Theory for Environmental Ethics. *Environmental Ethics* 31 (4) (2009): 339–357.

Clark, John. Marx's Inorganic Body. *Environmental Ethics* 11 (1989): 243–258.

Crist, Eileen. Against the Social Construction of Nature and Wilderness. *Environmental Ethics* 26 (1) (2004): 5–24.

Cronon, William. *Changes in the Land: Indians, Colonists, and the Ecology of New England.* New York: Hill & Wang, 1983.

Cronon, William. The Trouble with Wilderness, or Getting Back to the Wrong Nature. In *The Great New Wilderness Debate*, ed. Callicott and Nelson, 471–499.

Cronon, William, ed. *Uncommon Ground: Rethinking the Human Place in Nature.* New York: Norton, 1996

Deleuze, Gilles, and Félix Guattari. *A Thousand Plateaus.* Trans. Brian Massumi. Minneapolis: University of Minnesota Press, 1987.

Denevan, William. The Pristine Myth: The Landscape of the Americas in 1492. In *The Great New Wilderness Debate*, ed. Callicott and Nelson, 414–442.

Derrida, Jacques. Différance. In *Margins of Philosophy.* Trans. Alan Bass. Chicago: University of Chicago Press, 1982.

Dobson, Andrew, and Robyn Eckersley, eds. *Political Theory and the Ecological Challenge.* Cambridge: Cambridge University Press, 2006.

Dryzek, John. Green Reason: Communicative Ethics for the Biosphere. *Environmental Ethics* 12 (3) (1990): 195–210.

Elliot, Robert. Environmental Ethics. In *A Companion to Ethics*, ed. Peter Singer, 284–293. Oxford: Blackwell, 1993.

Elliot, Robert. Faking Nature. *Inquiry* 25 (1) (1982): 81–93.

Elliot, Robert. *Faking Nature: The Ethics of Environmental Restoration*. London: Routledge, 1997.

Elster, Jon. The Market and the Forum: Three Varieties of Political Theory. In *Deliberative Democracy*, ed. James Bohman and William Rehg, 3–33. Cambridge, MA: MIT Press, 1997.

Feinberg, Joel. The Rights of Animals and Unborn Generations. In *Philosophy and Environmental Crisis*, ed. William T. Blackstone, 43–68. Athens: University of Georgia Press, 1974.

Foster, John Bellamy. *Marx's Ecology*. New York: Monthly Review Press, 2000.

Frey, R. G. Rights, Interests, Desires and Beliefs. *American Philosophical Quarterly* 16 (3) (1979): 233–239.

Friskics, Scott. Dialogical Relations with Nature. *Environmental Ethics* 23 (4) (2001): 391–410.

Gardiner, Stephen. Are We the Scum of the Earth? In *Ethical Adaptation to Climate Change: Human Virtues of the Future*, ed. Thompson and Bendik-Keymer, 241–259.

Gardiner, Stephen M. *A Perfect Moral Storm: The Ethical Tragedy of Climate Change*. Oxford: Oxford University Press, 2011.

Gardner, Gerald T., and Paul C. Stern. *Environmental Problems and Human Behavior*. Needham Heights, MA: Allyn & Bacon, 1996.

Glover, Jonathan. It Makes No Difference Whether I Do It. Part I. *Proceedings of the Aristotelian Society*, Supplementary Volumes, 49 (1975): 171–209.

Gobster, Paul H., and R. Bruce Hull, eds. *Restoring Nature: Perspectives from the Social Sciences and Humanities*. Washington, DC: Island Press, 2000.

Goldblatt, David. *Art and Ventriloquism*. New York: Routledge, 2005.

Goodpaster, Kenneth. On Being Morally Considerable. *Journal of Philosophy* 75 (6) (1978): 308–325.

Grundmann, Reiner. *Marxism and Ecology*. Oxford: Clarendon Press, 1991.

Guha, Ramachandra. Radical Environmentalism and Wilderness Preservation: A Third World Critique. In *The Great New Wilderness Debate*, ed. Callicott and Nelson, 231–245.

Habermas, Jürgen. *Legitimation Crisis*. Trans. Thomas McCarthy. Boston: Beacon Press, 1975.

Habermas, Jürgen. *Moral Consciousness and Communicative Action*. Trans. Christian Lenhardt and Shierry Weber Nicholson. Cambridge, MA: MIT Press, 1990.

Habermas, Jürgen. *On the Pragmatics of Communication*, ed. Maeve Cook. Cambridge, MA: MIT Press, 1998.

Habermas, Jürgen. *The Philosophical Discourse of Modernity*. Trans. Frederick Lawrence. Cambridge, MA: MIT Press, 1987.

Habermas, Jürgen. *The Theory of Communicative Action*. Vol. 1. Trans. Thomas McCarthy. Boston: Beacon Press, 1984.

Habermas, Jürgen. *The Theory of Communicative Action*. Vol. 2. Trans. Thomas McCarthy. Boston: Beacon Press, 1987.

Hacking, Ian. *The Social Construction of What?* Cambridge, MA: Harvard University Press, 1999.

Haraway, Donna. The Promises of Monsters: Reproductive Politics for Inappropriate/d Others. In *Cultural Studies*, ed. Larry Grossberg, Cary Nelson, and Paula Treichler, 295–337. New York: Routledge, 1992.

Hardin, Garrett. The Tragedy of the Commons. *Science* 162 (3859) (1968): 1243–1248.

Hegel, G. W. F. *Phenomenology of Spirit*. Trans. A. V. Miller. New York: Oxford University Press, 1977.

Hegel, G. W. F. *Science of Logic*. Trans. A. V. Miller. New York: Humanities Press, 1976.

Heidegger, Martin. *Being and Time*. Trans. Edward Robinson and John Macquarrie. New York: Harper and Row, 1962.

Heidegger, Martin. Building Dwelling Thinking. Trans. Alfred Hofstadter. In *Poetry, Language, Thought*, 141–161. New York: Harper Colophon, 1971.

Heidegger, Martin. *The Question Concerning Technology and Other Essays*. Trans. William Lovitt. New York: Harper & Row, 1977.

Held, Virginia. Can a Random Collection of Individuals be Morally Responsible? *Journal of Philosophy* 67 (14) (1970): 471–481.

Heyd, Thomas, ed. *Recognizing the Autonomy of Nature*. New York: Columbia University Press, 2005.

Hobbes, Thomas. *Leviathan*. New York: Collier Books, 1962.

Honneth, Axel, Judith Butler, Raymond Geuss, and Jonathan Lear. *Reification: A New Look at an Old Idea*, ed. Martin Jay. Oxford: Oxford University Press, 2008.

Horkheimer, Max, and Theodor Adorno. *Dialectic of Enlightenment*. Trans. Edmund Jephcott. Stanford: Stanford University Press, 2002.

Hulme, Mike. *Why We Disagree about Climate Change*. Cambridge: Cambridge University Press, 2009.

Hume, David. *A Treatise of Human Nature*. Oxford: Clarendon Press, 1975.

Hunt, W. Murray. Are *Mere Things* Morally Considerable? *Environmental Ethics* 2 (1) (1980): 59–65.

Ihde, Don. *Heidegger's Technologies*. New York: Fordham University Press, 2010.

Ingold, Tim. *The Perception of the Environment: Essays in Livelihood, Dwelling and Skill*. London: Routledge, 2000.

Jackson, Frank. Group Morality. In *Metaphysics and Morality*, ed. Philip Pettit, Richard Sylvan, and Jean Norman. Oxford: Basil Blackwell, 1987.

Jamieson, Dale. *Morality's Progress: Essays on Humans, Other Animals, and the Rest of Nature*. Oxford: Oxford University Press, 2002.

Jamieson, Dale. When Utilitarians Should Be Virtue Theorists. *Utilitas* 19 (2) (2007): 160–183.

Johnson, Baylor L. Ethical Obligations in a Tragedy of the Commons. *Environmental Values* 12 (3) (2003): 271–287.

Jordan, William. *The Sunflower Forest: Ecological Restoration and the New Communion with Nature*. Berkeley: University of California Press, 2003.

Katz, Eric. Further Adventures in the Case against Restoration. *Environmental Ethics* 34 (1) (2012): 67–97.

Katz, Eric. The Liberation of Humanity and Nature. In *Recognizing the Autonomy of Nature*, ed. Heyd, 77–85.

Katz, Eric. *Nature as Subject: Human Obligation and Natural Community*. Lanham, MD: Rowman & Littlefield, 1997.

Kawall, Jason. Rethinking Greed. In *Ethical Adaptation to Climate Change: Human Virtues of the Future,* ed. Thompson and Bendik-Keymer, 223–239.

Kidner, David. Fabricating Nature: A Critique of the Social Construction of Nature. *Environmental Ethics* 22 (4) (2000): 339–357.

Kirkman, Robert. *Skeptical Environmentalism: The Limits of Philosophy and Science*. Bloomington: Indiana University Press, 2002.

Kohák, Erazim. *The Embers and the Stars: A Philosophical Inquiry into the Moral Sense of Nature*. Chicago: University of Chicago Press, 1984.

Krebs, Angelika. *Ethics of Nature*. Berlin: Walter de Gruyter, 1999.

Krieger, Martin H. What's Wrong with Plastic Trees? *Science* 179 (4072) (1973): 446–455.

Latour, Bruno. *Love Your Monsters*. Breakthrough Institute, Kindle, 2011.

Latour, Bruno. *Pandora's Hope: Essays on the Reality of Science Studies*. Cambridge, MA: Harvard University Press, 1999.

Latour, Bruno. *Politics of Nature: How to Bring the Sciences into Democracy*. Trans. Catherine Porter. Cambridge, MA: Harvard University Press, 2004.

Latour, Bruno. *We Have Never Been Modern*. Trans. Catherine Porter. Cambridge, MA: Harvard University Press, 1993.

Lee, Keekok. Awe and Humility: Intrinsic Value in Nature. Beyond an Earthbound Environmental Ethics. *Royal Institute of Philosophy Supplement* 36 (1994): 89–101.

Lee, Keekok. Is Nature Autonomous? In *Recognizing the Autonomy of Nature*, ed. Heyd, 54–74.

Lee, Keekok. *The Natural and the Artefactual*. Lanham, MD: Lexington Books, 1999.

Leopold, Aldo. *A Sand County Almanac*. New York: Oxford University Press, 1966.

Lewis, C. S. *Studies in Words*. Cambridge: Cambridge University Press, 1960.

Light, Andrew. Ecological Restoration and the Culture of Nature: A Pragmatic Perspective. In *Restoring Nature: Perspectives from the Social Sciences and Humanities*, ed. Gobster and Hull, 49–70.

Lo, Yeuk-Sze. Natural and Artifactual: Restored Nature as Subject. *Environmental Ethics* 21 (1999): 247–266.

Locke, John. *An Essay Concerning Human Understanding*, vol. 1. New York: Dover, 1959.

Locke, John. *Two Treatises of Government*. Cambridge: Cambridge University Press, 1988.

Louv, Richard. *Last Child in the Woods: Saving Our Children from Nature-Deficit Disorder*. Chapel Hill, NC: Algonquin Books, 2008.

Lukács, Georg. *History and Class Consciousness: Studies in Marxist Dialectics*. Trans. Rodney Livingstone. Cambridge, MA: MIT Press, 1971.

Maniates, Michael, and John M. Meyer. *The Environmental Politics of Sacrifice*. Cambridge, MA: MIT Press, 2010.

Mann, Charles. *1491: New Revelations of the Americas before Columbus*. New York: Vintage Books, 2006.

Marcuse, Herbert. *Counterrevolution and Revolt*. Boston: Beacon Press, 1972.

Marx, Karl. *Capital*. Vol. 1. New York: International Publishers, 1967.

Marx, Karl. *Das Kapital*. Vol. 1. Frankfurt: Verlag Marxistische Blätter, 1976.

Marx, Karl. *Grundrisse: Introduction to the Critique of Political Economy*. Trans. Martin Nicolaus. New York: Vintage Books, 1973.

Marx, Karl, and Frederick Engels. *Collected Works*. Vol. 3. New York: International Publishers, 1975.

Marx, Karl, and Frederick Engels. *Collected Works*. Vol. 5. New York: International Publishers, 1976.

Marx, Karl, and Friedrich Engels. *Die Deutsche Ideologie*. Berlin: Dietz Verlag, 1953.

Marx, Karl, and Friedrich Engels. *Gesamtausgabe*. Vol. 2. Berlin: Dietz Verlag, 1982.

Maser, Chris. *The Redesigned Forest*. San Pedro, CA: R&E Miles, 1988.

McCarthy, Thomas. *Ideals and Illusions: On Reconstruction and Deconstruction in Contemporary Critical Theory*. Cambridge, MA: MIT Press, 1991.

McKibben, Bill. *The End of Nature*. New York: Anchor Books, 1989.

Midgley, Mary. Duties Concerning Islands. In *Environmental Ethics*, ed. Robert Elliot, 89–103. Oxford: Oxford University Press, 1995.

Mill, John Stuart. Nature. In *Collected Works*. Vol. 10. Toronto: University of Toronto Press, 1963.

Mills, Stephanie. *In Service of the Wild: Restoring and Reinhabiting Damaged Land*. Boston: Beacon Press, 1995.

Nabhan, Gary Paul. Cultural Parallax in Viewing North American Habitats. In *The Great New Wilderness Debate*, ed. Callicott and Nelson, 628–641.

Nash, Roderick. *Wilderness and the American Mind*. 3rd ed. New Haven, CT: Yale University Press, 1983.

Nilsen, Richard, ed. *Helping Nature Heal: An Introduction to Environmental Restoration*. Berkeley, CA: Ten Speed Press, 1991.

Nolt, John. How Harmful Are the Average American's Greenhouse Gas Emissions? *Ethics, Policy and Environment* 14 (1) (2011): 3–10.

Nordhaus, Ted, and Michael Shellenberger. *Break Through: From the Death of Environmentalism to the Politics of Possibility*. New York: Houghton Mifflin, 2007.

Norton, Bryan G. *Toward Unity among Environmentalists*. New York: Oxford University Press, 1991.

Oelschlaeger, Max. *The Idea of Wilderness*. New Haven, CT: Yale University Press, 1991.

O'Neill, John. *Markets, Deliberation, and Environment*. London: Routledge, 2007.

O'Neill, John. Who Speaks for Nature? In *How Nature Speaks: The Dynamics of the Human Ecological Condition*, ed. Yrjö Haila and Chuck Dyke. Durham, NC: Duke University Press, 2008.

O'Neill, John, Alan Holland, and Andrew Light. *Environmental Values*. London: Routledge, 2008.

Ostrom, Elinor. *Governing the Commons: The Evolution of Institutions for Collective Action*. New York: Cambridge University Press, 1990.

Parfit, Derek. *Reasons and Persons*. Oxford: Clarendon Press, 1984.

Peterson, Anna. Environmental Ethics and the Social Construction of Nature. *Environmental Ethics* 21 (4) (1999): 339–357.

Plato. *Phaedrus*.

Plumwood, Val. *Environmental Culture: The Ecological Crisis of Reason*. London: Routledge, 2002.

Plumwood, Val. *Feminism and the Mastery of Nature*. London: Routledge, 1993.

Price, Jennifer. Looking for Nature at the Mall: A Field Guide to the Nature Company. In *Uncommon Ground: Rethinking the Human Place in Nature*, ed. Cronon.

Regan, Tom. *Animal Rights, Human Wrongs: An Introduction to Moral Philosophy*. London: Rowman & Littlefield, 2003.

Rolston, Holmes, III. *Environmental Ethics: Duties to and Values in the Natural World*. Philadelphia: Temple University Press, 1988.

Rolston, Holmes, III. Nature for Real: Is Nature a Social Construct? In *The Philosophy of the Environment*, ed. T. D. J. Chappell, 38–64. Edinburgh: University of Edinburgh Press, 1997.

Rolston, Holmes, III. *Philosophy Gone Wild*. Buffalo, NY: Prometheus Books, 1986.

Routley, Richard (Sylvan). Is There a Need for a New, an Environmental Ethic? In *Environmental Ethics*, ed. Andrew Light and Holmes Rolston III, 47–52. Malden, MA: Blackwell, 2003.

Routley, Val (Plumwood). On Karl Marx as an Environmental Hero. *Environmental Ethics* 3 (3) (1981): 237–244.

Sagoff, Mark. On Preserving the Natural Environment. *Yale Law Journal* 84 (2) (1974): 205–267.

Sandberg, Joakim. "*My* Emissions Make No Difference": Climate Change and the Argument from Inconsequentialism. *Environmental Ethics* 33 (3) (2011): 229–248.

Sandler, Ronald. Beware of Averages: A Response to John Nolt's "How Harmful Are the Average American's Greenhouse Gas Emissions?" *Ethics, Policy and Environment* 14 (1) (2011): 31–33.

Sandler, Ronald. *Character and Environment: A Virtue-Oriented Approach to Environmental Ethics*. New York: Columbia University Press, 2007.

Sandler, Ronald. Ethical Theory and the Problem of Inconsequentialism: Why Environmental Ethicists Should Be Virtue Oriented Ethicists. *Journal of Agricultural and Environmental Ethics* 23 (1–2) (2010): 167–183.

Sandler, Ronald, and Philip Cafaro, eds. *Environmental Virtue Ethics*. Landham, MD: Rowman & Littlefield, 2005.

Shapiro, Jeremy J. The Slime of History. In *On Critical Theory*, ed. John O'Neill, 145–163. New York: Seabury Press, 1976.

Siipi, Helene. Dimensions of Naturalness. *Ethics and the Environment* 13 (1) (2008): 71–103.

Sinnott-Armstrong, Walter. It's Not *My* Fault: Global Warming and Individual Moral Obligations. In *Perspectives on Climate Change: Science, Economics, Politics, Ethics*, ed. Walter Sinnott-Armstrong and Richard B. Howarth, 285–307. Burlington, VT: Emerald Group Publishing, 2005.

Smith, Adam. *The Wealth of Nations*. Baltimore, MD: Penguin Books, 1970.

Soper, Kate. *What Is Nature?* Oxford: Blackwell, 1995.

Soulé, Michael E., and Gary Lease, eds. *Reinventing Nature? Responses to Postmodern Deconstruction*. Washington, DC: Island Press, 1995.

Stevens, William K. *Miracle under the Oaks: The Renewal of Nature in America*. New York: Pocket Books, 1995.

Stone, Christopher. Should Trees Have Standing? *Southern California Law Review* 45 (1972): 450–501.

Taylor, Paul. *Respect For Nature: A Theory of Environmental Ethics*. Princeton, NJ: Princeton University Press, 1986.

Thompson, Allen, and Jeremy Bendik-Keymer, eds. *Ethical Adaptation to Climate Change: Human Virtues of the Future*. Cambridge, MA: MIT Press, 2012.

Toadvine, Ted. Limits of the Flesh: The Role of Reflection in David Abram's Ecophenomenology. *Environmental Ethics* 27 (2) (2005): 155–170.

Turner, Frederick. The Invented Landscape. In *Beyond Preservation: Restoring and Inventing Landscapes,* ed. Baldwin, De Luce, and Pletsch.

Verbeek, Peter-Paul. *What Things Do: Philosophical Reflections on Technology, Agency, and Design.* University Park: Pennsylvania State University Press, 2005.

Vitousek, Peter M., and Harold A. Mooney. Human Domination of Earth's Ecosystems. *Science* 277 (5325) (1997): 494–499.

Von Frisch, Karl. *Animal Architecture.* New York: Harcourt Brace Jovanovich, 1974.

Wapner, Paul. *Living through the End of Nature: The Future of American Environmentalism.* Cambridge, MA: MIT Press, 2010.

Warnock, G. J. *The Object of Morality.* New York: Methuen, 1971.

Weisman, Alan. *The World without Us.* New York: Thomas Dunne Books, 2007.

Index